MANAGEMENT, CONTROL AND ACCOUNTABILITY IN NONPROFIT/ VOLUNTARY ORGANIZATIONS

GW00371863

For Seán

Management, Control and Accountability in Nonprofit/ Voluntary Organizations

TREASA HAYES
Dublin City University Business School
Dublin City University
Dublin

Avebury

Aldershot • Brookfield USA • Hong Kong • Singapore • Sydney

100367291

361.763068
HAY

© T. Hayes 1996

All rights reserved. No part of this publication may be reproduced, stored in a retrieval system, or transmitted in any form or by any means, electronic, mechanical, photocopying, recording or otherwise without the prior permission of the publisher.

Published by
Avebury
Ashgate Publishing Limited
Gower House
Croft Road
Aldershot
Hants GU11 3HR
England

Ashgate Publishing Company
Old Post Road
Brookfield
Vermont 05036
USA

British Library Cataloguing in Publication Data

Hayes, Treasa
    Management, control and accountability in
    nonprofit/voluntary organizations
    1. Nonprofit organizations - Management 2. Associations,
    institutions, etc. - Management
    I. Title
    361.7 ' 63 ' 068

    ISBN 1 85972 207 5

Library of Congress Catalog Card Number: 96-83713

Printed and bound in Great Britain by
Ipswich Book Co. Ltd., Ipswich, Suffolk

Contents

Figure and Tables

Acknowledgements

I wish to express my gratitude to all those who offered their assistance in various ways in the course of my research. In particular I would like to thank Dr. David Billis for his valuable guidance and encouragement. To Mr. Roger Acton, CEO of the Union of Voluntary Organisations for the Handicapped and the forty respondents affiliated to UVOH who gave freely of their time in the course of the main fieldwork, I offer my sincere appreciation which also extends to all those who contributed to the earlier field research. On the administrative side, I am most grateful to my colleague in Dublin City University, Mr. Billy Kelly, who came to my assistance frequently as I tried to grapple with the complexities of word processing. Finally, my warmest thanks are due to my husband, Seán and my children, Eoin, Conor and Cillin for their continued support and patience throughout the entire project.

Part I
THE VOLUNTARY SECTOR

1 Introduction

The research presented in this work is centred on an exploratory study of management, control and accountability in Irish voluntary organizations. The broad objective of this opening chapter is to introduce the research topic and provide an overview of the complete study. It commences with a brief background sketch of voluntary activity, by way of establishing its relevance as an area of academic enquiry. The necessity for research in an Irish context is then validated. This is followed by an outline of the approach used in undertaking the current study. The research questions used to guide the enquiry and the structure of the entire study are then presented in sequence.

Brief overview of the voluntary sector

Over the past ten years or so, there has been a dramatic upsurge of interest in voluntary sector activities, at an international level (Anheier & Knapp 1990; Billis & Young 1990). There seems to be a growing acceptance that voluntary agencies have the ability to be sensitively attuned to specific needs in a manner that evades the wide embrace of the welfare state. In the UK, disenchantment with the welfare state has given rise to the notion of welfare pluralism (Brenton 1985; Gladstone 1979; Hinton & Hyde 1980-81). Gaining courage from their heightened profile,

> voluntary organisations are showing a new audacity. . . . The apologetic tone which has dominated discussion of the role of the voluntary sector during much of the life of the welfare state is now muted. . . . We have

entered a phase of positive and ambitious thinking about the role and influence of voluntary organisations. (Leat et al 1981:1)

The Wolfenden Report (1978) on the UK voluntary sector, which presented evidence of the substantial input from voluntary organizations, considerably strengthened the sector's significance. Writing some years later, Billis (1984a:74) commented on the progress that had been achieved, observing:

> The nature of non-governmental voluntary agencies is now rightly receiving greater attention. . . .Politicians of all parties, spurred on by financial stringency, continually affirm the benefits of voluntary involvement in the welfare service.

Mindful of the growing EC dimension in voluntary action for member states as the single market becomes a reality, ECAS (Euro Citizen Action Service) has been established as a Brussels-based information and advocacy service aiming "to strengthen the voice of voluntary sector associations within the European Community" (ECAS 1990:1).

The voluntary sector is of particular importance in the US where the terms "nonprofit" or "third" sector are used to describe it. In comparison to the UK, the US nonprofit sector "bears a larger share of total responsibility for the provision of welfare" (Harris & Billis 1985:7) and currently, it has a very strong profile, having "grown tremendously in the last two decades" (Drucker 1989:89). The work of the Filer Commission (1975), named after its chairman John Filer, represents a benchmark in nonprofit sector activity in America (O'Connell 1983).

At a global level, the contribution of the voluntary sector is in evidence. For instance, the rising ecological consciousness of recent decades is attributable in no small measure to voluntary groups who were first to create heightened public awareness of the issues (Douglas 1987; Patton 1990). An indication of the success of these organizations can be gleaned from the operations of one major player in the environmental field, Greenpeace. This organization has over a thousand fulltime staff members operating from 24 countries and five million supporters worldwide, all committed to protecting the environment and the delicate ecological balance that exists in the world (Greenpeace 1992).

In keeping with this higher profile now being enjoyed by voluntary/ nonprofit organizations, a concomitant increase in scholarly interest in voluntary action is discernible. Much of the writing which has emerged in recent years offers a fresh, exciting foundation for further study in this nonprofit field. The pluralism that is the hallmark of the nonprofit sector (Simon 1989) is reflected in the eclectic nature of academic contributions to the debate, providing numerous perspectives on voluntary action.

In their guide to the literature relating to organising voluntary agencies, Harris & Billis (1985:6) state that their search for useful material entailed moving across "the traditional academic disciplines". Likewise, Hodgkinson & Lyman (1989:xiii), in their publication on the nonprofit sector, present a gathering of academic disciplines which includes "law professors, economists, philosophers, experts in public administration, historians, statisticians, psychologists, sociologists, marketing people, geographers, and educationalists". This confirms the interdisciplinary nature of academic interest in the nonprofit field and also points to the rapid growth of serious research in the nonprofit arena. Derrickson's (1989) bibliography on the literature of the nonprofit sector, with an impressive total of 4,992 entries, is indicative of the now considerable outpouring of scholarly works relating to voluntary activity.

The current volume of academic output on the sector endorses its importance in terms of both interest and debate. Support for this development has been strengthened by the setting up of various nonprofit programmes in universities. One early example is the Program on Non-Profit Organizations, an interdisciplinary programme started in 1976 at the Institute for Social and Policy Studies at Yale University. Its goals consist of: "studying the role, character, organization and impact of the voluntary sector in the United States and abroad and of building a substantial body of information, analysis, and theory relating to nonprofit organizations" (Powell 1987:xi). Now over 300 colleges and universities in the US have similar programmes on offer (Wish 1990). These centres have established nonprofit activity as a distinctive area of academic interest.

The publication of two new international journals in 1990 which focus on the nonprofit world - *Nonprofit Management & Leadership* and *Voluntas*, augments the evidence of academic endeavour in the nonprofit field and facilitates the wider dissemination and application of the varied research undertaken. This brief overview establishes that the voluntary sector "is seeking more elbow room" (Patton 1990:9) at both an operational and research level, arising from its recently reclaimed vantage point of renewed interest from both academics and practitioners in the field.

Need and opportunity for the present study

The generally raised profile of the voluntary sector is mirrored in an Irish context. Some recent developments at governmental level endorse this heightened interest in the Irish voluntary sector. As part of a commitment given in the Irish government's Programme for Economic and Social Progress (PESP 1991) the Minister for Social Welfare is currently preparing a Charter and a White Paper on the role of voluntary organizations in social services in order to "set out a clear policy framework for partnership between government and voluntary organisations" (PESP 1991:24).

Somewhat earlier, in 1989, specific concerns about fundraising in the Irish voluntary sector led to the establishment of a government committee to investigate this area. The appointment of a High Court judge, the Hon. Mr. Justice Declan Costello, to chair this committee is indicative of the government's concern in relation to fundraising activities in support of voluntary action. The ensuing report issued by this committee (Report on Fundraising 1990) recommended considerable changes in current practice, all pointing in the direction of more stringent legislative controls over fundraising for charitable purposes (Report on Fundraising 1990:cht 5).

Towards the end of 1991 an influential religious umbrella body, the Conference of Major Religious Superiors (CMRS), commissioned a wide ranging study on voluntary sector activity in Ireland (Faughnan & Kelleher 1991). In their draft proposal for this study the two researchers contrast the accepted significance of the sector with its low research profile:

> In Ireland the importance of voluntary sector activity in a wide range of institutional provisions is widely acknowledged. Despite this, there has been remarkably little systematic research undertaken. (Faughnan & Kelleher 1991:1)

The present study is set within this climate of current interest in the Irish voluntary sector and the identified lack of a commensurate level of research. Its focus on management is likewise apposite as no detailed analysis of management practice in Irish voluntary agencies has been undertaken to date. Preliminary probings by the writer (detailed in chapter 9), undertaken as a prelude to the main study, produced very positive responses on the usefulness of carrying out research with a management focus.

Accountability was chosen as one of the central themes, in view of the current concerns about fraud in voluntary sector activity and the perceived need for accountability both at government level (Report on Fundraising 1990) and within the voluntary sector itself. For example, a document drafted by a group representing over sixty Irish voluntary organizations suggests that the sector should "further develop its accountability"(CWC 1992:3). (The chapter on accountability - chapter 7 - details this debate.)

Control (discussed in depth in chapter 6) is another specific focus and is closely related to accountability. Meeting demands for external accountability presupposes internal control: if an organization does not have internal control over the funding it receives, or on how this money is spent, then it is difficult to present an accurate account to external constituents.

Overall approach to the research

The initial point of departure for this study consisted of "poking around in relevant places" (Mintzberg 1979:585) in order to gain a broad perspective on voluntary action in an Irish context and to examine the feasibility of undertaking field research. (This preliminary fieldwork is detailed later in chapter 9.)

Encouraged by the positive responses at this early stage, the research process began in earnest. It commenced with an extensive review of the literature on the nonprofit sector. Computerised data bases provided one useful source of tracking down the wide spread of relevant publications. Then the background information for the Irish dimension to the study was assembled. The insights gained from the literature review facilitated the move to the major fieldwork. It was decided to undertake a qualitative study, based on a series of forty intensive interviews, spread over ten voluntary organizations. The broad conceptual framework used for the study entailed viewing an organization as an open system, interacting with its environment (Daft 1986; Kast & Rosenzweig 1985). Management, control and accountability were explored in the context of this framework.

Research questions and contribution

The following questions, shaped by the preliminary reading, were used to guide this exploratory study of management, control and accountability in Irish voluntary organizations.

- How do environmental characteristics impact on management in voluntary organizations?

- How do organizational characteristics impact on management in voluntary organizations?

- What are the profiles of management in Irish voluntary organizations?

- What is the approach to control in Irish voluntary organizations?

- How is accountability perceived and responded to in Irish voluntary organizations?

- How does the combination of environmental and organizational characteristics impact on management, control and accountability in voluntary organizations?

- How does this research contribute towards a fuller understanding of the processes of management, control and accountability in voluntary organizations?

As there has not been any research undertaken to date on management in the Irish voluntary sector, the study presents a first step in remedying this deficiency. It is intended to contribute to one area of the on-going wider debate on voluntary sector activity and to afford new insights into understanding the practice and problems associated with management, control and accountability in voluntary organizations.

Organization and overview of research

The overall logic of the research is to start by taking a broad view of voluntary action, and then to focus on the Irish dimension of the study. With this backdrop in place, the actual fieldwork is then detailed.

The work is divided into four main parts. The remaining chapter in Part I sets the main study in its broader perspective by exploring definitions, typologies, theories and roles of voluntary organizations. The Irish dimension of the research is introduced in the two chapters (3 and 4) which constitute Part II of the thesis. A socio-economic overview of Ireland is presented in chapter 3 in order to outline the wider context in which Irish voluntary organizations operate. Chapter 4 commences by examining the contribution made by Irish voluntary organizations in the past and then goes on to describe the contemporary scene in relation to the Irish voluntary sector.

Part III presents a review of the literature related to the central themes of the field research - management (chapter 5), control (chapter 6), and accountability (chapter 7).

The final major section of the study, Part IV, is devoted to the fieldwork. It begins with a chapter (8) on research methodology. The preliminary fieldwork for the research is then described in chapter 9. In addition, this chapter introduces the ten participant organizations which constituted the purposive sample for the main fieldwork. Research findings are presented in chapter 10 and interpreted in chapter 11. Finally, the remaining chapter (12) concludes the study by synthesising the main findings and presenting an outline model which emerges from the research.

Summary

This opening chapter provides an introduction to the complete study. The brief excursus into voluntary sector activity, although of necessity selective, serves the purpose of establishing the resurgence of interest in nonprofit activity at both an operational and scholarly level.

As the fieldwork is set in an Irish context, the need for the present study was established against a background of heightened interest in the voluntary debate and enthusiasm for relevant research in Ireland. This confirmed the appropriateness of the research task.

Having outlined the approach to undertaking the study, the specific research questions used to guide the enquiry were detailed. Finally, the organization of the entire work was described.

2 The Voluntary Sector: Definitions, Typologies, Theories and Roles

The purpose of this chapter is to provide some general background information on the voluntary sector by examining four significant dimensions relating to nonprofit activity - definitions, typologies, theories and roles.

Definitions

Although the term "voluntary organization" is widely used, its precise meaning is not so clear. The general literature relating to the voluntary sector contains terminology such as "third sector", "independent sector", "non-statutory organizations", "nonprofit" or "not-for-profit" organizations, all of which tend to compound rather than ameliorate the confusion. Some of these terms are examined, in an effort to grapple with the "terminological tempest" (Anheier & Knapp 1990:3) surrounding the sector.

Voluntary organizations in society

One starting point in defining this sector is to examine where voluntary organizations fit, in meeting the recognised needs of society. The Wolfenden Report (1978) adopts this approach, identifying four main avenues for meeting social need - the statutory, commercial, voluntary and informal. Regarding statutory sources, Fearns (1984:47) explains:

The aim of government departments and local authorities are laid down by statute, and each organization within the public sector has legal obligations to provide certain services.

Cumulatively, this very wide range of services, provided under the welfare state, constitutes provision in the statutory sector.

Services made available on a profit making basis fall within the ambit of the commercial sector. A privately run, fee paying nursing home is one example of a service provided in this manner.

The informal sector encompasses help and support from family, friends and neighbours. A family which cares for a sick relative or a neighbour who shops for a pensioner are examples of informal intervention. Billis (1987:5) refers to it as the "personal world" where "the overwhelming character of these relationships is that they are inexplicit. . . . Problems are responded to without recourse to categorising either those who have the problem or those who respond".

Yet, these characteristics do not take from the overall importance of such informal intervention. For example, one Irish study carried out by the National Council for the Aged (1988) estimated that 66,300 elderly people received a significant amount of care at home from family members whose role was unrecognised and unsupported by the State. Although it applies to only one area, this example serves to indicate the significant scope of informal input, both in terms of numbers and service provided. Brenton (1985:7) indicates its overall importance, referring to it as "the hidden part of the iceberg of which the state and voluntary sector services are only a small visible tip".

However, the distinguishing feature of informal care is that it is not organised in any structured sense. This contrasts with organised forms of voluntary action, which constitutes the voluntary sector in society. Organizations in this sector are the focus for the present study. As they include a large cast of many players engaged in bewildering variety of roles which permeate many aspects of society, one precise definition covering all these organizations proves elusive. Some of the available approaches to defining organised voluntary activity are now examined.

Exploring definitions of the voluntary sector

A succinct definition is provided by Gladstone (1979:4): "voluntary action typically involves a group of individuals who freely associate, without a commercial motive, to further their own welfare or the welfare of others". Whereas this definition has the merit of brevity, it is also rather general. Other writers (Brenton 1985; Hatch 1980; Johnson 1981) tackle the task of definition by identifying the cluster of features which characterise voluntary organizations.

According to Hatch (1980:15),

> it is necessary to define them as (i) being organizations, not simply informal groups; (ii) not established by statute or under statutory authority and not directly controlled by a statutory authority; and (iii) not commercial in the sense of being profit-making or (like much of the private sector in health and education) being mainly dependent for their resources on fees and charges paid by private individuals.

The negative elements of this definition render it less than ideal and it is also somewhat cumbersome. Yet it is broadly in line with the four criteria cited by Johnson (1981) in formulating a definition, namely method of formation, method of governance, method of finance, and motive. Brenton's (1985) approach is to present an ideal type model. The key elements of her model are that a voluntary body should be "a formal organization, constitutionally separate from government, self-governing, non-profit distributing, . . . and of public benefit" (Brenton 1985:9). This description has the advantage of being more concise and less negative in tone than that put forward by Hatch (1980).

Therefore, while there is no one clearcut definition of a voluntary organization, an ideal type model has five characteristics. It should be: a formal organization; formed independently of the state; self-governing; non profit distributing; of public benefit.

The other labels that arise in the "voluntary" vocabulary are now explored in some detail.

The third sector

This title is used frequently in the American literature. The idea that voluntary organizations belong neither to the public nor to the private sectors underpins the use of this term. Levitt (1973) took issue with the conventional division of society into two sectors - public and private. The latter referred to business, leaving "all else" under the "public" label which Levitt considered to be too broad. So he introduced the third sector to refer to that wide variety of organizations whose general purposes are broadly similar - "to do things business and government are either not doing, not doing well, or not doing often enough" (Levitt 1973:49).

Van Til (1988) reviews this sector in the US and its interrelationships with business and government. He notes that the third sector constitutes 6% of the US national economy (Van Til 1988:3), thus establishing its significance in national terms. Sometimes the title "independent sector" is used as an alternative to the third sector, in order to indicate its freedom from constraints of profits and politics.

"Nonprofit" and "not-for-profit" labels

These labels are also associated with North American literature, as well as being employed in a more general context. A nonprofit organization "is an organization whose goal is something other than earning a profit for its owners" according to Anthony & Young (1988:49). Another writer in the field, McLaughlin (1986:3) views a nonprofit organization as "one that exists to meet the goals of the public at large or of the subset of the public that support it." He states that nonprofit organizations comprise 20% of the US economy (McLaughlin 1986:3). The discrepancy between this figure and Van Til's (1988) 6% for the third sector is explained by the inclusion of governmental organizations under the wider "nonprofit" umbrella. In fact Van Til (1988:3) gives a figure of 14% for the governmental sector, thus reconciling the overall arithmetic.

Whereas it is clear from the foregoing discussion that "nonprofit" (or the hyphenated alternative "non-profit") can have a wider embrace in the US literature than merely voluntary endeavour, the term is used by many other writers (e.g. Kramer 1981; Van Til 1988; Ben-Ner & Van Hoomissen 1990) as being interchangeable with the "voluntary" label.

It is worth noting that some writers have taken issue with the term "non-profit". A sign in a Birmingham shop window, sighted by Observer in the *Financial Times*, encapsulates their reservations. It read as follows: "This is a non-profit making organization. That is why we are closing" (quoted in *Readers' Digest* 1990:53). The objection, of course, is based on the fact that casualties in the commercial cast can arguably come under this "nonprofit" banner. Hofstede (1981:193), one of the objectors, makes this very point and opts for the terms "for profit" and "not-for-profit" to "stress the intent of making a profit or not".

In contrast, Ramanathan (1982:10), in his book on management control in nonprofit organizations, states: "the adjective "nonprofit" signifies that the pursuit of profit is not a goal of the organizations we are concerned with in this book." Therefore, even though "nonprofit" could be construed as being misleading, if one wishes to interpret it in a literal sense, its common usage in referring to "not-for-profit" organizations makes it an acceptable and slightly less cumbersome label.

Another variation used by American writers such as Hall (1987:3) and Hodgkinson & Weitzman (1984:11) is the "private nonprofit" tag, to distinguish between government and other nonprofit organizations in an American context.

In sum, perhaps Kramer (1981:1) captures the considerable terminological diversity in referring to voluntary organizations when he states that such undertakings are "known variously as the private, independent, philanthropic, non-profit or third sector - after government and business".

Having explained the different interpretations that can arise, depending partly on the particular national context, in this study the terms "voluntary" and "nonprofit" are used interchangeably, in keeping with general practice in the field, and also in the interest of providing some variety.

Moving on from the arena of definitions, typologies are now examined, bearing in mind that a fundamental element in the development of a scientific body of knowledge is the availability of a widely accepted and usable classification scheme (Hempel 1965; Haas & Drabek 1973).

Typologies

The noted Irish statesman and orator, Edmund Burke, observed that "good order is the foundation for all things" (quoted in Tripp 1976:449). This quest for order arises when conducting any form of scientific inquiry. Crowson (1970:1), a biologist, even goes so far as to conclude that "classifying things is perhaps the most fundamental and characteristic activity of the human mind and underlines all forms of science".

Typologies address this need for classification. They play an important role in theory development because "valid typologies provide a general set of principles for scientifically classifying things or events" (Mills & Margulies 1980:255). Their usefulness stems from the fact that a typology should "allow us to combine a number of variables into a single construct, and thus allow us to deal with extremely complex phenomena in a relatively simple fashion" (Mechanic 1962:58).

This need to find a common basis for categorisation is also relevant in the study of organizations (Carper & Snizek 1980) as "organizations are not unlike any other phenomena. They possess certain common characteristics as well as unique idiosyncrasies" (Mills & Margulies 1980:255). This section explores some of the literature relating to classification of organizations in general, before moving on to the classification of voluntary organizations.

Organizational classification

The need to group organizations into various categories has been addressed by many writers in the domain of organizational theory, as evidenced in the ensuing discussion. Despite their cumulative efforts, McKelvey (1975:509), in an article which reconfirms the importance of taxonomy, notes that "the study of organizational classification is at such a primitive stage that there is not even agreement about terms, let alone agreement about a theory of classification".

The terms most frequently used are "typology", "taxonomy" and "classification". The ensuing semantic confusion is referred to also by Carper & Snizek (1980) who present a comprehensive and critical review of both theoretical and empirical approaches to the topic. They summarise 18 of the most frequently cited works, distinguishing theoretically and empirically constructed typologies or taxonomies. These range from Weber's (1947) patrimonial/feudal/bureaucratic divide of social domination to more modern contributions such as Blau & Scott"s (1962) typology based on the principle of cui bono, to that of Thompson (1967) which focuses on technology. In their overall assessment it is noted that while theoretically based schemes tend to neglect the fit between theory and reality, the empirically constructed taxonomies have tended to be problem specific, thus lacking broader applicability.

Yet another approach is that adopted by Mills & Margulies (1980) who isolate two basic categories which they label the grand typologies and the mid-range typologies. The former attempt to devise a typology capable of embracing all organizations. Blau & Scott's (1962) model, referred to above, and Etzioni's (1961) classification based on three control systems - coercive, utilitarian and normative - are representative of the "grand" category, as is Van Riper's (1966) six-category model which focuses on the degree of power exercised from the top. The authors conclude that "because of the complexity of the phenomenon being analyzed, however, there are limitations in the use of these typologies" (Mills & Margulies 1980:258).

Their second broad category of mid-range typologies adopts a more restrictive approach. It refers to typologies specific to work organizations. The technology structure approach of both Woodward (1965) and Thompson (1967) and Jurkovich's (1974) environmental approach based on Lawrence & Lorsch's (1967) earlier work, are cited as examples in this category. Yet these midrange typologies, while narrowing the field, "appear to have typed primarily industrial or manufacturing organizations" (Mills & Margulies 1980:259).

The foregoing brief review of organizational typologies indicates the range of approaches advanced by writers in the field of organization theory. However, "the problem is that there are countless ways of grouping organizations, and therefore almost any taxonomy can be supported by pointing out these groupings" (McKelvey 1975:511). The situation at present seems to be that "organization science has a long way to go before it establishes a comprehensive taxonomy that even begins to approach the precision of its biological counterpart" (Carper & Snizek 1980:73).

Having established the usefulness of classification and highlighted the difficulties regarding classification of organizations in general, categorization in the voluntary sector is now reviewed. It is our chosen field of inquiry.

Classification of voluntary organizations

Here again, the task is not easy. Writing in a voluntary sector context, Mason (1984:7) comments that "scholars have had difficulties with definitions and classifications". In a sociological review of voluntary associations, Sills (1968:366) says that "the range of variation is probably greater than that which exists among government and business organizations", while, according to the Wolfenden Committee (1978:189), voluntary organizations are "as different from each other as the ant is from the elephant or the whale from the hermit crab." This tremendous range and diversity renders classification difficult. Some of the approaches that have been adopted are now examined.

Parsimony of categories is achieved by Eisenberg (1983) who merely bisects the sector into voluntary organizations that promote self-betterment (which he sees as essentially private) and secondly, organizations chiefly concerned with societal problems. This is similar to Gordon & Babchuk's (1966:27) instrumental/ expressive functional variable which is also used later by Gatewood & Lahiff (1977:133). It relates to whether activities are directed towards the needs of nonmembers or of members.

Murray (1969:4-5), in a typology confined to voluntary organizations in the social welfare field, postulates three categories, adding pressure groups to the self-help and caring categories. Aiming for a relatively modest number of broad categories of nonprofit organizations, classified according to their single most central purpose, Smith et al (1980:1-4) present an 18-category breakdown. Geographical spread is the basis used by Johnson (1978:87) for his typology of voluntary social service organizations. He distinguishes between local and national levels of operation. Four variables are identified -

17

an entirely local organization; an entirely national organization; a national organization with local branches and finally, a national association with local affiliates. While this may be of interest in ascertaining the various territories covered, it tells us little else. In fact, all of the foregoing are broadly-based classifications which tend to sacrifice depth for simplicity.

Having considered the merits of various typologies, Brenton (1985:11) comments on the "almost impossible task of devising mutually exclusive categories for the multiform organizations of the voluntary sector." Stating that the crucial element is to identify what voluntary organizations actually do, she suggests a five-fold functional typology, distinguishing between service provision, mutual aid, pressure groups, resource and co-ordinator functions (Brenton 1985:11-12). A broadly similar typology is proposed by Handy (1988:11) who admits to "a lot of overlap" between sectors, particularly in the areas of service and advocacy. From these functional groupings, one can readily grasp the wide range of activities encompassed by the voluntary sector as a whole.

Questions concerning staffing and funding are addressed by Hatch (1980:35-6) in his typology of voluntary undertakings. Firstly he distinguished between organizations in terms of whether the work is carried out primarily by volunteers or paid staff. For the former, he then sub-divides them according to those which provide services for their own members (mutual aid associations) and those which offer a service to a distinctly separate group of clients (volunteer organizations). For organizations employing paid staff, he distinguishes according to source of income - whether they are almost exclusively government grant funded (special agencies), or rely to a considerable extent on donations and charges (funded charities). Hatch himself acknowledges the limitations of his classification which "does not fit all organizations perfectly and unambiguously" (Hatch 1980:36). For instance volunteer organizations also require funding, and donations and charges seem rather disparate sources to be grouped together.

In an attempt to grapple with the problem of devising exclusive categories, Mawby & Gill (1987) come up with an interesting solution. They suggest the use of a continuum. Opting for four issues, voluntary bodies can be located appropriately on each continuum. The four issues are: the relationship to conventional statutory agencies; source of funding; goals; and finally, the relationship between the helper and the helped. At one extreme lie conventional statutory welfare agencies, while the antithesis is an agency which provides a radical critique of statutory provision. Yet again, the authors admit that "these four issues are not exhaustive" (Mawby & Gill 1987:75).

It has been established that, at a general level, classification of organizations presents profound difficulties which have yet to be surmounted. As Carper & Snizek (1980:74) conclude from their review of the relevant literature on organizational taxonomies, "we have a long way to go in formulating a workable classification system for organizations". The voluntary sector, with its tremendous variety of activities, poses similar challenges in classification. Gerard (1983:35) counsels that "the simple division into ideal types is unlikely to reflect the diversity apparent in the real world." The Wolfenden Committee (1978:12) found that "different patterns of classification were useful for different purposes", a stance echoed by Johnson (1978:87). The "patterns" used to classify Irish voluntary organizations are detailed later in chapter 7.

Another important and indeed fundamental question in relation to the voluntary sector is: why do voluntary organizations exist? This query is now addressed by taking a look at some of the main theories that have been advanced regarding the existence of nonprofit organizations.

Some theories of the voluntary sector

Several theories have been put forward to explain the economic roles of nonprofit organizations. Some of these are demand-side theories, i.e., they present reasons why consumers choose to patronise nonprofits in preference to for-profit organizations in certain circumstances. One broad theory, Weisbrod's (1975, 1977, 1988) "public goods" theory, comes under this rubric. Issues of contract failure and trust are dominant in a second broad theory on the sector advanced by Hansmann (Hansmann 1980, Easley & O'Hara 1986, Krashinsky 1986). Two other contributors, Salamon (1987) writing in an American context, and James (1987) who adopts a broader international perspective, note the importance of the role of government in developing and financing the nonprofit sector, and put forward theories which are compatible with this reality. These approaches are now reviewed, starting with Weisbrod's "public goods" theory.

Public goods theory

The broad theory advanced by Weisbrod (1975, 1977, 1988) suggests that nonprofits serve as private producers of public goods. As Eckstein (1967:8) explains, public goods are

. . . goods and services that simply cannot be provided through the market. They have two related qualities. First, they inevitably have to be supplied to a group of people rather than on an individual basis. Second, they cannot be withheld from individuals who refuse to pay for them.

. . . There is no way of withholding the service, of creating a market which separates those who pay from the freeloaders. In fact, in this type of situation, rational consumers who are interested only in economics will never pay since they will get the benefit in any event. In the case of ordinary private goods, this difficulty does not occur.

A lighthouse is a classic example of a public good (Anthony & Young 1988:277). The collective quality of these goods is sufficient to rule out for-profit firms. This leaves provision to either government or nonprofits.

The public sector can and does provide public goods, using taxation as a funding mechanism. However, government provision tends to be at a level that satisfies the median voter, due to what Douglas (1987:46) calls the "categorical constraint". This leaves supra-median or heterogeneous demand unsatisfied. Nonprofits step in to meet this residual unsatisfied demand for public or collective goods. In essence, for Weisbrod, the issue is one of institutional choice. As collective goods fall outside the for-profit domain, due to the free-rider problem, this narrows the institutional choice to either government or nonprofits. Government provision, meeting median demand, is augmented by nonprofit provision to cater for the residual excess and also for diverse demands (Douglas 1987; Simon 1987).

However, nonprofit organizations also provide private goods, e.g., day care and nursing homes. Weisbrod's theory does not explain this aspect. Another contribution to the debate, Hansmann's "contract failure" theory, goes some way to addressing this problem.

Contract failure

Hansmann's (1980; 1987) theory concentrates on issues of contract failure and trust. In situations where consumers find it difficult to assess what they purchase, for-profit firms may have an incentive to increase profits, at the expense of downgrading quality. It is argued that as nonprofit firms lack these incentives, they are more trustworthy.

Observations on the quality and service in day-care provide the backdrop to this theory. Nelson & Krashinsky (1973) noted that the quality of service offered by a day-care centre can be difficult to judge. Consequently, they suggested, parents might opt for a service provider in whom they could place more trust, rather than using a for-profit firm which could take advantage of the situation and provide service of an inferior quality. They argued that the strong presence of nonprofit firms in the day-care industry could possibly be explained as a response to this demand.

This theme is expanded by Hansmann (1980) who suggests that nonprofits typically arise in situations where consumers feel unable to evaluate accurately the quantity or quality of the service a firm produces for them. In these circumstances for-profit firms have both the incentive and opportunity to take advantage of customers by producing services of inferior quality. In contrast, nonprofit organizations, owing to the non-distribution constraint whereby "those who control the organization are constrained in their ability to benefit personally from providing low quality services" (Hansmann 1987:29), there is less incentive to short-change customers.

The "contract failure" tag arises because ordinary contractual mechanisms do not provide consumers with adequate means of policing producers. In these situations of assymetric information between consumers and producers, the non-distribution constraint of the nonprofit form offers some assurance to individuals, as "most commonly nonprofit firms have . . . been assumed to maximise the quality and/or quantity of the services they produce" (Hansmann 1987:37). Models of nonprofit firms that pursue one or both of these goals have been developed for nonprofits in general by James (1983).

The nub of Hansmann's theory is that in certain circumstances, especially where the consumer is not the same as the purchaser, such as in care of the aged or of children, the normal mechanisms of the market do not obtain. This gives rise to the issue of trust, thus making nonprofit organizations more acceptable, as they are unconstrained by issues of profitability and concomitant possibilities of reducing quality.

Noting that, in the American context, government has become the single most important source of income for most types of nonprofit agencies, Salamon (1987) takes issue with the theories of both Weisbrod and Hansmann. "In neither of these theories is there much hint that the nonprofit sector should play as substantial a role as it does" (Salamon 1987:109). A closer scrutiny of Salamon's theory now follows.

Another theory of the voluntary sector

Referring specifically to Weisbrod's (1977) theory, Salamon (1987:109) is of the opinion that "government support to nonprofit organizations has no theoretical rationale" under this rubric where the nonprofit sector is viewed as a substitute for government, providing services that the wider community has not endorsed. Likewise bearing in mind that most government programmes involve a substantial amount of regulation, which is at variance with a high degree of trust, Hansmann's (1980) theory "provides little rationale for government reliance on nonprofits" (Salamon 1987:109).

To incorporate the reality of government as the major financial actor on the nonprofit stage, Salamon (1987) comes up with a new theory explaining its existence. First of all he views the extensive pattern of government support for nonprofits as part of what he terms "third-party government" which relates to "the use of nongovernmental . . . entities to carry out governmental purposes" (Salamon 1987:110). Given the extensive pattern of third-party government, widespread reliance on nonprofit organizations is "not an anomaly but exactly what one would expect" (Salamon 1987:111). In these circumstances Salamon (1987) suggests that instead of demoting the voluntary sector to a derivative role, it should be seen as the preferred mechanism for providing collective goods, with government assuming the residual role.

He then proceeds to identify four voluntary-sector failures which justify government involvement. These are labelled as "philanthropic insufficiency" which concerns the inability of the sector to generate sufficient income; "philanthropic particularism" which describes the tendency of voluntary organizations to focus on particular sub-groups, with the drawback that it might not favour all equally; "philanthropic paternalism" where those in control of resources can determine direction which may be less democratic and retain a "lady bountiful" image; and finally "philanthropic amateurism" relating to difficulties in attracting professional personnel.

However, Salamon (1987:113) notes that, felicitously, "the voluntary sector's weaknesses correspond well with government's strengths, and vice versa." Given this situation, he considers that collaboration between government and the nonprofit sector is both logical and theoretically sensible.

Changing the setting to the international scene, James (1987:387) agrees with Salamon (1987) regarding the importance of government funding, commenting that "from a worldwide point of view private philanthropy is insignificant, whereas governmental subsidies are a major source of funds, particularly in countries where the nonprofit sector is large." Krashinsky (1990) also highlights the importance of government funding in the context of the Canadian voluntary sector and once again queries the omission of this aspect in existing theories on nonprofits. Building on these observations, some international perspectives on the sector are now presented.

Grounded on gleanings from a range of countries, James(1987) offers an alternative theory on the voluntary sector, based on input characteristics. Noting that "universally, religious groups are the major founders of nonprofit service institutions" (James 1987:404), she considers that this has important implications for nonprofit theory.

These religious-based institutions do not have the objective of maximizing profits, but rather some other non-monetary objective. Also service provision is an effective way for them to gain entree and goodwill in a society. Thus, having advantages in terms of perceived trustworthiness, low-cost voluntary labour and donated capital, inter alia, "the religious motive for founding provides a powerful supply-side explanation for where nonprofits are found, why the nonprofit form is used" (James 1987:405).

Why do governments choose to use nonprofits, rather than produce the commodities themselves? James (1987) offers three explanations. Firstly, certain groups want control over certain services and their support can be gained by contracting out. Secondly, in exchange for this control, these groups are prepared to absorb some of the costs incurred. Thirdly, nonprofits have access to volunteer labour or cheaper labour which can reduce overall costs. On this latter point, Kraskinsky (1990:48) refers to the ability of nonprofit suppliers in Canada to dilute union power as being a contributory factor in keeping wage costs down. He also mentions the appeal of nonprofits in permitting government to distance itself from politically awkward decisions, citing the sensitive area of abortion as an example.

At this stage, insights into some demand and supply theories on the voluntary sector have been provided. While individual theories shed some light on the existence of voluntary organizations, no one theory is sufficient to give a total explanation of their existence.

Roles of voluntary organizations

Voluntary organizations are credited with a range of attributes which justify and underpin their continued existence. Many writers, including Brenton (1985), the Filer Commission (1975), Gerard (1983), Gladstone (1979; 1982), Knapp et al (1988), Kramer (1981; 1987) and Leat et al (1986), offer comment on the roles and functions of nonprofit organizations in society. "These agencies are expected to be innovative and flexible, to protect particular interests, to provide volunteer citizen participation and to meet needs not met by government" (Kramer 1981:4). Gladstone (1982) endorses these sentiments when he points to the unique, experimental and innovative qualities of services provided by voluntary organizations.

The pluralist approach to services offered by the voluntary sector which "can more readily lend itself to experiment, innovation and adaptation over time" is seen as desirable by Hinton & Hyde (1980-1:13). An array of independent sector virtues is cited by Lynam (1983:371) who stresses "its contribution to pluralism and diversity, its tendency to enable individuals to participate in civil life . . . its encouragement of innovation and its capacity to act as a check on the inadequacies of government."

How valid are all these claims? To explore this question in a systematic way, some of the sector's attributes are evaluated, focussing in turn on each of the following:

- consumer choice
- specialisation
- cost effectiveness
- flexibility
- innovation
- advocacy
- participation.

Consumer choice

In the commercial sector, market researchers spend considerable time, effort and money on discerning consumer tastes and preferences for goods (Pride & Ferrell 1987) thus acknowledging that requirements are by no means homogeneous. Rather, different tastes can be fashioned by considerations such as income, culture, ethnic, political or other variations. Likewise in the service arena consumers" tastes and preferences can vary (Lovelock 1984) and the voluntary sector is seen as having the capacity to respond to these diverse demands (Kotler 1982).

As Gerard (1983:29) sees it:

> Clearly governments lack centrally the variety of responses to satisfy the differentiated needs of individual citizens. They react therefore by endeavouring to reduce variety in the system, rather than by expanding their capacity for sensitive and varied response.

Public provision, with its lack of a "varied response", can create a niche for voluntary organizations to fill. This is not a new phenomenon. Writing in

1859, John Stuart Mills contrasted government and voluntary approaches in this regard: "Government operations tend to be everywhere alike. With . . . voluntary associations, on the contrary, there are varied experiments, and endless diversity of experience" (quoted in Hopkins 1980:6).

Another problem in public provision is that "statutory functions alone can never hope to fulfill people's expectations for care, support and security in a modern society" (Hadley et al 1975:4). Writing from a broader perspective, Kramer (1981:5-6) puts it another way: "it is widely believed that the welfare state inevitably generates more demand for social services than it can realistically (financially and politically) provide." Overall, given the limitations of public provision and its tendency towards homogeneity in services on offer, an important function of the voluntary sector is to bring back variety to the social system by offering alternative systems of values, free from, or at least less constrained by, political considerations.

However, it must be remembered that whatever their limitations may be, welfare states endeavour to make available basic levels of provision for all citizens. In contrast, voluntary organizations tend to focus on particular areas of interest, i.e., they operate in a more specialised way. This aspect of their activity is now considered.

Specialisation

"The first salient attribute of a voluntary agency is . . . specialization in a problem, a group of people, or a method of intervention" (Kramer 1981:359). In contrast to the wide lens of the welfare state, beamed on the full spectrum of societal needs, voluntary organizations tend to adopt a more specific focus. This approach is not new. Over forty years ago, Lord Beveridge (1948:26) commented that "the philanthropic motive is in practice a specialist motive; it drives men to combat a particular evil, to meet a particular need that arouses their interests".

These views are echoed by Kramer (1987:250), writing almost four decades later:

> As interest groups, voluntary agencies are intrinsically particularistic and selective in contrast to the more universal scope of governmental agencies. . . . Like a brand name, specialization contributes to the preservation of organizational identity and enables a voluntary agency to claim jurisdiction over a domain such as the mentally retarded, Catholic youth or Jewish aged.

The voluntary sector seems at ease with this role as, according to the Barclay Committee (1982:82), it is "prepared to concentrate unashamedly on certain people and certain areas".

Examples of the specialist role of voluntary organizations are not scarce. Groups that may have low visibility or low priority within the broad sweep of statutory services such as "paraplegics, deaf alcoholics, autistic children, or persons with multiple sclerosis, muscular dystrophy or cerebral palsy" (Kramer 1981:242-3) can have recourse to relevant voluntary provision. Accommodation for alcoholics, drug addicts, ex-mental patients and ex-offenders, all provided on a voluntary basis, feature in Hatch's (1980) study of voluntary agencies in three English towns. Minority causes can be taken on board also by the nonprofit sector (Filer 1975; Gerard 1983) when the needs they cherish are either ignored or rejected by the majority.

Another important feature of voluntary agencies centres on their integrative role. Kramer (1981:260) captures this aspect, noting that "because they can often more readily serve the whole person, voluntary agencies are also able to put together what governmental agencies fragmentize through departmentalization." In an Irish context the problem of homeless children provides a good example of official "fragmentization". As a spokesperson for Focus Point, a Dublin-based voluntary crisis service for young homeless, describes it, "there is still no co-ordination between the three departments involved in childcare - Justice, Education and Health - and they are all evading responsibility" (quoted in O"Meara 1991). Confronted with this official bureaucratic tangle, voluntary agencies have to shoulder the brunt of the responsibility in attending to the needs of these displaced children, as "the long-awaited provision of extra residential places for male and female juvenile offenders" (O"Meara 1991) is still outstanding.

Specialisation can also have some shortcomings. "Voluntary organizations represent particular sectional interests and the voluntary sector as a whole does not equally represent every interest" (Leat et al 1981:102). The problem arises because some needs can have more appeal than others. For example, Salamon (1987) suggests that subgroups such as gays, the disabled and Hispanics have found difficulties establishing a niche in the voluntary system. A related problem regarding provision is "an uneven geographical distribution of voluntary organizations" identified by the Wolfenden Committee (1978:57). The case of refuges for battered women also highlights this point, as refuge provision "has never approached the level of need" (Mawby & Gill 1987:76).

In sum, specialisation provided by voluntary organizations proves useful in addressing specific needs which are sometimes neglected or underserved by the wider embrace of statutory provision. Yet shortcomings are apparent both in terms of groups served and geographical cover.

Cost effectiveness

In an adverse economic climate which necessitates government cut-backs, facilities with possibilities of presenting a cheaper alternative have a compelling attraction. Voluntary organizations have been cast in the role of being "frequently more cost-effective" (Hinton & Hyde 1980-1:13). But how true, in fact, is this statement? In order to respond to this question, it is necessary to explore how this cost advantage might arise.

Gladstone (1979:119) sees self-help, volunteering, private giving and the absence of "extensive administration" as contributory factors in reducing costs, compared with statutory provision. In their field research Leat et al (1981) found a willingness on the part of statutory providers to allow voluntary agencies handle cases with which they seemed able to deal adequately, one reason being that this saved resources. A research study reported by Hatch & Moycroft (1979) which compared voluntary meals-on-wheels services with public sector equivalents, showed significant cost advantages of between 50% and 90% in favour of the voluntary services. So there is some evidence to suggest that the voluntary sector may be more cost-effective, particularly in cases where there is a high volunteer input.

Of course, it must be remembered that nonprofits also use paid employees. In such circumstances the Wolfenden Committee (1978:155) stated that "it is much more difficult to tell whether voluntary organizations are more cost-effective than local authorities when both are relying on paid staff." Delving more deeply reveals possible savings in the staffing area. For instance, Preston (1990:15) notes that "wages in nonprofits are on average 10 to 15 per cent lower than they are in the for-profit sector, when employees with otherwise identical observed characteristics are compared." An even higher differential of 32 per cent in full-time income is cited by Mervis & Hackett (1983), while Weisbrod (1983) found as much as a 20 per cent gap between earnings of nonprofit lawyers and comparable for-profit lawyers.

All these examples are taken from a US setting. However Mellor's (1985) research in the UK regarding staffing in the voluntary sector supports these findings. He reports that often employers have relied on goodwill to the degree that they have contravened the employment laws. The foregoing information relating to paid staff in the voluntary sector indicates that savings may be gained, but that, at times, this may involve less than equitable treatment of staff, in comparison to their counterparts working in the commercial sector.

Due to the tremendous variations in voluntary sector organizations, particularly with regard to use of volunteers and paid staff, it is not possible to generalise about the cost-effectiveness of the sector as a whole. This eliminates sweeping assertions about "cheaper alternatives" in the voluntary sector. Yet the possibility of saving on labour costs, through the use of volunteer labour, must be acknowledged.

Flexibility

Contemporary society is engulfed in an era of rapid social and economic change (O Murchu 1987). The accompanying turbulence can give rise to new needs and, in turn, responding to them can demand a flexibility of approach. This flexibility is cited as yet another virtue of the voluntary sector, when compared to bureaucratic responses which "only squeeze citizens into the rigidly structured services of the public sector" (Knapp et al 1988:12-3). Based on their research findings, Leat et al (1981:106) report that the "different nature of voluntary bodies was repeatedly said to have advantages over statutory provision in terms of flexibility, lack of bureaucracy and informality." Similar sentiments are expressed by Gladstone (1979:119) when he states that voluntary organizations can "generate the diversity necessary for adaptation both to rapid change and to varying local circumstances", a point endorsed in a later study by Leat et al (1986:37).

The growth and development of refuges for battered women provides some interesting examples of flexibility. Awareness of this problem of violence in the home arose initially in 1972 when a group from the Women's Liberation Movement, who were engaged in an unrelated task of campaigning for price restraint, encountered battered victims in the course of their campaign (Mawby & Gill 1987). At that time the shape of welfare service development, with its focus upon welfare for the family unit, meant that statutory provisions were "inimical to the needs of the battered wife" (Mawby & Gill 1987:75).

However, those who encountered the problem took action to address it, the response being to establish the Chiswick Women's Aid, a refuge aimed at meeting the short-term needs of battered women. The concept blossomed so that by 1978 there were 150 refuges catering for some 1,000 women and 1,700 children (Binney et al 1985). This example, together with the story of Rape Crisis Centres and Victim Support movements (Mawby & Gill 1987) indicate how voluntary flexibility, untrammelled by statutory constraints, can counter perceived inadequacies in state response, or indeed lack of response, to some identified need.

Sometimes instances can arise where flexibility is fashioned for purely pragmatic reasons. For example, in the arena of grantsmanship, programme flexibility can veer towards meeting funding requirements, rather than client needs (Mills et al 1983). However, the results of such expenditure may be shortlived and independence may be sacrificed "for what turns out to be carrots for only one meal" (Mawby & Gill 1987:82).

The general position seems to be one where voluntary organizations, being less constrained by bureaucratic rules and procedures, do have the potential to be more flexible. However, to quote Knapp et al (1988:13), "at the end of the day we are left with limited evidence of the flexibility of voluntary organizations".

Innovation

Another ascribed advantage of the voluntary sector, again of added import in times of rapid change, is its innovative capacity. Nonprofits are "the first birds off the telephone wire" in terms of ideas, according to Gardner, as they have the freedom "to let a hundred ideas bubble up, sift the ones that speak to the condition of the time, and let the rest evaporate" (quoted in Nielsen 1983:369).

Comment on innovation is plentiful, some supportive and some more cautious of its endorsement in relation to voluntary organizations. According to Knapp et al (1988:14):

> The pioneering characteristic of voluntary organizations has been cited so frequently as to become legendary. But like all the best legends the truth has sometimes been colourfully embellished to make a better story.

This "story" is now scrutinised.

A solid consensus emerges in support of voluntary action's "tradition of innovation" (Gladstone (1979:63). Commentators as far apart in time as the Webbs (1912) and the Wolfenden Committee (1978) have endorsed this trait. In the US, the Filer Commission (1975) notes the sector's contribution in promoting minority causes and also its more general success in instigating new initiatives which "once successfully pioneered by nonprofit groups . . . can be, and often have been supported and expanded by government" (Filer Commission [1975](1983:308)). Another American writer, Nielsen (1983:369) views voluntary organizations as "the seedbeds from which most important reforms in our country have begun" and cites civil rights, environmentalists and the women's movement as examples, as does Rockefeller (1983). The "greater facility for experimentation possessed by the voluntary nonprofit sector" (Douglas 1987:48) probably accounts for this precursor role.

In an English context, Johnson (1981) sees developments such as advice and information services, and refuges for battered women as displaying the capacity to uncover needs which were previously either unrecognised or neglected. Overall, as he sees the situation, "both their past record and their present performance support the view that voluntary organizations are an important source of experimentation and innovation in social services" (Johnson 1981:38).

Commenting that "their genesis has been largely recent", Richardson & Goodman (1983:3-4) rate self-help groups as "innovative beacons, directing the way to newer kinds of helping." Initiatives instigated by the voluntary sector are viewed as contributing to the "present cornucopia of services" (Leat et al 1986:38) available in the country, according to statutory-sector officers interviewed by Leat and her colleagues in their research.

Yet, some commentators sound a discordant note in this harmony of praise. For instance, the Wolfenden Committee (1978) speculates on how long the innovative era lasts: "it is interesting to question how far voluntary organizations continue to act in a pioneering role, once their opening phase is over" (Wolfenden Committee 1978:47). A quote from the Toronto Rape Crisis centre indicates how atrophy can set in over time:

An idea becomes a movement

The movement becomes an organization

The organization becomes an institution

And there lies the death of an idea. (quoted in Amir & Amir,1979:255)

Even Gladstone, an ardent advocate of welfare pluralism, concedes that "there exist voluntary associations whose practice owes more to Victorian times than any desire to experiment with new approaches" but balances this observation by referring also to "a host of encouraging initiatives" (Gladstone 1979:115). In keeping with this Victorian image is Eisenberg's (1983:317) comment about the "fossilization of traditional practices" in cases where organizations have not adjusted to recent developments, thereby substituting intransigence for innovativeness. Bodies like the Salvation Army have been criticised for pursuing nineteenth century "innovation" to meet late twentieth century needs, in building large impersonal hostels (Walker 1981).

The interpretation of what passes for "innovation" is queried by Kramer (1981; 1987). In his view sometimes innovation can be merely "a ploy in the game of grantsmanship as agencies describe minor modifications . . . as original breakthroughs in order to compete for funding" (Kramer 1981:189). In other cases Kramer also regards the innovative content as being of dubious quality in programmes that are" essentially small-scale, uncontroversial, . . . incremental improvements or extensions of conventional programs with relatively few original features" (Kramer 1987:249).

So far, it has been shown that the voluntary sector has an historical legacy of being positioned at the experimental edge. Examples from the more recent past endorse this image. Yet, in some instances, the innovative content may be of dubious value, especially in cases where the innovation is of the "pseudo" variety and is, in fact, merely used as a funding device. In these circumstances, innovation is degraded as a virtue in itself.

Advocacy

This has been termed the "quintessential function" of the voluntary sector (O"Connell 1976). Advocacy has been described as "pursuing causes in the corridors of power" (Mellor 1985:61) or as "the mission of defending and articulating the interests of underserved populations at risk" (Kramer 1981:261). The advocacy role is not of recent origin. Thane (1982:19), in a review of charities in Britain in the 1870-1900 period notes that "some charities combined pressure group activity with practical action". Moving on to the inter war period, she records that "voluntary organizations, however, retained an important innovative role in providing and agitating for groups neglected by public policy, such as unmarried mothers and their children" (Thane 1982:171). Stressing the importance of advocacy, Jordan (1983:403) states that a voluntary organization which neglects this role "forces itself into the position of being a band-aid dispenser for a sick society."

Advocacy can be relevant at two levels - personal and public. Knapp et al (1988:15) label these "citizen advocacy" and "policy advocacy". The former is offered by organizations such as citizen's advice bureaux, legal advice centres and specialist agencies dealing with disabilities, unemployment, youth, problem families (Johnson 1981). Policy advocacy represents the campaigning role of nonprofits. While some agencies view their role as essentially political, others focus on providing a service for those needing help. However, many combine both functions and so advocacy features on the agenda of numerous voluntary organizations, to a greater or lesser extent.

One organization with a balanced focus is MADD (Mothers Against Drunk Driving), founded in California in 1980 by Candy Lightner, following the death of her daughter in an accident caused by a drunk driver. This organization combines pressure group activity with direct help for individual victims (Harris 1986). Spouse battering and rape are other areas which incorporate both provision and advocacy. Pizzey (1974), in her book *Scream*

Quietly or the Neighbours Will Hear, put the issue of battered women on the political map, while refuges mushroomed in the 1970s, as already mentioned, to cater for the related practical needs (Binney et al 1985). The problems of rape victims emerged also in the 1970s as part of the feminist wave of that era. The Rape Crisis Centres which were set up in response have a political role, being "committed to educating and informing the public about the reality of rape" (London Rape Crisis Centre 1984:ix). But their primary aim is "to provide a place where women and girls who have been raped . . . can talk with other women" (London Rape Crisis Centre 1984:ix).

While Kramer (1981) and Mellor (1985) report successful pressure group activities in the social services area, self-help groups also include advocacy in their range of functions (Katz & Bender 1976; Richardson & Goodman 1983).

Looking at the situation in general, one can conclude that the advocacy role of voluntary organizations is well established. One area of concern is the ability of the sector to maintain its critical stance in the light of increased reliance on statutory funding. While evidence from research by writers such as Kramer (1981), Leat et al (1981) and Mellor (1985) does not indicate that government funding poses a major threat to independence, nonetheless common sense would counsel caution when criticising the "hand that feeds".

Moving on from the advocacy aspect of nonprofits, the final function ascribed to the sector is examined. It centres on the opportunities for participation afforded to volunteers who offer their services to others.

Participation

Voluntary organizations are credited as being a vehicle for altruistic action and citizen participation. They afford opportunities to citizens to become involved by contributing money, time and skills towards providing a range of services and activities. In addition to benefitting the recipient organizations, this can also benefit the donors themselves.

In his widely-quoted book *The Gift Relationship*, Titmuss(1971) expresses concern about the diminished opportunities in the welfare state for altruistic behaviour where one can "exercise a moral choice to give in non-monetary form to strangers" (Titmuss 1971:31). Later he states: "If it is accepted that man has a social and a biological need to help then to deny him opportunities to express this need is to deny him the freedom to enter into gift relationship" (Titmuss 1971:243). Titmuss was not the first to focus on the provision of opportunities for participation. Writing over one hundred years earlier, John Stuart Mill highlighted its importance:

Although individuals may not do the particular thing so well, on the average, as the officers of government, it is nevertheless desirable that it should be done by them, rather than by the government, as a means to their own mental education - a mode of strengthening their active faculties, exercising their judgement, and giving them a familiar knowledge of the subjects with which they are thus left to deal.

(quoted in Hopkins 1980:6)

Returning to contemporary commentators, many endorse the merits of participation which volunteering provides. As Nielsen (1983:366) sees it, the third sector serves as a humanising force in every sphere of American society "by providing outlets for the nearly universal impulse to altruism . . . the means of expression for all those spiritual, social and creative needs of individuals that government, the army, the office, the store, the factory and the farm cannot satisfy." By affording opportunities for personal involvement, the voluntary sector "becomes the cement that binds our society together" (Jordan 1983:402). Another merit of involvement is that it can overcome alienation by allowing ordinary people to have a greater say in decisions affecting their lives (Gladstone 1979; Hinton & Hyde 1980-1; Gerard 1983).

Support for voluntary participation has also come from the statutory side. Various reports have indicated the possibility and desirability of weaving the various strands of voluntary action into the fabric of social welfare provision. The Seebohm Report (1968) expressed the view that it would become necessary for local authorities to enlist the services of volunteers to complement the teams of professional workers. A similar stance was taken by the Aves Report (1969) which also recommended the formation of a national volunteer centre to co-ordinate and encourage the use of volunteers in social services. More recently the Barclay Report (1982) also pressed the case for volunteers. The distinctive contribution of voluntary workers in the personal social services is explored and evaluated by Darvill & Munday (1984).

How do volunteers themselves view their involvement? A cluster of contributors in Hatch (1983) provides a good overview of volunteers and their various motives. Regarding motivation, Handy (1988:31) observes that "the calculus is personal to each one of us." Research by Sherrott (1983) supports this view: "No simple classifying of explanations can do justice to the complexity of life experiences that have, for all our volunteers, resulted in volunteering" (Sherrott 1983:139). Respondents in Sherrott's (1983) study listed tangible benefits such as making friends, providing leisure activity and employment benefits, in addition to offering moral and normative explanations for their involvement, e.g., the belief that you should help your neighbour.

These findings are in broad agreement with those of Qureshi et al (1983) who, in a study of forty helpers in a community care scheme also discovered "mixed motives" for volunteering.

In the arena of self-help, participation is of a special kind. Self-help organizations involve "groups of people who feel they have a common problem and have joined together to do something about it" (Richardson & Goodman 1983:139). The role of the person who has already lived through the experience is considered critical for helping others (Gartner & Riessman 1977). Self-help groups facilitate this process. Alcoholics Anonymous (AA), founded in 1934 by a Newark salesman, William Wilson (Robinson 1979), is probably the best known example. Legions of individuals have benefitted from the "12 Steps" recovery programme of the AA. "No amount of money could buy the caring relationship of one human being for another that exists within all chapters of AA, nor could any government bureau ever do the job so effectively" (Rockefeller 1983:358). Despite this generous praise, some cavil with the AA's "spiritual" approach. To facilitate these dissenters, a new organization - SOS (Secular Organizations for Sobriety, popularly known as Save Our Selves) has been founded by James Christopher which offers "a friendly alternative" to AA (Christopher 1991:4).

"Recovery", the oldest self-help organization in the mental health field, this year celebrates the centennial of the birth of its founder, Dr. Abraham Low (Sachnoff 1991). In more recent times the enormous growth of self-help groups has become "the focus of increasing interest, arising in part from the simple fact of their proliferation" (Richardson & Goodman 1983:1).

Although this brief overview of voluntary participation is not intended to cover the topic in a comprehensive manner, none the less it is sufficient to establish that the participatory aspect of voluntarism can be beneficial both to volunteers themselves and to the organizations in which they offer their services.

Summary

This chapter began by focussing on definitions of voluntary organizations. It established that, due to the tremendous diversity in the voluntary sector, an overall neat, concise definition proves elusive.

Difficulties in organizational classification were reviewed, both in relation to organizations in general, and also concerning the nonprofit sector. In the absence of "one best way", a contingency approach to classification of voluntary organizations is considered most appropriate, i.e., one which fits the particular situation under review. Classification of Irish voluntary organizations is presented later in chapter 7.

Some theoretical perspectives on the sector were then presented. Two major economic theories explaining the existence of the voluntary sector in society were reviewed, namely Weisbrod's (1977) "public goods" theory and Hansmann's (1980) "contract failure" approach. Taking on board Salaman's (1987) reservations about these two theories, given the dominance of public funding in the sector, his own theory of the voluntary sector was examined. Another alternative to the conventional theory of nonprofit formation, put forward by James (1987), was also reviewed. Cumulatively these approaches show that it is necessary to take both demand and supply side theories into account when trying to understand why voluntary organizations exist.

Finally the functions of the voluntary sector were reviewed, covering seven broad areas - consumer choice; specialisation; cost effectiveness; flexibility; innovation; advocacy and participation.

This overview of the nonprofit sector has provided an understanding of important aspects of voluntary action at a general level, as part of the wider context of the main fieldwork. Next, as the fieldwork for the research was undertaken in Ireland, the Irish dimension of the study is introduced.

Part II
THE IRISH DIMENSION

3 Ireland: A Socio-Economic Overview

Ireland occupies a singular place among the nations, and this singularity manifests itself in various ways. . . . Half way between the developed countries and those which are striving with increasing difficulty to industrialise, Ireland tends to defy classification. (Peillon 1982:1)

Part Two of the research focuses on the Republic of Ireland, providing some general background data, in addition to information on the Irish voluntary sector. To set the study of Irish voluntary organizations in its broader context, this chapter looks at socio-economic data, bearing in mind that voluntary organizations are part of a wider system and are "inescapably dependent on their environment" (Kramer 1981:289). Also, in line with the overall conceptual framework of viewing organizations as open systems interacting with their environment (Daft 1986; Kast & Rosenzweig 1985), it is necessary to examine the context in which voluntary organizations operate as it is relevant to their management, as well as to issues of control and accountability. (These aspects are detailed later in chapters 5, 6 and 7).

To begin this chapter, basic demographic data are presented, followed by an economic review. Next some social inequalities are considered. The chapter concludes with a brief overview of Irish religious and political values as these also can impact on the operational climate of voluntary organizations.

Ireland: demographic facts

The Republic of Ireland is a small country with a relatively low population. A recent publication by the Central Statistics Office (CSO 1988), Population and Labour Force Projections 1991 - 2021, shows that this country had a population of 3.541 million in 1986 (CSO 1988:6). Slightly under half of the total (46 per cent) was less than 25 years of age (CSO 1988:41), indicating that Ireland has a young population which, in turn, has implications for voluntary organizations involved in youth work.

Population projections, compared with the base of 3.54 million for 1986 and assuming net outward migration of 25,000 per annum in 1986-1996 and 20,000 per annum in 1996-2001, suggest a slight downward trend to 3.47 million in 2001 (CSO 1988). While the annual outward migration figure appears high, it reflects reality as the estimated annual rate for the 1986-1996 period was equal to the average estimated for the three most recent years available (CSO 1988:15).

Based on the same assumptions, the dependency ratio is projected to fall from 0.66 in 1986 to 0.51 in 2001 (CSO 1988:27), due essentially to the decline in the young dependency ratio, heralding a striking middle-ageing of the population by the turn of the century. Although the old dependency ratio (relating those 65 and over to those aged 15-64) is projected to decline from 0.18 in 1986 to 0.17 in 2001, the population in the 65 and over group is estimated to increase from 384.4 thousand in 1986 to 395.1 thousand in 2001. In the context of voluntary organizations, this projected increase needs to be considered by groups dealing with the elderly.

Again using the same medium migration assumption, the labour force is projected to grow by 62,000 between 1986 and 1996 (CSO 1988:37). This will place severe demands on the need for job creation and further exacerbate the present acute unemployment problem which is detailed in the next section.

The Irish economy

By international standards, Ireland is not a poor country, ranking twenty fourth among 120 countries surveyed by the World Bank (1989) in its World Bank Development Report 1989. This Report shows that Irish gross national product (GNP) per capita reached 6,120 dollars during 1987, putting Ireland slightly ahead of Spain (6,010 dollars) in the league table of international living standards. Ireland's national income per head of population was sufficiently

40

high to place it among those economies categorised as high income economies, by world standards.

However, if the analysis is confined to the European Community (EC) arena, Ireland's position is not so favourable as it ranks near the end of the EC league ahead of only Spain, Portugal and Greece (World Bank 1989). Britain, in comparison, had a per capita GNP of 10,420 dollars (World Bank 1989). So it seems fair to conclude that "by European standards Ireland's level of economic development is modest" (Commission on Social Welfare [CSW] 1986:78). A review of Ireland's internal economy now follows which reveals a lower level of economic prosperity than the global comparisons cited above might suggest.

At present the Irish economy is burdened by two major difficulties - debt and unemployment. In 1976, Ireland's indebtedness amounted to 3.6 billion pounds, a ratio of 78.2 per cent of GNP (National Income and Expenditure 1985). In the succeeding twelve years, a further 21 billion pounds was added to this figure so that by the end of 1988 the national debt had reached almost 25 billion pounds, a ratio of 134 per cent of GNP (Central Bank 1989). The cost of servicing this debt is a major drain on government resources. The Budget Book (1989) provides some comparative figures. In 1976 the national debt pre-empted one-sixth of the government's day-to-day spending on goods and services. By 1985 the increased level of debt servicing had risen to one quarter of government outlay. At this level almost all income tax revenue (93.5 per cent) was destined for debt servicing.

Recent figures issued by the Central Bank (1992:11) indicate a total exchequer borrowing requirement (EBR) for 1992 of 592 million pounds or 2.4% of GNP, which represents an increase of 91 million pounds over the 1991 out-turn. Future prospects are not encouraging either, as the Central Bank predicts that, "looking beyond 1992, a number of factors seem likely to produce an uncomfortably large opening position for the EBR next year"(Central Bank 1992:7).

By pre-empting an ever-increasing share of current government outlay, escalating debt service payments deny cash to other areas of government spending. The debt crisis has heralded a period of stringent cutbacks by successive governments in recent years. Yet, despite these efforts to curtail spending, the debt crisis remains unsolved (Central Bank 1992). This debt problem and the related cutbacks in government spending also have implications for the Irish voluntary sector, in particular for the many voluntary organizations which rely on statutory funding to finance their operations.

Turning to the second major problem, unemployment, the number out of work at the end of July 1989 stood at 230,000 (CSO 1989). Subsequent efforts to reduce this very high rate of unemployment have yielded negative results. In fact, by July 1992, the position had deteriorated even further when the CSO figures showed that the number out of work had risen to 289,200, accounting for over 17% of the workforce (Boland 1992). This means that Ireland's registered unemployment level is the highest in the EC which has an overall unemployment rate of 9.5% (Canniffe 1992).

In a challenging discussion on unemployment and its implications within a global context, O Murchu (1987:177) reminds us of the human reality behind the statistics when he states that "unemployment is about people and not jobs". He compares the experience of being jobless to "a form of death" (O Murchu 1987:168) and uses the Kubler-Ross (1969) grieving model as a useful method of understanding the plight of the unemployed. These general observations obviously apply also in an Irish context. The personal trauma of unemployment and its ripple effect on family life and the wider society all have implications for the voluntary sector which is called upon to address various demands emanating from the jobs crisis. The voluntary group Support, started in an unemployment black spot in Cork city five years ago and now providing a range of services for the local unemployed, is just one example of a voluntary sector response to this major problem (Hand 1992).

The continuing mass unemployment also poses considerable financial burdens on the Exchequer. To put it in perspective, the Commission on Social Welfare (CSW 1986:79) notes that "in 1985, the total estimated annual cost of the main unemployment payments is 629 million pounds, second in magnitude only to old age pensions." The financial impact of high unemployment is simultaneously to increase expenditure on the relevant payments, and to reduce the taxation base from which these payments can be financed. So, obviously, it has a negative impact on the national debt.

The demographic projections reviewed earlier showed that an increase in the labour force is forecast in the 1986-1996 period. Therefore it is unrealistic to assume any significant decline in unemployment. Rather, its upward curve is likely to continue unabated, creating further pressures on the already over-stretched public purse. In addition it has major social implications, as indicated previously. Both the fiscal and social aspects of unemployment can impact on the Irish voluntary sector in terms of the drain on state funding and creating demands for relevant services to the unemployed.

Social inequality

Rottman et al (1982) undertook a major study relating to the distribution of income in the Republic of Ireland. They concluded that "social class differences are so deeply implanted in Irish society as to be self-perpetuating" (Rottman et al 1982:181). The study shows that income and living standards are clearly linked to class position, as their analysis of 1973 data indicates that direct income of heads of households in large proprietor households was over three times the direct income in unskilled working-class households (Rottman et al 1982:77). At the conclusion of their report they note that by 1978 "the distribution of income as we have described it for 1973 remains valid. . . . Prospects for basic changes in the 1980s are rendered almost nil by social group differentials in educational participation" (Rottman et al 1982:181).

A number of studies comment on this differential in education by social group. For instance Clancy (1983) has shown that educational participation rates vary considerably according to social class position, despite efforts to reduce inequalities by introducing "free" schooling at secondary level and a grant system at third level, as discussed by Barlow (1981). Whelan & Whelan (1984) suggest that the educational system generates a social structure with little opportunity for social mobility. "The current middle class domination of the upper levels of secondary and of all third level education . . . needs to be challenged" according to Rottman et al (1982:182), while the Commission on Social Welfare (CSW 1986:91) concludes that "the educational system is, in effect, a gatekeeper to social classes".

Poverty is another issue closely related to social class and unemployment and "is a major part of the present Irish reality" according to Reynolds & Healy (1988:5) in their introduction to the proceedings of a major conference on poverty. The Commission on Social Welfare (CSW) refers to an earlier conference on the same theme held in Kilkenny in 1971 and notes that "it constituted a watershed. It was at this conference that poverty in Ireland was "rediscovered" and subsequently became the subject for public and political debate" (CSW 1986:26). The title of Kennedy's (1981a) book *One Million Poor* indicates the magnitude of the problem, in an overall population of 3.5 million. A more recent study undertaken by the Economic and Social Research Institute (ESRI) on behalf of the Combat Poverty Agency provides evidence to endorse this title.

> The results, based on data collected from some 3,300 households and 8200 individuals, reveal a range and depth of financial poverty that is alarming in a society that has long claimed to be concerned about inequality. (Combat Poverty Agency 1988:i)

As poverty is a relative term, that study used a poverty-line approach, with cut-off points of 32, 42 and 48 pounds per week for a single person. In a summary of its findings it is stated that

> the Agency is of the opinion that anyone living on incomes below any of these three lines is in poverty. This means that at least one in three of the population is now living in financial poverty. (Combat Poverty Agency 1988:ii)

These findings have been disputed by politicians and other commentators. For instance, Barrett (1989) is of the opinion that the report overestimates the level of poverty by not including non-cash benefits. However, the authors of the original report refute Barrett's argument, saying that he did not understand the issues involved (Callan et al 1989).

The Combat Poverty report identifies the three main groupings vulnerable to poverty as being: households headed by the unemployed; families with several children, and farming households. It notes that "the first key issue that emerges is the incontrovertible relationship between unemployment and poverty" (Combat Poverty Agency 1988:vii) as the findings show that one third of all households at the 50 per cent poverty line (based on a percentage of the average industrial income) were headed by an unemployed person. This extensive level of poverty has implications for the voluntary sector, particularly for voluntary organizations which deal with the alleviation of poverty, e.g., the Society of St. Vincent de Paul and the Catholic Social Service Conference (CSSC).

So far, this chapter has reviewed demographic, economic and social aspects of Irish society, indicating how they can impact on the voluntary sector. The next section takes a brief look at religious and political values in Ireland.

Some Irish values

Fogarty (1984), in his introduction to the Irish report of the European value systems study (EVSS) comments that

> Ireland is different from other European countries. . . . But the difference is largely in a   conservative direction: conservative in religion, in morality, in politics, in views on work and marriage and family.
>
> (Fogarty et al 1984:2)

Some of these values are now explored. On religion, Inglis (1987), in a study of the Catholic Church in Ireland, notes that

> what makes the Republic of Ireland different from other Western European societies is the high level of adherence to the Roman Catholic Church. More than nine in ten of the population identify themselves as Church members and of these more than eight in ten attend Mass at least once a week.
>
> (Inglis 1987:11)

The findings in the EVSS study are similar: they show that 95 per cent of the whole population is Catholic, compared to 57 percent for "all Europe" (Fogarty et al 1984:125). Peillon (1982:113) comments that "the Catholic Church has unambiguously declared its interest in certain sectors such as education and social policy." So it is evident that this Church has been and still is a powerful force in Irish society. Its significant role in relation to voluntary organizations is discussed in the next chapter.

In the area of politics "Irish people . . . are much more likely than Europeans in general to identify themselves as being on the political right" (Fogarty et al 1984:68). Fianna Fail and Fine Gael are the two main political parties in the Republic of Ireland. Peillon (1982:120) notes that Fianna Fail, the biggest political party, "appears to receive support from almost all social forces in Ireland." In the context of social legislation, Curry (1980:5) comments that "the differences in social policy between Labour and Conservatives in Britain appear to be much greater than between Fianna Fail and Fine Gael in Ireland." He echoes an earlier observation by Coughlan (1966:4) who points out that "the political parties have differed in emphasis on social service policy, not in basic principles."

Summary

This chapter provides some socio-economic data on Ireland. It records that the Republic of Ireland has a population of just over 3.5 million which is projected to remain fairly static, assuming that present rates of outward migration continue. Economically, while Ireland rates comfortably by global standards, it tumbles towards the bottom in the EC league. Currently, the Irish economy is labouring under a large national debt and chronic high unemployment. Both factors have implications for the Irish voluntary sector in relation to government funding for the sector and demands for relevant services.

4 Voluntary Organizations in Ireland

The broad objective of this chapter is to present an overview of the Irish voluntary sector. The opening section briefly traces voluntary action in Ireland over the past two centuries in order to explore the background to its present operation. Then the voluntary sector, as it currently functions, is described. This includes a dual classification of voluntary organizations, followed by an assessment of some of the Irish sector's strengths and weaknesses. Next, the focus is on those involved in volunteering. Finally, voluntary/statutory relationships are investigated.

Voluntary action in Ireland: a brief history

Voluntary action is not new in Ireland. As Kennedy (1981:88-9) observes:

> Ireland has never been without a very impressive vigorous voluntary service. . . . Historically, if not statistically, there is plenty of evidence of neighbourliness in Ireland through the generations.

Various writers such as Brody (1974) refer to the prevalence of "cooring" in rural Ireland. In his study of change and decline in the west of Ireland, Brody explains that "cooring" is in fact a nineteenth century anglicisation of the Irish word "comhar" which means co-operation. He continues:

> Neighbours once established in a "cooring" relationship looked to one another for help when their own household could not provide sufficient

47

labour for a task: when the harvest work was onerous or hurried, when the turf had to be hauled in a few fierce days. (Brody 1974:134-5)

Another Irish word, "meitheal" meaning "a working party" denotes a similar concept. Arensberg & Kimball (1968) refer to it in the context of a group of men or women acting together to perform a task like haymaking, threshing or spinning. Their study was undertaken in the late 1930s, but a more recent study of Irish rural families at the beginning of the 1970s found that mutual aid was still practised (Hannan & Katsiaouni 1977). It seems reasonable to conclude therefore that the people of rural Ireland were imbued with a spirit of providing voluntary assistance to one another. Kennedy (1989:1) observes that "until the 1960s the Irish economy was predominantly an agricultural one with a majority of families still rural based", thus providing a suitable milieu for voluntary action. Some of the fruits of this action prior to the foundation of the State in 1921 are now examined.

Voluntary organizations before 1921

In the last century, statutory provisions, based mainly on the Poor Law, were minimal. Binchy (1967:254) reports that, in the absence of state input, religious groups set up their own institutions "to rescue various types of people from the dreadful conditions in the workhouse" Writing in the 1860s, Taylor (1867) gives numerous examples of specialised institutions set up by religious orders, catering for orphans, lunatics, the blind and the deaf.

Voluntary efforts were not confined to the Church. Dublin's oldest charity, now known as The Sick and Indigent Roomkeepers Society, was founded in 1790 and still functions, although on a much smaller scale. Tutty (1959) gives an interesting account of its work which sought to assist "persons who had never begged abroad, industrious mechanics, and indigent roomkeepers" (Tutty 1959:1).

Another major lay religious voluntary organization, the Society of Saint Vincent de Paul, also has roots in Ireland going back nearly 150 years. Its aim is to help those in need, irrespective of creed or class (Society of St. Vincent de Paul 1987). Today it has a membership of about 10,000, spread throughout the country (Society of St.Vincent de Paul 1987).

Many other charities developed during the nineteenth century. When George Williams (1902) published his register of Dublin charities in 1902, he listed 401. Home nursing was pioneered by a number of voluntary organizations. Money raised in Ireland to celebrate Queen Victoria's jubilee was used to establish the "Jubilee nurses" who visited the sick poor at home (Barrington

1987). Various religious orders pioneered similar home nursing schemes (Kennedy 1981).

New developments 1921-1960

The Legion of Mary, another major lay Catholic voluntary organization, was founded in 1921 by Frank Duff, a civil servant. He had been a member of the Society of Saint Vincent de Paul which, at that time, excluded female members from its ranks. When a group of women sought a more organised approach to their work of visiting the cancer wards in the South Dublin Union, Frank Duff scheduled a meeting for 7 September 1921. In effect, this was the first meeting of the Legion of Mary (Dunleavy 1989). The focus of the organization was to provide non-material relief by doing works of service (Legio Mariae 1969:222).

Dunleavy (1989:15) charts some of the early work of the Legion:

> The new group began work at once. . . . In July 1922 Sancta Maria, the first Legion hostel for street girls was opened. March 1923 saw the beginnings of the Legion's work in Bentley Place, a renowned red-light area. . . . In 1927 the Morning Star hostel for down-and-out men was opened and in 1930 the Regina Coeli hostel for unmarried mothers and their children.

The latter two hostels still operate today, run entirely by voluntary staff. The organization expanded both at home and overseas and now operates world-wide. Inglis (1987) lists its Irish membership at 10,000. The dominant female membership pattern established at the outset still remains.

An interesting expansion in the area of community development occurred in 1931 when Fr. John Hayes founded Muintir na Tire (the People of the Land) which developed into a movement for the social uplift of the Irish countryside (Rynne 1960).

Shortly after taking up office as Archbishop of Dublin in November 1940, Dr. John Charles McQuaid started the Catholic Social Service Conference (CSSC) early in 1941 to meet "the grave social needs of Dublin's poor for food, fuel and clothing in the grim conditions that had developed since the beginning of the 1939 War" (Burke-Savage 1965:303). The CSSC still plays a prominent, although slightly different, role today (CSSC 1988).

Archbishop McQuaid also took other initiatives during his term of office. Burke-Savage (1965) highlights how he encouraged various orders of nuns and brothers to establish or improve on existing facilities for the elderly, the

49

mentally handicapped, the deaf and the blind. This shows the archbishop's tremendous reliance at that time on Church-based voluntary organizations for the provision of social services.

Voluntary ventures 1960 onwards

The early 1960s saw the initiation, entirely by voluntary effort, of an important social experiment, the Kilkenny Social Services. It provided a comprehensive community-based service in the area (Kennedy 1981), and was started by the local Catholic bishop, Dr. Birch.

Costello (1985) documents another new voluntary venture begun in 1968 by Sr. Concilio, a Sister of Mercy, in a disused convent dairy! Its aim is to rehabilitate alcoholics, using Glasser's (1975) reality therapy as its approach (Costello 1985). A custom-built home was opened in Athy in 1973. Since its inception, over 16,000 people have been treated at the Athy centre. Due to the dramatic increase in the numbers at Athy, another centre was opened in County Limerick in 1976 and the Northern Ireland Health Authorities helped fund a third centre in Newry, County Down in 1982.

Curry (1980) notes developments in the voluntary sector from the late 1960s onwards. He comments: "Despite the improvement in the provision of statutory social services the role of voluntary organizations in the social services field has not diminished. In fact there has been an upsurge in the activity of such bodies in recent years" (Curry 1980:13). Examples cited include FLAC (Free Legal Advice Centres) established in 1969 and ALLY, set up in 1971 to assist single mothers. The Simon Community and the Samaritans established bases in Dublin in 1969 and 1970 respectively, modelled on their British counterparts. ALONE, an organization to meet the needs of the elderly in Dublin, was set up in 1977 by William Bermingham, a Dublin fireman (Bermingham & O'Cuanaigh 1978).

Voluntary self-help groups are not new in Ireland. Well known groups such as the AA (Alcoholics Anonymous) have been operating here for many years. In recent times there has been a noticeable upsurge in new self-help groups. Many of these are ailment based, helping sufferers of widespread disorders such as depression, estimated to have 20,000 sufferers for whom the AWARE organization caters. Also support is offered to those inflicted with rarer diseases such as arthrogryposis, a rare neuromuscular disorder, or M E (myalgic encephalomyelitis), a difficult disease to diagnose. Female interests are well catered for through groups such as AIMS (Association for Improvement in the Maternity Services); infertility, miscarriage and caesarean support groups; WHBA (Women Hurt By Abortion); and AFTERCARE for women who have placed children for adoption.

Other groups such as the Bethany support group for the bereaved which was established in 1984, and Beginnings Experience for those who are separated, are there to assist people cope with various personal traumas.

Historical summary

This brief overview of voluntary effort shows the considerable contribution made by both Church-based and lay voluntary organizations in the past and indicates a long tradition of voluntary action which is still active in contemporary Irish society.

Moving from the distant and more recent past to the present, the current contribution of Irish voluntary organizations is now described, in order to indicate their impact on Irish society and thereby establish their significance as an important area of research.

Irish voluntary organizations: the contemporary scene

Difficulties in detailing the current scope of voluntary activity in Ireland can be gathered from the pertinent observation made by the NSSB (1982:12) that "information on the overall extent and effectiveness of voluntary services in Ireland is surprisingly patchy". Butler, a former information officer with the NSSB, starts on a more optimistic note when he declares that "there are thousands of voluntary organizations in the Republic of Ireland. . . . Hundreds of thousands of Irish people devote some of their free time to working with these voluntary organizations" (Butler 1981:16). However, he also observes that "in reality, the voluntary sector, in the sense of an identifiable and quantifiable entity, can scarcely be said to exist" (Butler 1981:16). Bearing these constraints in mind, the available information on the sector, however "patchy", is now presented.

Classification of Irish voluntary organizations

The Irish voluntary sector "is made up of a large number of diverse bodies and organizations concerned with a range of issues, organised in a multiplicity of ways" (Lee 1987:1). This heterogeneity and the fact that few systematic studies of the Irish voluntary sector as a whole have been undertaken, pose

51

University
of Ulster
LIBRARY

added difficulties in devising a single classification of Irish voluntary organizations, in addition to those discussed earlier in chapter 2, in a more general context. Therefore, in line with the Wolfenden Committee's (1978) suggestion of having different patterns of classification for different purposes, a two-pronged approach to classification is used in order to capture (a) the broad scope of Irish voluntary sector activities, with a view to identifying what they do (Brenton 1985; Handy 1988); and (b) organizational aspects of the sector in Ireland, to indicate the range of organizational types involved.

Irish voluntary organizations grouped by activities

As part of its preliminary work on the proposed White Paper and Charter for Irish voluntary organizations (PESP 1991), the Department of Social Welfare (DSW) uses five broad headings to categorise voluntary activity in Ireland (DSW 1992:2-3). These may be summarised as follows:

- Community development/local development organizations are involved in mobilising the community to achieve some particular goal for its common good.
- Mutual support and self-help organizations are concerned with a wide range of activities, from sharing advice and information, providing services and support networks, to lobbying for improved state provision.
- Resource and service providing organizations are engaged in providing services within the community in response to recognised social problems.
- Representative and co-ordinating organizations have an advocacy role. They undertake research and seek to inform public opinion, influence policy-making and change existing legislation.
- Funding organizations provide back-up support to individual voluntary groups.

This indicates the wide scope of voluntary activity in Ireland and the classification is in line with that used by Faughnan (1990) in relation to the Irish voluntary sector. The different types of organizations involved in undertaking these activities are now reviewed.

Irish voluntary bodies grouped by organizational type

O'Mahoney (1985:159-62) presents a six-fold classification of organizational types in the Irish voluntary sector. She distinguishes between national and local voluntary bodies, in line with Johnson (1978), and for each of these two groupings identifies three categories:

- voluntary body
- professional voluntary body
- intermediary body

This gives a total of six categories. Each one is now considered in more detail and some examples are provided in the various categories.

(i) National voluntary body

This type of organization relies on volunteers to achieve its aims, but may employ a small administrative staff. Examples include the Society of St. Vincent de Paul, with 980 branches and a total active membership of 10,000 spread throughout the country (O'Leary 1988:37); the Catholic Marriage Advisory Council (CMAC) which has 55 centres in Ireland staffed by 1,327 counsellors (CMAC 1987:4).

(ii) National professional voluntary body

Organizations run mainly by professionally employed staff are in this category, with voluntary input primarily on management committees and fundraising. Childcare agencies such as the Irish Society for the Prevention of Cruelty to Children (ISPCC) and Barnardo's are examples. The term "non-statutory welfare body" is used by the NSSB (1982:27) to refer to such bodies which it includes as part of the voluntary system (NSSB 1982:9). A similar categorisation is referred to by the National Economic and Social Council (NESC 1987:38).

(iii) National intermediary voluntary body

Umbrella-type organizations whose main beneficiaries are other affiliated voluntary bodies form this group. For example the National Association for the Mentally Handicapped of Ireland (NAMHI) has almost 150 affiliated organizations (O'Morain 1989), while the National Youth Council of Ireland (NYCI) represents over half a million young Irish people in 46 voluntary bodies.

These three are national groupings. The NSSB's directory of national voluntary organizations (NSSB 1985) which lists over 450 national bodies ranging over the three categories, indicates the combined strength of the voluntary sector at national level.

(iv) Local voluntary body

Smaller voluntary groups providing services for a particular client group form this category. A local care of the aged committee is a typical example.

(v) Local professional voluntary body

Organizations in this category are similar to those in group (ii) except that their activities are confined to a specific area. Western Care, which provides services for the mentally handicapped in the County Mayo area is an example.

(vi) Local intermediary body

Organizations in this group focus on the co-ordination of the voluntary sector at a local level. Larger social service councils such as the one described by Kennedy (1981) are representative of this category.

While it is recognised that both these classifications, covering activities and organizational types, are rather broad, it is considered that they do have the virtue of putting some order on the "plethora of voluntary bodies" (Kennedy 1981:106) operating in Ireland. In addition, the classifications indicate the tremendous diversity of undertakings, in terms of activities and organizational types. Yet, all these organizations, irrespective of their size or activity, share a common need for management as "managers must manage organizations in order to accomplish their objectives" (Baird, post & Mahon 1990:5). (This management aspect is discussed in more detail in the next chapter.)

Strengths and weaknesses of Irish voluntary action

Irish voluntary bodies, in common with organizations in other sectors of the economy, have both strengths and weaknesses. Their contribution to Irish society is highlighted by the CSSC (1988:11) when it notes:

> The State has always depended on the voluntary sector to operate social supports at local levels, to cater for the needs of particular groups and to do a whole range of activities which the State either could not or would not do.

The National Social Service Board (NSSB 1986:16-7) identifies a more specific list of positive attributes in relation to Irish voluntary endeavour which can be summarised as follows:

- voluntary bodies are adept at identifying needs and offering appropriate means of meeting them, often providing a degree of choice in services
- their flexibility enables them to respond quickly to changing needs
- by pioneering new services they can contribute to social change
- they stimulate self-help initiatives
- at a community level they harness resources both in terms of funding and skills and enhance social awareness.

Some concrete examples of these attributes are now presented. Regarding the identification of needs, a survey of the elderly living alone, undertaken by the Society of St. Vincent de Paul (Power 1980), identified sub-standard housing as a problem. The Society responded by initiating a building programme for the elderly. As a result, by 1987 200 people were housed in developments built by the Society (Society of St. Vincent de Paul 1987:6). In response to other identified needs the same Society has set up a pilot project for disadvantaged youth in Dublin's inner city; it has started pre-schools for the children of travellers and has instigated a major home management programme for mothers of low-income families (Society of St. Vincent de Paul 1987). Children at Risk in Ireland (CARI) is another example of a group started to meet an identified need. It was launched in September 1989 in response to the major increase (66 per cent) in confirmed cases of child abuse (Cummins 1989) and aims to provide a range of support services for those affected.

Responses to the present AIDS epidemic indicate how voluntary organizations can show flexibility in addressing new areas of need. By March 1992 there were 293 confirmed cases of AIDS in Ireland and a further 1,265 had been diagnosed as having the HIV virus (Kennedy 1992). This disease has posed new challenges for existing agencies in the voluntary sector. For instance the CSSC set up an AIDS project "to facilitate various responses to the problems associated with AIDS" (CSSC 1988:20). This project is trying to co-ordinate the various other groups involved and helps to train volunteers working with AIDS victims. CSSC has also set up a befriending group whose members offer support to sufferers (O'Sullivan 1990).

Irish Voluntary organizations are also credited with pioneering roles. "Homestart" is one example. It is a novel scheme started by a former social worker which offers support to mothers who are housebound with young children. The first pilot scheme has started in the Blanchardstown area of

Dublin (Irish Times 1989). Another innovative move was the opening of an MS care centre which offers MS sufferers and those who care for them a much-needed break (O'Morain 1989a). The concept of providing for the needs of both sufferers and carers is a new departure.

The previous section referred to the many support groups which exist in Ireland for those with a common interest or ailment. There is a very discernible upward trend in this self-help area in recent years.

As detailed earlier in chapter 3, the severe unemployment problem has prompted action at community level in many areas. The fortunes of sixteen community groups are recounted in a report published by the Independent Poverty Action Movement (IPAM 1986). The CSSC states that a fundamental principle of its work is "to empower people in deprived communities to do things for themselves" (CSSC 1988:32). It has established schemes in two deprived areas of Dublin, Blanchardstown and Neilstown, to further this aim. An earlier study by Lavan (1981) details developments in community social services in Tallaght, another deprived area in County Dublin.

The foregoing provides examples of the perceived positive attributes of Irish voluntary organizations, as identified by the NSSB (1986). Other commentators have made similar positive observations about the Irish voluntary sector. For instance, the Task Force on the Child Care Services, in its final report, comments that "voluntary organizations have been established to meet new needs. . . . In fact, in many instances, very useful services are more effectively provided by voluntary organizations than by statutory agencies" (Task Force on the Child Care Services 1980:93).

Curry (1980) highlights the limits of State intervention which he sees as providing a niche for voluntary action.

> Irrespective of the number of services provided by the state there will always be cases which defy help channelled through official agencies. Voluntary bodies can provide the flexibility to pick up such cases. (Curry 1980:215)

The important role of voluntary organizations as pressure groups "which focus attention on existing needs or gaps in existing services" is also noted by Curry (1980:215). Numerous examples of such pressure groups exist. For example CARE (Campaign for the Care of Deprived Children) was established to promote the welfare of these children and actively seeks improvements in children's services and legislation. The problems of homelessness are tackled by Focuspoint, while Threshold seeks relevant reforms of both law and housing policy.

Other service organizations such as the CSSC and the Society of Saint Vincent de Paul also adopt an advocacy role in addition to their main focus. "Through speaking out on issues and lobbying for change, the agency's priority is to raise the level of public awareness on issues of poverty, unemployment and social welfare" (CSSC 1988:37). The Society of St. Vincent de Paul makes an annual pre-budget submission to the government, "speaking on behalf of the poor who themselves have no voice",(Society of St. Vincent de Paul 1987:5) and the CSSC prepares a similar document, in an effort to influence government policy.

In addition to having positive attributes, the Irish voluntary sector is also seen to have some shortcomings: "It would be wrong to suggest, however, that the voluntary sector is without failures, faults and weaknesses" (NSSB 1986:17). Lack of co-ordination is one difficulty which is highlighted. According to Curry (1980:218):

> In general, voluntary bodies operate as free agents without any central direction. This situation may lead to the futile expenditure of energy, funds or skills which are in short supply. Duplication can easily arise.

The need for co-ordination is also emphasised in the Independent Poverty Action Movement report (IPAM 1986:23) and Kennedy (1981:33) notes that "lack of co-ordination was the salient feature of voluntary bodies in most communities". Reviewing constraints in the voluntary sector, Lee (1987:3) refers to fragmentation of services and "unhelpful competition between bodies for resources and public support". She suggests that "voluntary organizations need to start trusting one another a little more and pay somewhat more attention to the needs of their users than to ideological disputes and differences" (Lee 1987:6).

Another perceived shortcoming in the voluntary sector relates to patchy provision of services. The National Economic and Social Council (NESC) report on community care observes that "the level and pattern of voluntary services is very uneven, with some voluntary organizations/voluntary services prominent in some areas and absent in others" (NESC 1987:6-7). Some surveys endorse this aspect of uneven coverage. For instance Power's (1980) study of the elderly shows that 49 per cent of old people who live alone in the Republic do not receive regular visits from social service agencies, whether voluntary or statutory (Power 1980:87). (This finding highlights the limitations of statutory provisions also - separate figures for voluntary and statutory involvement are not provided in that study.)

Whelan & Vaughan (1982) carried out a survey on a national random sample of the elderly. Regarding the availability of aid in the case of illness, for those living alone "only about 0.7 per cent mentioned help from a state social service agency and 0.3 per cent help from a voluntary organization. Indeed the latter was not mentioned at all in rural areas" (Whelan & Vaughan 1982:91). Once again this shows the unevenness of both statutory and voluntary provisions.

The NSSB (1982:17) makes a more generalised negative comment in relation to voluntary organizations:

> The reality is not uniformly good. For example it is argued that many voluntary organizations very quickly become institutionalised, that they become dependent on statutory grant aid, that they lose the ability to look critically at themselves and at the society with which they work.

To summarise this section, an appraisal of the Irish voluntary sector by various commentators suggests that it has both strengths and shortcomings at an operational level. Once again, these are factors which need to be taken into consideration in the management of voluntary organizations, as they are part of the wider system in which individual organizations operate.

Who is involved?

The Irish report of the European Value Systems Study (EVSS) by Fogarty et al (1984) provides information on the overall level of voluntary action in Ireland. The relevant details are provided in Tables 19 and 20 of the report (Fogarty et al 1984:179-84). Summarising the results, Fogarty comments:

> One person in five in the Republic as in Britain and Europe as a whole claims to be a voluntary worker, but the distribution of these volunteers across types is uneven and different from the European average. . . . Overall it is clear that much the largest part of voluntary activism in Ireland is concentrated in religious, charitable, and youth work.
>
> (Fogarty et al 1984:35-6)

Eight per cent of the Irish population does voluntary work for religious organizations, compared to an European average of 6 per cent; the figure for both welfare charity and youth work is 7 per cent here and 5 per cent and 3 per cent respectively for Europe as a whole (Fogarty et al 1984:179). Regarding age of volunteers, for Ireland, as for Britain there is some truth in the cliche that volunteers tend to be middle-aged and middle- class. . . Except in the case of youth work, people over 45 provide more than their share of organization activists. So do people educated to 19 or over, and especially "graduates" and professionals or managers.   (Fogarty et al 1984:36)

Similar observations have been made elsewhere. For instance the NSSB, in a discussion document on voluntary social services notes that "organised voluntary activity is still largely a middle class activity" (NSSB 1982:7). According to Peillon (1982) the term "middle class" may be used to designate a certain ensemble of characteristics one of which is "a tendency to join voluntary organizations" (Peillon 1982:30). Regarding the age of volunteers, a specific study of nearly 1,000 volunteers attached to the Kilkenny Social Services showed that "the highest proportion (43 per cent) are in the 40-60 age group"   (Kennedy 1981:96).

Voluntary / statutory relations

Tributes to the work of voluntary organizations have been paid by politicians at all levels. At the opening of a Clarecare Centre in Ennis in 1988, the former President of Ireland, Dr. Hillery said that the voluntary sector had a very important role to play in Irish society and he mentioned the sector's ability to identify local needs and organise appropriate responses (Quinlan 1988). Similar sentiments were expressed by the Minister for Social Welfare, Dr. Woods at the launch of the Centrecare social agency report in Dublin in the same year. He said he "firmly believed that Church bodies and voluntary groups had a major role to play in identifying and meeting social needs" (Yeates 1988:10).

Ireland's first woman President, Mary Robinson, who was sworn in on 3rd December 1990, showed considerable interest in the voluntary sector during her pre-election campaign (O'Faolain 1990). She substantiated this interest when elected to office by appointing Quintin Oliver, Director of the Northern Ireland Council for Voluntary Action, as a member of her Council of State (Duffy 1991). Another of her appointees, Donal Toolin, is a founder member of the voluntary group Forum of People with Disabilities (O'Keeffe 1991) and is himself confined to a wheelchair. In his capacity as a freelance journalist he contributes to the ongoing debate on the voluntary sector (e.g., see Toolin 1992).

In the past, many commentators have lamented the lack of a clear overall policy framework for voluntary organizations. For example, Butler (1981:16) noted that "there is no clearly enunciated social policy which spells out, among other things, precisely how voluntary organizations are meant to fit into the overall scheme of things". The NSSB made a similar observation: "No clear policy exists in the area of voluntary service or in the area of voluntary/statutory co-operation" (NSSB 1982:12), a point echoed more recently by Lee (1987):

> There has been no real attempt by successive Governments to translate their generally shared social policy aims into clearly defined, manageable objectives which would provide the basis for a framework within which the voluntary sector could plan and deliver its services in a coherent and co-ordinated way.
>
> (Lee 1987:2)

Various governments have given indications of good intent on the matter. The National Economic and Social Council (NESC) report on community care services states that "the value of voluntary services has repeatedly been stressed, notably by successive Ministers for Health and in official-reports throughout the 1960s" (NESC 1987:33). As far back as 1971, a government White Paper on Local Government reorganization clearly recognised the potential of voluntary organizations for local development and referred to the need for a partnership between voluntary and statutory authorities.

In 1979 the then Minister for Health referred to the intention of his department to draw up a policy document on the relationship between the Health Boards and social service councils in the provision of social services (Dail Debates 1979:374). A decade after the 1971 White Paper, the Fine-Gael/Labour coalition government's Programme for Government 1981-86 (1981) contained a commitment to a charter for voluntary services which would provide a framework for the relations between statutory and voluntary agencies. With the fall of that government, this charter did not materialise.

Another influential body, the CSSC, notes that concern about the statutory/voluntary relationship is not new:

> The relationship between the State and the voluntary sector has always been a difficult one. Often the State is in a position of dominance as the funding agent yet despite the responsibility and experience of the voluntary sector, rarely does the State consult it in policy decisions.
>
> (CSSC 1988:11)

Recent developments indicate that the present government is now prepared to address this issue. As mentioned previously, its Programme for Economic and Social Progress (PESP 1991) incorporates a specific proposal to this effect as the Programme's section on social reform acknowledges that closer links need to be developed with voluntary organizations. To enable this to occur, the government proposes a charter for voluntary social services in Ireland which will set out a clear framework for partnership between State and voluntary bodies (PESP 1991:24).

The Department of Social Welfare is currently preparing this charter, together with a White Paper outlining the government's proposals in the area. In June 1992, the then Minister for Social Welfare, Mr.Charles McCreevy, announced the setting up of an interdepartmental Task Force to assist in preparing these documents, in order to ensure "the active participation of all government departments who have a role in relation to the voluntary sector" (DSW 1992:2). In addition, he proposed the setting up of an Expert Group "drawn from people with wide experience of voluntary activity" (DSW 1992:3), as a means of facilitating consultation with the voluntary sector.

Future developments in this area of voluntary/statutory relationships will have considerable implications for voluntary sector management, as they will determine the wider climate in which voluntary organizations operate.

Summary

This chapter commenced by presenting a brief history of voluntary activity in Ireland. This established the long tradition of voluntary action by both church-based and lay voluntary organizations. An overview of the current position of voluntary organizations in Irish society was then presented. It was noted at the outset that detailed studies on the topic are scarce. The two broad classifications presented indicated the wide range of activities included in Irish voluntary action and the main organizational types in the voluntary sector. The need for management in all voluntary organizations, whatever their size or activity, was highlighted. The perceived strengths and shortcomings of this sector were also reviewed.

The limited evidence available indicates that Ireland has a voluntary sector comparable to that of Britain and Europe as a whole, but with more input in religious, charitable and youth sectors. Lastly it was seen that statutory/voluntary relationships posed difficulties in the past. One perceived major drawback, the absence of a general social policy framework, is now in the process of being addressed by the proposed voluntary charter and White

Paper on the voluntary sector being prepared by the Department of Social Welfare. This development, as it impacts on the broader operational context of voluntary action, can have implications for its management.

Part III now follows and is concerned with examining the literature relating to three broad areas - management, control and accountability - as a prelude to the field research which is focused on these areas in the context of the Irish voluntary sector.

Part III
MANAGEMENT, CONTROL & ACCOUNTABILITY

5 Management in Voluntary Organizations

The core purpose of this chapter is to explore some aspects of management in voluntary organizations. Before focussing on a nonprofit setting, organizations and their management are considered in a more general context. Attention is then directed to management in the voluntary sector. Finally, some characteristics of nonprofit organizations and their implications for management are reviewed.

Organizations and management

Organizations play a major and continuing role in the lives of all of us as "we live in an organizational world. Organizations of one form or another are a necessary part of our society and serve many important needs" (Mullins 1985:xi). Before progressing further in this discussion on organizations, the concept itself is clarified. One definition by Reeser & Loper (1978) has the merit of simplicity. As this duo sees it, "an organization is a collection of people who are joined together in some common bond" (Reeser & Loper 1978:9). The organizational theorist, Richard Daft (1986:9) couches his definition in the context of systems theory, viewing organizations as "social entities that are goal directed, deliberately structured activity systems with an identifiable boundary". How do these social groupings impact on our lives?

The all-pervading nature of organizations on modern life is graphically captured by Etzioni (1964:1):

We are born in organizations, educated by organizations, and most of us spend much of our lives working for organizations. We spend much of our leisure time paying, playing and praying in organizations. Most of us will die in an organization.

In effect, as Kast & Rosenzweig (1985:4) observe, this means that "all of us, except hermits, are involved in a variety of groups and organizations. . . . They are inextricably interwoven into our daily lives".

The second and related concern in this section is management. Organizations are set up with some purpose or goal in view. Just as , at a personal level, individuals have to manage their own affairs in order to achieve their objectives in life, "managers must manage organizations to accomplish their objectives" (Baird, Post & Mahon 1990:5). What exactly does management entail?

Definitions of management are plentiful. A widely-quoted and long-standing definition, attributed to the famous management philosopher Mary Parker Follet, views management as "the art of getting things done through other people". Gray & Smeltzer (1989:7) indicate the need for management in all types of organizations when they define it as

an authorised activity that is inherent in all formal organizations, whether they be business firms, government agencies, hospitals, churches, armies, universities, fraternities, or Girl Scout troops.

Another definition provided by Pearse & Robinson 1989:4) sees management as "the process of optimizing human, material and financial contributions for the achievement of organizational goals". The open systems nature of organizational life is acknowledged by Baird, Post & Mahon (1990:6) when they define management as "the process of setting and accomplishing goals through the use and coordination of human, technical, and financial resources within the context of the environment". Kreitner (1989:9) makes a similar point, referring to the need to take cognisance of "a changing environment" in the process of management. In addition, he stresses the need for management expertise in organizations, counselling that "a solid grounding in management is essential in successfully guiding today's large or small, profit or not-for-profit organizations through rapidly changing times" (Kreitner 1989:xxiii).

So far, it has been established that organizations are inexorably interwoven into our daily lives and that, in order to function, they need to be managed. This brings the topic of management to the fore. Prior to looking at management in a voluntary sector context, a brief overview of the development of management thought is provided, in order to get some measure of how the current focus on a systems and contingency approach evolved.

Management theory: a brief overview

Although the body of theory relating to management is of relatively recent origin, management at an operational level is not new. Baird, Post & Mahon (1990:xxviii) recount how "the basic principles of management had their beginnings in the birth of civilization, when people first began to live in groups and first sought to improve their lot in life". These authors cite as an example King Nebuchadnezzar of Babylon who, on deciding over 2,500 years ago to turn his desert kingdom into an oasis, had to co-ordinate human, technical and financial resources to accomplish his goal.

Another writer on management, Robbins (1988:30), using as examples the Egyptian pyramids and the Great Wall of China, also concludes that these ancient and remarkable achievements necessitated the process of management in their execution:

> Regardless of what managers were called at the time, someone had to plan what was to be done, organize people and materials to do it, lead and direct the workers, and impose some controls to ensure that everything was done as planned.

Yet, even though organizations and ideas about how to manage them have been around since antiquity, Hampton (1986:43) reports that developments in management theory are of relatively recent origin:

> Until the twentieth century, the legacy of management practice is far more in evidence than the legacy of management thought. . . . A body of writings on management began to take shape early in the twentieth century.

Even though the systematic study of management was far behind its practical implementation, judging by the "veritable mountain" (Kreitner 1989:53) of outpourings on the subject, management theorists have not been slow in making up the lost ground. Summing up the current situation, Kreitner (1989:55) concludes that "there is so much information on management theory and practice today that it is difficult, if not impossible, to keep abreast of it".

67

Next, some of the main threads from the various theories put forward over time are explored. The discussion divides into two parts, the diversified approaches which developed in the earlier part of the century and the more recent integrated approaches preferred.

Robbins (1988:32) tells us that "the first half of this century was a period of diversity in management thought". Four main approaches to management can be identified in this period - scientific, general administrative, behavioural and quantitative (Robbins 1988).

Scientific management was pioneered by Taylor (1911). Essentially, he sought production efficiencies by searching for "the one best way" to do each job. The general administrative theorists sought principles of management that applied to the entire organization. The most prominent of these theorists was Henri Fayol who designated management as a universal set of functions, specifically planning, organising, commanding, coordinating and controlling (Fayol [1916] 1949). Fayol's functions have withstood the test of time as "the classical functions still represent the most useful way of conceptualizing the manager's job" (Carroll & Gillen 1987:48). Max Weber's theory of bureaucracy, characterised by division of labour, a clearly defined hierarchy, detailed rules and regulations and impersonal relationships (Weber 1947), was another major administrative theory.

The study of management that focuses on human behaviour is categorised as being part of the behaviourist approach. Probably the most important contribution to this school emerged from Elton Mayo's Hawthorne studies which are detailed by Roethlisberger & Dickson (1939). Mayo's work led to a new emphasis on the human factor in the functioning of organizations as did later work in the 1950s and 1960s by behaviourists such as Chris Argyris (1957) and Douglas McGregor (1960).

Finally, in this period of diversity in management thought, there was the quantitative approach which is used in decision making and includes techniques such as linear programming and simulation (Reeser & Loper 1978).

A relevant analogy to these four approaches to management is the old Indian tale of the six blind men and the elephant, which is cited by Morgan (1986) to indicate the complexities of organizations. In essence it describes how each of the blind men touched a different part of the elephant, so that what they "saw" depended on where they stood, e.g., the man who touched the leg felt it was a tree, whereas the one who touched the side felt it was like a wall. Yet they were all touching the one elephant. Similarly, each of the four perspectives on management has validity, but is a limited view of a larger "animal".

The limitations in these diverse approaches led to efforts at developing a more unified framework, "beginning in earnest in the early 1960s" (Robbins

1988:43). Systems and contingency approaches represent these more recent perspectives on management (Kast & Rosenzweig 1985). The systems approach defines a system as "a set of interrelated and interdependent parts arranged in a manner that produces a unified whole" (Robbins 1988:44). An organization is seen as an open system as it "acquires inputs from the environment, transforms them and discharges outputs to the external environment" (Daft 1986:10). The need for inputs and outputs reflects the dependency on the environment. Its interrelated elements means that people and departments depend on one another and must work together (Kast & Rosenzweig 1985).

Formally defined, "the contingency approach is an effort to determine through research which managerial practices and techniques are appropriate in specific situations" (Kreitner 1989:75). This explains its alternative label of "situational management" (Lawrence & Lorsch 1967).

From this precis on the evolution of management thought it can be seen that it evolved "in bits and pieces" (Kreitner 1989:83) over the years. Earlier perspectives such as scientific management, behavioural, administrative and quantitative approaches, have been supplemented in more recent times by the two more modern approaches of systems and contingency theory.

This section has provided some general insights into organizations and their management, together with an overview of the development of management thought. Now management in the voluntary sector is explored.

Management in the voluntary sector

Voluntary organizations, in common with all other undertakings, are established with some purpose or goal in view. The achievement of this goal necessitates management. Although the previous section established that literature on the topic of management abounds, most of it relates to the business sector. In fact, "management as a process, profession and function was born in the commercial sector" (Zaltman 1979:122). Not surprisingly then, Cyert (1975:7) comments that management scholars "have tended to emphasize the business firm without looking for the possible transfer of knowledge." Even more recently, similar observations have been made. "Most management books and programs address the objectives of private profit-oriented organizations rather than nonprofit organizations" according to Grayson & Tompkins (1984:vii), while Stewart & Ranson (1988:13) comment that "in the field of management the private sector model dominates thinking".

However, there is evidence to suggest that the tide is turning, given the growing awareness of both the lack of management competence and the need for appropriate management in the voluntary sector. The Wolfenden Committee (1978) refers to management in the voluntary sector. Suggesting a five-yearly self examination of voluntary organizations, it observes that "one area in which such an operation might be particularly productive is that of management" (Wolfenden Committee 1978:191), diplomatically indicating the need for improvement in the area. This identified need had not been addressed some years later, according to Gerard (1983:3) who reported "indications . . . of complacency and a lack of awareness of the need to improve management competence".

About the same time, to address this perceived deficiency, ARVAC organised a conference on the theme of management in voluntary organizations, as "there were very few resources put into the management sphere, despite its evident importance" (Knight 1984:i). Similar concerns are expressed by Billis (1984:14) who suggests that "management is a vital missing link in voluntary sector research" and later refers to the genuine management complexity of voluntary agencies (Billis 1989:25). Another writer in the field of organization theory, who has contributed widely to the debate on the voluntary sector, postulates that "any wholesale rejection of the idea of management must be naive" (Handy 1988:19).

The catalogue of failures chronicled by Landry et al(1985) in their analysis of unsuccessful libertarian projects endorses this management deficiency. Their final assessment concludes: "we are in no doubt at all, there is a lot to be learned from management thinking" (Landry et al 1985:63). On a more positive note, Butler & Wilson (1990:161) consider that "since the mid 1980s the voluntary sector overall has moved away from concerns of its own survival and legitimacy to the more individualistic concerns of efficient and effective management of specific organizations".

In the US, concern has also been voiced about voluntary sector management. Van Til (1988:174) considers that "from the point of view of management authorities, the voluntary sector often appears to be a poor and weak sister". The romanticised role of the voluntary sector is referred to by Gardner (1979) which he feels confers on it a virtually faultless image. Personally he dissents from this view, opining that some organizations are so badly managed as to make a mockery of any good intention they might have had, thus agreeing with Vladeck (1976). Another contributor (Eisenberg 1983:317) endorses this criticism of the sector: "many social agencies and volunteer groups continue to serve their clients, old and new, as they have for years, irrespective of changing circumstances and the need for modern strategies and special skills".

70

There is evidence now that change is occurring. "Human service organizations in the current economy of scarce resources and efficiency-minded funding sources have come to realise the importance of good management" (Young 1985:xi). Texts have been produced on both sides of the Atlantic focussing specifically on management in the voluntary sector, e.g., Borst & Montana (1987), Butler & Wilson (1990), Cyert (1975), Grayson & Thompkin (1984), Mason (1984), McLaughlin (1986), Moyer (1983), Young (1985), Zaltman (1979).

In Britain the work of the Centre for Voluntary Organization at LSE is broadly in the field of organization and management. Also the Open University instituted a voluntary sector management programme in April 1988 with the aim of promoting the understanding and use of management principle and practice appropriate to the sector. According to its publicity pamphlet, the programme is seen as contributing to the understanding of managerial ideas and activity in "a hitherto neglected area".

To summarise, in view of the fact that all organizations, including nonprofits, have to be managed, management is now recognised as being important in the voluntary sector. Its neglect in the past is acknowledged. Progress in remedying this deficiency is now discernible, as there is a growing literature relating to voluntary sector management. Yet it is still modest in relation to other aspects of this sector. For instance Layton (1987:xv), in her annotated bibliography on philanthropy and voluntarism, observes that "from a disciplinary perspective, scholarship in philanthropy is dominated by history", and of over 1,600 works cited, merely six refer specifically to management.

In order to understand why "the task of managing a non-profit organization differs considerably from that of managing a for-profit organization" (McLaughlin 1986:22), some characteristics of the voluntary sector which set it apart from business are now examined.

Characteristics of nonprofit organizations

The relevant literature indicates that voluntary organizations exhibit certain characteristics which need to be considered in relation to their management. Gerard (1983:20) notes that "whilst management techniques developed for use in the commercial sector can be adapted for use in voluntary organizations, charities do exhibit a number of characteristics which, though not unique, require special consideration". It is claimed by Handy (1988:11) that whereas "it does not make any sense at all to try to formulate an all-embracing theory in practice for all voluntary organizations, nevertheless there are things in common". Business faculties now consider special courses in not-for-profit management "which implies that significant distinctions exist" (Newman & Wallender 1978:24). Therefore, the belief that business management concepts can be applied readily to not-for-profit enterprises needs qualification.

What are these "unique constraints and opportunities" (Butler & Wilson 1990:2) which arise in not-for-profit management? Mason (1984:21-2) presents a formidable list of fourteen distinguishing features, while Anthony & Young (1988:54) summarise their attributes under ten main headings. Many other writers present what they consider to be special features of the sector. Drawing on the above views and based on an analysis of the main characteristics highlighted by various authors, this writer has identified the following six broad areas which need to be considered in relation to management in the voluntary sector:

- the nonprofit nature of their operations
- a tendency to be service organizations
- two distinct management systems
- governance issues
- staffing patterns
- environmental characteristics.

Each one is now discussed in more detail. It should be noted at the outset that whereas all these characteristics are not unique to the voluntary sector, they do have a particular impact on management in the sector and are reviewed in that context.

The nonprofit nature of voluntary organizations

Profit is "the common measure of success, transcending boundaries of geography, language, currency and relative economic status" (Maloney 1989:467). This makes profit an extremely useful tool in management as it can give a broad indication of how successful a business organization is in achieving its mission. Nonprofit organizations, by their nature, fall outside the ambit of this guiding concept. The fact that such organizations do not have a profit and loss criterion with which to measure their overall performance is emphasised as one of their major distinguishing characteristics. Anthony & Young (1988:55-7) detail the advantages of the profit measure. To summarise their analysis, this measure:

- provides a single criterion for evaluation which serves as a focus for decision-making
- permits quantitative analysis of proposals, whereby inputs and outputs can be compared directly
- serves as a single broad measure of performance, incorporating many separate aspects
- facilitates decentralisation to individual managers whose performance can be measured in terms of their contribution to the overall goal of the organization
- enables comparison of performance between entities that are heterogeneous functions, and so facilitates comparing the effectiveness of different units.

These very useful facilities are not available to management operating in a nonprofit setting. The lack of any overall performance measure gives rise to difficulties as "success or failure cannot be measured in strictly financial terms" (Lovelock & Weinberg 1977:3). This, in turn, raises the question of what measure can be substituted for profitability in evaluating the efficiency and effectiveness of voluntary organizations? There are no easy answers to this problem. "When such a measure as profit is absent from the operating environment . . . the measure of success and achievement will be exponentially more difficult to establish" according to Ryan (1980:6). Having elaborated on the measurement difficulties posed by the absence of the profit yardstick, the same author (Ryan 1980:6) concludes that "in comparing the nonprofit to the profit oriented organization, it is apparent that the ground rules to determine management performance must be different at least in the measurement used." He suggests that the nonprofit organization must seek a profit surrogate such as measurement of quality of service.

Problems of performance measurement in nonprofit undertakings are detailed by Kanter & Summers (1987:154-64). In their analysis they observe:

Financial measures are central in for-profit organizations . . . but the test in nonprofits is different: these organizations have defined themselves not around their financial returns but around their mission or the service they offer. . .It is this factor - the centrality of social values over financial values - that complicates measurement for nonprofit organizations.

(Kanter & Summers 1987:154)

Their solution is the adoption of a multi-constituency approach, suggesting that "the ideal performance assessment system in a nonprofit organization would acknowledge the existence of multiple constituencies and build measures around all of them" (Kanter & Summers 1987:164).

To conclude, it is clear that the absence of a profit measure in voluntary organizations leaves them without the benefit of this very useful measuring "tool" for judging their overall performance.

Service organizations

The focus on service provision in voluntary organizations, although not unique to this sector, is identified in the literature as a second major distinguishing characteristic. Both Newman & Wallender (1978) and Ryan (1980) head their list of operational differences between profit and nonprofit organizations with the service feature of the latter category. Also Handy (1981) and Gerard (1983) comment on the intangible nature of much of the work of voluntary organizations. Some of the difficulties associated with services, as opposed to tangible products, are outlined by Lovelock & Weinberg (1977:3):

> A physical good can be inspected and, if necessary, rejected before leaving the factory and reaching the user. However the simultaneous occurrence of production and consumption of many services means that a defective service . . . is experienced by the consumer.

McLaughlin (1986:117-8) presents and expands on a formidable list of fifteen inter-related attributes of services, covering, inter alia, intangibility, perishability and consequently the reduced role of inventory, quality control requirements, and various management problems related to service provision.

According to Newman & Wallender (1978:26), service difficulties are often compounded by the existence of multiple service objectives. This point is endorsed by Murray (1987:20) who suggests yet another complexity, namely that such multiple goals "may conflict with one another, with no "bottom line" as a final arbiter". To illustrate his point he cites the example of health related charities which frequently have to decide between committing resources to research, direct service provision, or education. While the for profit sector undoubtedly is not immune to dilemmas of a similar nature, profit considerations can facilitate prioritisation of resources, and this "tool" is not available in the voluntary sector, as discussed already.

The service web is woven with another strand of complexity when multiple evaluators are taken into account. McLaughlin (1986:126) advises that "the management of service organizations has to remain vigilant about the potential differences in evaluation among staff, consumers, potential consumers, and external evaluators such as funding sources".

In summary, the provision of services in the nonprofit sector creates various demands for management that add to those associated with the provision of physical products in the marketplace.

Dual management system

A for-profit company generates financial resources from sales of its goods and/or services. This provides a direct link between inputs and outputs. In contrast, many voluntary nonprofit enterprises receive a significant amount of financial support from sources other than fees for services. Such organizations have no direct connection between the services provided and the resources received, giving rise to two distinct managerial sub-systems, whereas in business the systems are integrated (Mason 1984:21; McLaughlin 1986:159). In other words, the voluntary sector manager has to be concerned about two quite different stakeholders and reconcile often conflicting demands.

On the input side, interests and priorities of funders need to be addressed. Constraints on this side might point to the need for a reduction in services. Yet, on the output side, particularly in service provision agencies, clients may seek more and better services. The manager, at the centre, is faced with the task of handling these conflicting demands, coping with "the divorce between funding arrangements . . . and the quality and relevance of service provision", as Gerard (1983:121) describes it. Making the same point, managers of charities are cast in the role of "broker" by Butler & Wilson (1990:2), in view of their intermediary position between donors and recipients.

Anthony & Young (1988) highlight another difference between commercial and voluntary concerns on the output side. Whereas additional customers present a positive opportunity in the business world, in contrast a voluntary organization operating on fairly fixed, limited resources may view more customers negatively if they place a strain on available funds. Indeed some voluntary organizations, e.g., in the rehabilitation field, are positively motivated to decrease their clientele, an idea "foreign to the thinking of for-profit managers"(Anthony & Young 1988:65).

To sum up the situation, it is suggested in the literature that the "divide" between input and output in voluntary organizations creates added difficulties for nonprofit managers.

Governance of nonprofits

There is a growing literature on the subject of governance of nonprofit organizations, e.g., Drucker (1990); Harris (1987); Middleton (1987) and Murray & Bradshaw-Camball (1990). Nonprofit organizations are usually governed by a voluntary board of trustees as, unlike business concerns, "in the nonprofit sector there are no shareholders, so there is no defined group to select board members" (McLaughlin 1986:217). Instead, "governing bodies constitute the highest point of authority in voluntary organizations" (Billis & Harris 1986:8).

It is noted by Harris (1987:1) that, "in practice, a number of problems surround the role of governing bodies in the voluntary sector". She reports on complaints about some management committees who "interfere" too directly in day-to-day matters, while others offer no "support" for staff (Harris 1987). Commenting on the situation in the US, Drucker (1990:7) states that in many nonprofits the "governance structure malfunctions as often as it functions". This is in line with Middleton's (1987:142) observation that "critics have castigated boards for their lack of expertise".

Gerard (1983:120) describes trustees of voluntary organizations as being "typically part-time and often remote from day-to-day operations", a point endorsed by Handy (1981). A perceived lack of management ability on the part of trustees is emphasised by MacCrimmon (1979:101) who also considers that nonprofit boards "can be woefully inexperienced and unable to cope with major organizational or financial problems". Political or financial considerations may dictate the selection of nonprofit board members, rather than their ability to exercise sound judgement, according to Anthony & Young (1988:67), while recruitment of board members is cited as a problem area by Mellor (1985:84). Murray (1987) speculates on why volunteer boards are so different from business boards and concludes that "the answer lies in some combination of poor selection and inadequate training of board members" (Murray 1987:21). So perceived problems in boards of nonprofits are seen to be associated with both their personnel and the way in which individual boards operate.

Turning to the functions of the board of a nonprofit organization, "it is responsible in the broadest sense for its well-being and for ensuring that it fulfills its stated purpose" (Middleton 1987:141). Although individual boards can vary, their broad concerns, as identified by McLaughlin 1986:219-20), can be summarised as:

- Defining the mission and policy of the organization
- Dealing with personnel matters, including policy, selection and overseeing of staff

- Maintaining the image of the organization among its constituen[
- Providing financial stability for the organization
- Maintaining the continuity of the board.

Ideally, individuals appointed to boards should reflect these con
(1980:16) suggests that the selection criteria for board member
knowledge of the field and a committed interest in it; speciali
relevant to the needs and the organization's programmes, and the time ana
inclination to attend meetings and to understand the existing and emergent
issues". When recruited, McLaughlin (1986:233) considers that training
sessions for board members can be helpful.

Another consideration in regard to board composition is the degree of change
of membership. Mellor (1985:96) feels that change is important in order "to
give the stimulus of new blood". The same author identifies the level of
attendance at meetings as another factor which is "vital to a committee being
effective" (Mellor 1985:108). All the organizations in his own study reported
over 50% attendance, while half of them recorded a turnout at meetings of
over 75% (Mellor 1985:97).

Overall, the situation regarding boards of nonprofits is that their importance
is now recognised in the literature and "old myths such as the belief that . . . a
group of trustees can meet a few times a year and give adequate direction and
guidance to the organization are being exposed" (Murray & Bradshaw-Camball
1990:25).

Staffing patterns

It is self-evident that staff are essential in any organization as "people are the
common denominator of progress" (Galbraith 1978:120). The staffing function
in the voluntary sector can give rise to some special problems. Pertinent issues
relate to the employment of professionals (although not unique to this sector),
the contribution from volunteers, and general staff needs in the sector.

Regarding professionals, many voluntary organizations now employ
personnel who have an affiliation to a professional body, e.g., social workers,
occupational therapists, to facilitate in service provision. Some of the problems
which may ensue are detailed by Anthony & Young (1988:66). They note that
professionals often have motivations that are inconsistent with good resource
utilization, being motivated by dual standards - those of their organization and
those of their professional colleagues. The latter may be inconsistent with
organizational objectives or "undermine their allegiance to the enterprise"
(Newman & Wallender 1978:26). In fact McLaughlin (1986:160) states it in

stronger terms: he considers that the importance of professional values is often detrimental to consumers.

Another problem identified by Kanter & Summers (1987:163) is that "professional standards can create rigidities and interfere with responses to changing constituency needs." Whereas the technical competence of professionals is accepted by MacCrimmon (1979:101), he points out its limitations in the field of management, stating that "there is however, no guarantee that technical training and competence will translate into administrative ability." In a similar vein, Anthony & Young (1988:66) note that professional education does not usually include education in management, and so the importance of the management function may be underestimated. Lacking this managerial expertise, the professional, because he "hears a different drummer", steps to "the music he hears" (Thoreau, quoted in Tripp 1976:312).

Murray (1987:20) also refers to the use of paid professionals and, linking it with the use of volunteers, refers to "the possibility of internecine conflict and rampant politicking" between the various factions.

Dependence on volunteers can add a further layer of complexity to manager's the job. Although nonprofit organizations vary tremendously in the extent to which they depend on voluntary input, the "volunteering" label of the sector is strongly connected with this characteristic. Mason (1984:21) sees voluntarism as "produced by persuasion" which can raise its own problems in the areas of recruitment, selection and maintenance of commitment (Gerard 1983; Handy 1981). Without "the carrot of pay and the stick of dismissal" that characterise "real" jobs, Murray (1987:21) maintains that

> the manager of volunteers must be an applied sociologist and a marketing expert who knows how to uncover the special networks of people who are potential volunteers and then make the idea of volunteering so fascinating that they can't resist.

In addition to problems relating specifically to professional staff and volunteers, staffing difficulties may arise also at a more general level in voluntary organizations. For example, due to funding constraints or uncertainties, there can be a lack of both security in employment and a career structure for paid staff, leading to a high staff turnover and a shortage of experienced staff (Gerard 1983:120).

A report of the threatened closure of a women's refuge for victims of domestic violence in Dublin in May 1990 provides concrete evidence of these concerns (Morgan 1990). Staff at the refuge were employed under a

Department of Labour special employment scheme (SES) which expired June 1990. In the absence of alternative funding, the refuge was not in a position to continue its service, although demand was buoyant. Morgan (1990) also pointed to the inadequate nature of the SES scheme which only covered an individual staff input of 20 hours per week and made no provision for sick pay or overtime. As a result the refuge had already lost three workers and could not get replacement staff, given the very low wage of 65 pounds per week. These circumstances, which are characteristic of many Irish voluntary organizations dependent on SESs, show that even minimal staff security is absent, while the longer term question of a career structure does not even enter into the equation. In such a hand-to-mouth operation, long-term manpower planning cannot even be contemplated.

Another staff payment problem arises from the unmeasurable nature of service activities. Given this constraint, it is not possible to link rewards and/or punishment directly to output (Young 1987:174). This makes the pay element of staff motivation more problematic (Newman & Wallender 1978).

To conclude, the staffing function entails "human resource planning, acquisition and development aimed at providing the talent necessary for organizational success" (Kreitner 1989:346). Its inherent complexities in for-profit organizations can be further compounded in the voluntary sector by the employment of professionals, the use of volunteers and funding-related staffing problems.

Environmental characteristics

As established earlier in this chapter in the overview of systems theory, an organization does not exist in a vacuum, but rather in its environment which provides both resources and constraints. In the language of general systems theory (Boulding 1956; von Bertalanffy 1968) an organization is viewed as an open system (Katz & Kahn 1978; Kast & Rosenzweig 1985) as it must interact with its environment to survive, and also respond appropriately to changes in this environment. According to Daft (1986:10):

> Open systems can be enormously complex. Internal efficiency is just one issue. . . . The organization has to find and obtain needed resources, interpret and act on environmental changes, dispose of outputs, and control and coordinate internal activities in the face of environmental disturbances and uncertainty.

t studies of strategic management, authors such as Pettigrew (1987)
ıasised the importance of the "inner and outer context". Voluntary
have no immunity from this open system organizational reality. On
ıde, financial resources have to be obtained. Very often this is a
k, as multiple sources of funding may have to be tapped, in the
ı single reliable and adequate source, giving rise to the need to
_ıc the special needs and demands of many different funders" (Murray
1987:20). Resource contributors may intrude on internal management,
according to Newman & Wallender (1978:24). Anthony & Young (1988:61)
make a similar point, highlighting how donors can impose constraints on goals
and strategies. The impact of government funding on the UK and US voluntary
sectors is outlined by Leat et al (1986), Rosenbaum (1981) and Salaman
(1987).

General economic conditions are another environmental variable to be taken
into consideration. The welfare state has been labelled the "residual beneficiary
of the growth State" (Klein 1974:1). However, in the UK, the economic tide
turned in the 1980s and the ensuing financial constraints heralded government
cutbacks in social expenditure. Jenks (1987:336) reports a similar situation in
the US where "nonprofits learned to their sorrow after 1980, government
largesse is subject to sudden, unpredictable fluctuations". This can give rise to
two problems in the voluntary sector - a funding problem for agencies heavily
reliant on government money, and an increased demand for services no longer
funded by the public purse.

To address both of these problems can necessitate procuring funding from
alternative sources. Not surprisingly therefore, there has been increased
competition for voluntary sector funding in recent times. In this context, Butler
& Wilson (1990:172) refer to "the increasingly competitive charitable market"
in the UK, a point made also by Irwin (1989). These views are endorsed by
Kramer (1990:36) who notes that the voluntary sector environment has now
become "more turbulent and competitive".

Other environmental issues include tax and legal implications (Anthony &
Young 1988). A supportive tax stance by the government can benefit the
voluntary sector in terms of tax savings on donations, making giving a more
attractive proposition for prospective donors. Exemptions from income and
property taxes are helpful in reducing costs. On the other hand, an example
from Action Aid shows how this advantageous position can be reversed even
by indirect government action. Irvine (1988:93) relates how Action Aid in the
UK had 600,000 pounds lopped off its annual income arising from changes in
the basic tax rates, showing how good news for individual taxpayers can
translate into bad news for charities.

The distinct legal standing afforded to nonprofit organizations in some countries enables them to avail of tax advantages from which for-profit enterprises are excluded. Rayney (1988) outlines how UK charities can minimise their exposure to tax. The reverse side of this coin is that legal constraints can give rise to demands for control and accountability. This aspect is discussed in more detail in the following two chapters.

Consumerism is another relevant concern in the voluntary sector. According to Leat (1988:12), it involves taking "the ordinary person into account" while Kramer (1987:251) see it as "the involvement of clientele in policy-making in an organization designed for their welfare". Hinton & Hyde (1980-1:13) also advocate a greater say for consumers, suggesting that "the consumer of services should be able to exercise his or her verdict with greater ease and directness and to better effect on what is provided".

This challenges voluntary organizations "to do things with others . . . instead of doing things for others" (Leat 1988:12). It can be seen as part of a wider social movement towards increasing participation which facilitates the expression of consumer views. For example, "closeness to the customer" was identified by Peters & Waterman (1982) as one of the attributes that characterised excellent companies. Very recently, in September 1992, a social policy conference organised in Dublin by the Conference of Major Religious Superiors (CMRS) discussed both participation in society in general and also in the voluntary sector (CMRS 1992). This suggests that consumerism is also relevant in an Irish context.

"Social, cultural, religious, political and philosophical attitudes are significant factors in an organization's environment" (Hicks & Gullet 1981:73). Although attitudes are intangible, their effects cannot be overlooked by voluntary sector management as they can have a major impact on the general climate of support for voluntary endeavour.

The cumulative effects of the foregoing are that "change and complexity in environmental demands has major implications for organizational design and action" (Daft 1986:80). Therefore it suggests that managers of voluntary organizations need to appreciate the "outer context" (Pettigrew 1987) of their operations.

Drawing together the material in this section (5.4), it is evident that voluntary organizations, in common with those in other sectors, operate as an open system and are "sub-systems of a broader supra-system - the environment" (Kast & Rosenzweig 1985:131). Internal organizational characteristics have been identified which need to be taken into account in managing voluntary organizations. In addition, environmental characteristics have been shown to impact on voluntary sector organizations and Kast & Rosenzweig (1985:131) counsel that an understanding of this process "is significant for the practicing manager". Overall, it can be seen that a complex set of factors, both internal and external, impinge on organizations in the nonprofit sector. Therefore, "the management of such agencies can with justification be regarded as more complex than governmental and business management" (Billis 1989:25). Yet the task of management in the voluntary sector involves coping with this complex reality.

Summary

This chapter has introduced the topic of management in the voluntary sector. It began by providing some general insights on organizations and their management, followed by an overview of the evolution of management thought. This exercise established, in turn, the pervasiveness of organizations in modern life and the need for management to facilitate the achievement of the objectives set by individual organizations. Then, tracing the developments in management theory, it was shown how early diverse approaches provided the groundwork for the more recent integrated systems and contingency theories which suggest the need for congruence between an organization, its sub-systems and its external environment (Kast & Rosenzweig 1985).

Turning to the voluntary sector, it was established that, although the majority of management texts assume a commercial context, a sharpened awareness of nonprofit management is now discernible. The organizational and environmental characteristics of nonprofit organizations were identified, indicating how they can give rise to management challenges either not encountered or else less prominent in the for-profit world. This means, in turn, that nonprofit management can be even more complex than its counterpart in the commercial sector.

6 Control in Organizations

This chapter focuses on various aspects of control in organizations. To open the discussion, some definitions of control are presented, followed by an examination of the need for control in organizations. Then the basic control process in organizations is outlined and different types of control are examined.

Various aspects of organizational activity need to be controlled, and these are identified in the next section. The human factor in the control equation is then considered as, in the final analysis, control is about the regulation of human performance (Reeser & Loper 1978:437). Following on from this general discussion on control, its implementation in a voluntary sector context is reviewed.

What is control?

An examination of the literature, e.g., Baird, Post & Mahon (1990), Gray & Smeltzer (1989), Koontz & Weihrich (1988), Kreitner (1989), Robbins (1988) and Reeser & Loper 1978), identifies control as one of the basic phases of management, following on from planning, organizing, staffing and leading. Control can be defined as "a process of monitoring performance and taking action to ensure intended or desired results" (Baird, Post & Mahon 1990:454).

Appreciation of the need for control in organizations is not new. Over seventy years ago, Fayol [1916](1949) identified control as one of the five constituents in his overall framework of management, positing that control "operates in everything, things, people, actions" (Fayol 1949:107). A landmark book, Barnard's (1938) *Functions of the Executive*, includes consideration of control. Another pioneering analyst, Goetz (1949:229), notes that "management control seeks to compel events to conform to plans". An interesting summary of other pioneer writers on control is provided by Giglioni & Bedeian (1974).

Moving to more contemporary contributors, Newman (1975:5) views control as "the series of steps a manager takes to assure that actual performance conforms as nearly as practical to plans." According to Child (1984:136) control in organizations is "a process whereby management and other groups are able to initiate and regulate the conduct of activities so that their results accord with the goals and expectations held by those groups." Acknowledging that there are no universally accepted definitions of "management" and "control", Hofstede (1981:193) states that "the connotation of "management control" is a pragmatic concern for results, obtained through people".

The discussion in the previous chapter (8) on the general theme of management noted that much of the relevant literature related primarily to the commercial sector. The same orientation applies to control:

> In the Western European literature, it is customary to speak of "management control" primarily in the context of the private . . . profit-oriented organization. . . . It is much rarer to find the "management control" concept applied to public or voluntary not-for-profit organizations.
>
> (Hofstede 1981:193).

A similar point is made by Anthony & Young (1988:4) who have tried to redress this imbalance by publishing a major work on management control relating specifically to the non-profit sector, covering both governmental and private non-profit organizations. Ramanathan (1982:7), whose text covers the same territory, notes that "the subject of management control is an evolving field of study. . . . We do not have an axiomatic set of principles that can provide unerring guides to practice". The control requirement in all types of organizations is stressed by Newman (1975:5) who claims that "the need for evaluation and feedback is just as pressing in charitable organizations as in profit-seeking corporations."

Why is control important?

"Organizations are rarely established as ends in themselves. They are instruments created to achieve other ends" (Morgan 1986:22). An organization can devise elaborate plans, create a suitable organization structure and engage motivated employees who are directed to achieve the set objectives of the enterprise. However, as the poet Robert Burns reminds us "the best laid schemes o' mice an' men/ gang aft agley" (quoted in Tripp 1967:475), so it is necessary to ensure that goals are, in fact, being achieved.

Control is the mechanism which establishes actual attainments. If these are out of line with plans, management can then take the necessary action to correct the deviations. In a nutshell, setting objectives is not sufficient as "the declaration of desirable goals is not enough to guarantee immortality" (Cyert 1975:10). There must be follow-up control also, to find out if the organizational system is achieving its intended results. Without this regulation, "organizations have no indication of how well they perform in relation to their goals. Control, like a ship's rudder, keeps the organization moving in the proper direction" Barney & Griffin (1992:379).

The control process

Gray & Smeltzer (1989:662) synopsize the basic control process as follows: "Whether it involves controlling a multinational corporation, a neighbourhood group, or a government agency, control involves four steps: establishing standards, measuring performance, comparing performance to standards and correcting deviations from standard". While the mathematics may vary slightly from being telescoped to three stages, by fusing measuring and comparing performance into one step (Rue & Byars 1986:299; Koontz et al. 1984:551) to being expanded to five by including feedback of measured performance as a separate step (Hitt et al.1986:494; Hampton 1986:626), the basic approach taken is quite similar in general management texts.

The dominant and oft cited analogy for this model is a thermostat (Hofstede 1978). Setting standards is analogous to setting the temperature. Measuring performance corresponds to measuring the actual temperature. Comparing performance to standards is like comparing actual to set temperature. Finally correcting deviations is analogous to the negative feedback signal in the thermostat cycle. It is basically a cybernetic model of control (Daft 1986:316).

Returning to the main stages, standards are derived from the objectives set at the planning stage. "Without objectives and plans, control is not possible, because performance has to be compared against some established criteria" (Koontz & Weihrich 1988:490). It is recommended also that "standards should be easy to measure and definite. The more specific and measurable an objective is, the more likely that it can be directly used as a standard" (Rue & Byars 1986:299). At the opposite extreme, Sizer (1977:131) and Anthony & Young (1984:95) emphasise that if objectives are vague or ill-defined, no system can measure their attainment.

Measuring actual performance is the next step. Two aspects must be considered - how to measure and what to measure. Four common sources of information frequently used by managers to measure actual performance are personal observations and statistical, oral and written reports. Each on its own has strengths and weaknesses (Robbins 1988:473-4), so a combination of them increases the probability of receiving reliable information.

What to measure is probably even more critical because the selection of the wrong criteria can give rise to serious dysfunctional consequences, as what is measured can dictate, to a large extent, the focus of people in an organization (Kerr 1975). (This human factor in relation to control is discussed later in section 9.6.) It should be noted too that the performance of some activities is difficult to measure in quantifiable terms. In this case a manager may have to resort to the use of subjective judgements (Hofstede 1981). When comparing actual performance to the set standard, an acceptable range of variation has to be determined.

In the final stage of correcting deviations, action can be immediate when possible, or sometimes may require a more long-term approach such as a fundamental change in organization structure (Reeser & Loper 1978).

Situations in which inputs are readily measurable and quantifiable lend themselves to this traditional approach to control. For example, if a standard of 15% increase in sales is set, actual results can be measured objectively and compared to this clear target. If it is not achieved, corrective action can be applied. However, as outlined previously in chapter 5, in not-for-profit service organizations, performance measurement is not always so readily quantifiable. Management control in these organizations "cannot be achieved by simple extrapolation from profit-oriented and production activities" (Hofstede 1981:194). In a comprehensive article, Hofstede (1981) highlights the limitations of the basic cybernetic model of control when it is applied to public and not-for-profit organizations, and illustrates the complexity of the control issue in such organizations.

To summarise this section, the basic control process involves setting standards which are derived from objectives, then measuring actual performance and, finally, taking corrective action. It is obvious that management control is easiest in a straightforward situation with unambiguous objectives and measurable outputs. In the real world this situation does not always apply.

Types of control

Different methods can be used to establish control in an organization. Some of these are now outlined. Categorising the many types of control systems in an organization is helpful in understanding the general strategies and limitations of these systems. In theory, a manager has three options in relation to control. It can be implemented either before an activity commences, while the activity is ongoing, or after the fact (Robbins 1988). The first type is called feedforward control, the second is labelled concurrent control, and the last is termed feedback control (Baird, Post & Mahon 1990). These controls operate at the input, process and output stages. Each one is now examined in a little more detail.

With feedforward control, also known as steering control (Newman 1975:6; Gray & Smeltzer 1989:671), results are predicted and corrective action taken to prevent anticipated problems (Koontz & Bradspies 1972). This control follows the adage that "an ounce of prevention is worth a pound of cure." Effective cash management provides an example of a feature that requires feedforward control. A cash budget predicts future inflows and outflows, enabling suitable action to be taken in advance to accommodate surpluses or shortfalls. Unfortunately feedforward control requires timely and accurate information that is often difficult to develop (Robbins 1988). As a result managers frequently have to resort to one of the remaining two types of control.

Concurrent control, as the name implies, takes place while an activity is in progress. It is also labelled "screening control" (Gray & Smeltzer 1989:672), or "yes-no control" (Newman 1975:6). When control is enacted while the work is being performed or with an insignificant time lapse, management can correct problems before they become too costly. For example, most computers are programmed to provide operators with an immediate response if an error is made. Quality circles are another example of concurrent control.

Finally, feedback or post-action control (Newman 1975:6) is historical in its focus. Its major drawback is that by the time information is available on a problem the damage has been done. However this is balanced by some advantages. It allows organizations to apply the wisdom of hindsight to future actions and so is useful for future planning. Also, post action control can be useful in providing a basis for rewarding employees (Newman 1975:26).

Focus of control

Control efforts can be directed at different areas in an organization. Robbins (1988:480) identifies five main areas: people, finance, operations, information and overall performance. Each of these areas is now reviewed.

People are vital to any organization as it is by working through others that managers accomplish the goals of the undertaking. Control over staff can be exercised through supervision on a day-to-day basis. In addition, managers can assess the work of employees in a more formal way by means of systematic performance appraisal, and reward the outcome appropriately . But it must be borne in mind that personnel can react to controls either positively or negatively. (This factor is discussed later in more detail in section 6.6.)

Financial controls, such as budgets, are an important tool for controlling costs in any organization, whether it is in the for-profit or nonprofit category. Budgets provide management with quantitative standards against which to measure and compare resource consumption. By pointing out the variance between standard and actual consumption, they become control devices. Anthony & Young (1988) provide detailed information on budgeting in nonprofit organizations. The issue is addressed also by Hofstede (1981:202) who notes that "money is usually the only common denominator for all activities in the organization which makes the budget system that tries to control the flow of money into a focal part of the management control system". He elaborates on input budget techniques such as Programming Planning Budgeting Systems (PPBS), Measurement by Objectives (MBO) and Zero Base Budgeting (ZBB) in relation to nonprofit organizations.

Operations control techniques are designed to assess the effectiveness and efficiency of organizations in producing goods or services. In a service organization the emphasis tends to be on quality of service (Pride & Ferrell 1987).

Managers need information to do their job effectively. Inaccurate, incomplete or delayed information can seriously impede performance. Therefore it is necessary to develop a management information system that provides the required data to the appropriate person in a timely manner. Advances in computer technology greatly facilitate information provision.

Finally, evaluations of an organization's overall performance or effectiveness are made by a number of constituencies. Managers are concerned with effectiveness, as are outside groups such as clients and customers on the output side and suppliers and investors on the input side. These various interests support the idea that managers should be concerned with control in order to maintain or improve overall performance.

The various types of control and the organizational areas in which they are applied have now been outlined. Another factor, sometimes left out of the equation when a mechanistic approach to control is adopted, is the human factor which is now considered.

Control and the human factor

The broad objective of the control function is to ensure that organizational resources are effectively employed in achieving objectives. However, Reeser & Loper (1978:572) comment that "of all the managerial functions, controlling has become the most mechanistic and indifferent to human concerns". Yet, as non-human resources depend on human efforts for their utilization, control, in the final analysis, involves the regulation of human performance. Therefore, "it is behavioural response, not the mechanics of control, that really -matter" (Newman 1975:43). Controls can have a considerable effect on the motivation and behaviour of the people whose performance they measure, and it is only by taking the behavioural responses into account that a discussion of control eliminates a "misleading fiction" (Hampton 1986:635).

There is a considerable literature dealing with the way certain control strategies are incongruous with the personal psychological needs of adults (Anthony & Young 1988; Argyris 1952; Cammann & Nadler 1976; Hofstede 1967; Newman 1975). Some of the issues which may surface as the human element is factored into the control equation are now addressed.

As controls "typically have a poor reputation at least in terms of their popularity with persons being controlled" (Newman 1975:143) they can give rise to resistance. "Control in an organization is not simply a process in which everyone shares with the same goal in mind; it is also a process in which there is resistance and counter control and pursuit of conflicting objectives" (Child 1984:136). While an employee may subscribe to the objective need for control in an organization, having one's own performance controlled is not as acceptable, as an individual's need for satisfaction may be threatened by the control system (Gray & Smelter 1989:683). "Not only are people's established informal ways of doing things threatened, but also they are likely to view the intervention of formal systems as an attempt to reduce their discretion" (Child

89

1984:155). The same author remarks that professional people "resent having administrative controls imposed on them" (Child 1984:164).

Measuring human behaviour can also give rise to problems. When managers collect data on organizational performance, "they trigger a chain of perceptual, cognitive, motivational, and behavioural events that are, at best, only partially controlled" (Hampton 1986:635). This arises because, as social scientists have long known, it is difficult or impossible to measure behaviour without affecting the behaviour being measured (Webb 1966).

Three important aspects of measurement in relation to its impact on control are identified by Lawler & Rhode (1976) - how complete or inclusive, how objective and how subject to influence it is. Based on these criteria, they conclude that completeness, objectivity and responsiveness to employee effort and performance are desirable qualities in a control system. Motivation is enhanced when effort is linked to performance. Complete measures help focus on all aspects of the job, rather than on merely measured ones. Objective measures avoid the risk of bias and subjective assessments.

In addition to its direct influence, measurement can have a latent influence on performance. An example cited by Blau (1963) illustrates the way these "latent" effects can occur. Briefly, it concerns a state employment office dealing with job placement for the unemployed. Initially, performance measurement of interviewers was related to the single criterion of number of interviews held. Under these conditions, there was some evidence of discrimination against black applicants, even though interviewers were not conscious of such prejudice. Then, for reasons unrelated to discrimination, a new set of performance measures was introduced, broadening the base to include the number of referrals and placements, as well as interviews. The elimination of discrimination against black applicants was a latent effect of these new measures, as placement of black clients, who were more willing to accept unattractive jobs, became instrumental to interviewers' efforts to perform well.

Management controls can give rise also to dysfunctional consequences. This occurs when control systems cause employees to behave in ways that look good, in terms of the control system measurements, but that are dysfunctional in relation to the broader goals of the organization, thus leading to goal displacement. This dysfunctional compliance can take a number of forms, including rigid bureaucratic behaviour and invalid data reporting (Lawler & Rhode 1976). A classic example of the former, cited by Hofstede (1967:23), is the sales office where all the salesmen were found to be sitting at their desks at the end of each month because their car expenses were not paid beyond the budget limit. While this may have contained car expenses, it also reduced sales and consequently impinged on profits.

"Cooking the books" can be another response to controls. An example from the Boy Scouts of America of falsified membership figures is instructive (Cammann & Nadler 1976). A drive to increase membership motivated people to increase the number of members reported, but had not motivated them to increase the actual number of Boy Scouts enrolled, which of course was the purpose of the exercise. These examples show how the control process can be subject to "psychological shortcircuiting" (Hofstede 1967:26).

This section has explored some of the difficulties related to the human factor in the control process. These behavioural aspects need to be taken into account in the design of controls if they are to achieve their purpose. As Littler & Salaman (1982:253) have put it, "control must be seen in relation to conflict and sources of conflict and in relation to the potential terrain of compromise and consensus".

So far the discussion has indicated the need for, and importance of, control in organizations in order to ensure that goals and objectives are, in fact, achieved. Now control is looked at in a voluntary sector context.

Control in voluntary organizations

The material presented so far in this chapter shows that control is a many faceted, complex area. Its implementation in the nonprofit area tends to be further complicated by the characteristics of this sector.

Relating back to the management characteristics of nonprofit organizations identified in the previous chapter (5), several constraints on effective control have been implied in this analysis. Heading the list are the lack of a profit measure and the service nature of voluntary enterprises. These two characteristics pose additional problems in the control area, due to the difficulties in measuring output. The basic cybernetic model of control starts by setting quantifiable standards, based on objectives. Very often in the nonprofit world, goals are ill-defined or ambiguous (Hofstede 1981) and so do not provide a useful basis for setting standards. When obstacles arise at the stage of setting standards, the further steps of measurement, comparing and correcting are not facilitated (Sizer 1977).

Even if this first hurdle is surmounted and objectives are clarified, the next step of measurement looms ahead. Service goals do not lend themselves to easy measurement. Even if the quantity of service can be measured the quality, which may be far more important, is "an abstract and elusive construct because of three features unique to service, intangibility, heterogeneity and inseparability of production and consumption" (Parasuraman, Zeithaml & Berry 1988:13). In a service based situation, Newman & Wallender (1978:30) consider that measurable aspects, such as numbers of people served, "tend to receive disproportionate attention merely because they can be measured." Making much the same point, Sayles (1972:30) issues a note of caution about "the tendency for easily quantifiable measures to drive out more subjective measures".

Despite the difficulties encountered in efforts to measure service, some progress has been made in this regard. For example, Parasuraman, Zeithaml & Berry (1988:13) suggest that "in the absence of objective measures, an appropriate approach for assessing the quality of a firm's service is to measure consumers" perceptions of quality". They have devised a multiple-item scale named SERVQUAL for assessing customer perceptions of service quality.

Another response to difficulties in measuring output is for the relevant organizations to focus on control over inputs, using budget mechanisms (Anthony & Young 1984). Also the difficulties in measurement in the context of service operations may be counterbalanced to some extent by a strong commitment to the broad objective or "cause" of the organization, which facilitates clan control (Daft 1986;Ouchi 1979).

In the previous chapter (5), two distinct management sub-systems were identified in voluntary organizations, one relating to input and the other to output (Mason 1984). Control difficulties may arise on the input side due to environmental uncertainty, particularly in the funding area. For example, Holmquist (1990) reports on a fundraising venture run by the Irish Heart Foundation (IHF) where the actual yield was only half the targetted amount. Such uncertainty makes budgeting a problematic exercise at best.

The governance of nonprofit organizations can give rise to further control problems (Murray 1987). Trustees may be remote from day-to-day operations and/or unfamiliar with financial matters (MacCrimmon 1979). A system of an approved list of registered trustees is suggested by Reed (1990) to counteract this shortcoming. In the meantime, existing trustees, with all their limitations, are ultimately responsible for the affairs of the organization. A manager who is motivated to exercise control may have to contend with a board of trustees who do not share or even understand his/her enthusiasm.

Turning to the human side of the enterprise, it was established that control systems have implications for employee behaviour. The involvement of different categories of staff, including professionals, volunteers and administrative employees, adds to the basic human constraints outlined. Professionals are known to resist control (Child 1984). Bearing this in mind, it

92

is suggested by Newman & Wallender (1978:30) that in organizations where professionals dominate, "a manager has to design his organization to appeal to prevailing professional norms." The impact of controls on volunteers, who are there by choice and without payment, must be considered. If both professionals and volunteers show a reluctance to accept controls, this may impact negatively on their application to administrative employees in the same organization.

Finally the management overview referred to the open-system nature of organizations. Consequently environmental influences have to be reckoned with in relation to control in the sector. Daft's (1986) contingency model of control includes environment in the control equation. Many voluntary organizations operate in a turbulent environment, with uncertainty regarding funding. Also demands from both funders and clients raise questions about accountability, which is addressed in the next chapter.

In conclusion, the foregoing discussion shows how control in voluntary organizations is influenced by both the particular organizational and environmental characteristics of the voluntary sector.

Summary

This chapter focused on control in organizations. It began by defining control and clarifying its importance in an organizational context. The basic control process of setting standards, measuring performance and taking corrective action was then detailed and, following this, various types of control were outlined.

Next, areas of the organization where the need for control may arise were identified. As control, in the final analysis, is dependent on human beings for its implementation, the human factor in relation to control was explored. The discussion moved then to consider control in relation to voluntary organizations where it emerged that the particular characteristics of this sector can have the effect of adding to the difficulties encountered in implementing control in the for-profit world.

Now that the literature relating to control has been explored, the next chapter considers accountability, another main focus in the field research.

7 Accountability in the Voluntary Sector

"Accountability is one of the fashionable words of our time" (Day & Klein 1987:1). Voluntary organizations have not escaped this fashionable focus for, as Van Til (1988:168) cautions, it must be remembered that their acts are not "necessarily clothed in a special robe of virtue" which might provide them with automatic exemption. Rather, accountability has become "a central dilemma" of the nonprofit sector (Hodgkinson & Lyman 1989:475). The fact that accountability was chosen as one of the two basic enquiries around which the initial research agenda for the Yale Nonprofit Program was grouped (Simon 1989) further endorses its importance.

This chapter explores various aspects of accountability, beginning with an examination of the concept. A review of fraud and malpractice in some nonprofit organizations is then presented, as this is a significant factor in the current concern about accountability in the sector. In addition, a number of other changes in the voluntary arena have led to accountability being factored into the voluntary sector equation. These are examined in some detail.

In keeping with the higher profile of accountability in the context of nonprofit activity, in recent times accountants have shown increased interest in addressing this agenda. Their contributions to the debate are explored. This is followed by an overview of some of the implications of accountability, specifically its impact on the independence of voluntary organizations and the cost of compliance with demands for greater accountability.

Finally, the topic of external accountability is linked to internal control in voluntary organizations.

Accountability: exploring the concept

Accountability is categorised by Day & Klein (1987:32) as a "chameleon word" while Kramer & Grossman (1987:40) observe that "definitions of accountability vary greatly". Kramer (1981:290) also admits to having problems grappling with the concept of accountability, judging from his comment that "its popularity in the human services is exceeded only by the lack of agreement about its meaning". This gives some indication of the complexity of the term.

Before examining it in more depth, it is worth noting that accountability is not a new concept. At a personal level, St. Matthew (xii 36) reminds us that we will all have to cope with giving an account of "every idle word" on the day of judgement, and his fellow evangelist, St. Luke (xvi 1-2) uses the concept in the parable of the unjust steward who was called to "give an account of his stewardship." Concern for accountability is discernible earlier still in pre-christian times, as Aristotle refers to the need for public accountability when large sums of public money are involved (Normanton 1966).

The career of the concept of political accountability is traced by Day & Klein (1987:4-31) who identify five main models - Athenian, feudal, transitional, simple modern and complex modern - and cover developments from a basic face-to-face Athenian model right through to the more complex models in contemporary society.

Regarding the voluntary sector, concerns about accountability are not new either. Fremont-Smith (1989:75-6) reports that the basic methods for ensuring accountability in nonprofit organizations

> were devised as long ago as the sixteenth century, when the common law dealing with charitable trusts was developed and a pattern for government supervision was devised to ensure responsible behaviour by the managers of these trusts.

Having touched on the long-standing concerns about accountability, both at a general level and in relation to the voluntary sector, the concept is now examined in more detail.

As Jackson (1982:220) sees it,

> accountability involves explaining or justifying what has been done, what is being done and what has been planned. . . . Thus one party is

accountable to another in the sense that one of the parties has a right to call upon the other to give an account of his activities.

A similar approach is adopted by Rutherford (1983) who views the concept as being the requirement to be answerable for one's conduct and responsibilities. Another view put forward by Hatch (1980:127) is that

accountability can refer to several things. In the narrowest sense it means avoiding malpractice and keeping the accounts properly. . . . More substantially, accountability refers to the effective use of resources for the purposes for which they were provided.

At a theoretical level, accountability can be viewed in terms of a relationship involving the "giving and demanding of reasons for conduct" (Roberts & Scapens 1985:447). Expanding on this relationship, "it is usually assumed that some individual has certain rights to make these demands . . . and another has some responsibility to supply this information" (Laughlin 1990:95). The labels "principal" and "agent" are used by Gray, Owen & Maunders(1987:2-3) to denote these two participants in the accountability relationship. "Rights" relate to some transfer of resources from a principal to an agent with some expectations surrounding the transfer and, in turn, it is these expectations which provide the terms of the accountability relationship (Gray 1983).

Contextual factors are another dimension of accountability. For instance, Birkett (1988:15) identifies three possible accountability practices, linked to three forms of relationship, which he terms "gemeinschaft" (a form of private and spontaneous association), "gesellschaft" (where relationships are contractually derived), and "bureaucracy" (when task accomplishment is supreme). Obviously accountability relationships vary in these three different situations. Birkett (1988) links relationships based on "gemeinschaft" with communal accountability; he sees contractual accountability arising in a "gesellschaft" context and, finally, he associates administrative accountability with "bureaucracy". In common with Gray (1983), Birkett's (1988) overall view of accountability extends to both the contractual form and the less formal communal context.

The point is made by Roberts & Scapens (1985:448) that in each system of accountability there is a moral relationship involved whereby an individual or group is exercising power over another to ensure that something, meaningfully defined, is done by that person or persons. In a similar vein, Day & Klein (1987:4) refer to the ethical considerations in accountability.

There are different "bases of accountability" (Stewart 1984:17). In a study of accountability in voluntary organizations, Leat (1988:36), in line with Robinson's (1971) earlier work, identifies four dimensions of the concept. She suggests that one can distinguish between fiscal, process and programme accountability, and finally accountability for priorities. Stewart (1984:17) labels this a "ladder of accountability".

Stated in simple terms, fiscal accountability is about "the proper use of money" (Leat 1988:36). The term "fiscal/regulatory accountability" is used by Day & Klein (1987:27) to cover the same territory which they consider to be about "making sure that money has been spent as agreed, according to the appropriate rules". Continuing, they view legal accountability as a counterpart to this "in so far as it is concerned to make sure that the procedures and rules of decision-making have been observed". Stewart's (1984:17) reference to the need for "accountability for probity and legality" which ensures, in the main, that funds are used properly and in a manner authorised, has a similar focus.

However, Laughlin (1990:94) acknowledges the limitations of fiscal accountability when he states that "financial accountability is, of course, only one area in which accountability issues arise and is thus a simplification of the accountability process". (The perceived limitations of financial accountability are discussed in more detail later in the section (7.4) dealing with accountants and voluntary sector accountability.)

Process accountability "is about making sure that a given course of action has been carried out, and that value for money has been achieved in the use of resources" (Day & Klein 1987:27). Stated more succinctly, it is about "following proper procedures" (Leat 1988:36).

Programme accountability focuses on the quality of an organization's work both at the level of individual projects and more generally (Leat 1988). According to Day & Klein (1987:27), who use the term "programme/effectiveness accountability", it is about "making sure that a given course of action or investment of resources has achieved its intended result".

Accountability for priorities, the fourth and final dimension, is concerned with the "relevance or appropriateness" (Leat 1988:36) of services offered by an organization. This is related to the need for an organization to take on board the "era of customer orientation" (Pride & Ferrell 1987:17) whereby client needs are identified and met appropriately. It contrasts with operating in what Leat (1988:12) describes as "the old paternalistic way", when voluntary organizations thought that "they didn't need to listen [to clients] because they already knew".

Leat (1988:36) explains that groups may differ in their interests in accountability: "some may be interested in only one, others may be interested in all four".

At this stage, some insights have been provided into the concept and dimensions of accountability. However, one of the reasons for the increased emphasis on accountability in voluntary organizations is the incidence of fraud in the sector which is now examined.

Concerns about fraud and malpractice

"While charity in Ireland might not quite cover a multitude of sins, trickster fundraisers, acting as middlemen for charitable agencies, are still operating scams for their personal profit" (McCarthy 1989). One recent example of fraudulent practice was highlighted in the Radio Telefis Eireann (RTE) consumer affairs programme "Look Here" (RTE 1992). It concerned a dubious operation, based in Youghal, Co. Cork, set up to build a village to provide holidays for the blind. The organization was run by the Cottrells, a husband and wife team. Fundraising for the project began in 1989 and consisted of selling tickets costing 25 pounds each. Yet, by 1992, the site for the proposed holiday village was described on the RTE programme as being "still an empty field" (RTE 1992).

Obviously the negative media exposure did not auger well for this Cottrell operation. So they switched their "charity" fundraising efforts to a Dublin-based operation, the "Cancer Control Society", again funded by way of tickets at 25 pounds each for a competition to be held in 1993! (Phoenix 1992). This move prompted the Irish Cancer Society to disassociate itself publicly from the Cottrell operation in a series of ads in the Irish Times (e.g., see Irish Times April 17 1992).

Ireland is not unique in having dishonest operators masquerading as models of charitable concern. DiGiovanni (1992) reports on the increasingly tarnished image of some fundraising charity events in the UK. She recounts how a charity ball, held to raise funds for the Save the Children Fund, resulted in the charity receiving a mere 2,100 pounds of the 80,000 pounds which sponsors had paid.

Somewhat earlier in the UK, Irvine (1988:92) notes that even during the major famine in Ethiopia which prompted a profusion of generosity and goodwill, "not even the fact that the world's eyes were fixed on Ethiopia could prevent a sour note creeping in, with accusations of fraud and double dealing".

America too has had its share of shady operations in the voluntary sector. In the US in February 1990, the Rev. Bruce Ritter was forced to resign his position as CEO of Covenant House, the US's largest privately funded and operated shelter system for young runaways, amid allegations of financial impropriety (Time 1990:70). This does not appear to be an isolated incident, as Hopkins (1980:18) paints a more general scene of the US where "abuses appear to be on the increase, triggering greater governmental regulation". Another investigation into the multi-billion dollar charity sector in the US has an appositely labelled chapter entitled "Fake, Hoax and Charity" (Bakal 1979).

Of course fraud is not unique to nonprofit organizations. However, Ellman (1982:1018) explains why it seems to give rise to more disquiet in this sector than in a commercial context:

> Theft or embezzlement by a pastor, a March of the Dimes organiser, or a Salvation Army Santa Claus evokes a distinctive outrage. That same feeling is not generated by the self-dealing of a business corporation director, reprehensible as we may believe it is. The difference lies in the special insult we feel when everyday evil, which we may learn to watch for, sneaks up on us disguised as virtue.

The former Chief Charity Commissioner in England, Robin Guthrie, attempts to give some perspective to the issue: "We do not know how much abuse there is. It is, I suspect, less than some journalists would have us believe and more than charitable and unsuspecting members of the public would wish (Guthrie 1988:11). He goes on to identify five abuses, ranging from misapplication of funds by trustees and internal disputes, to tax evasion and fundraising abuse. The National Council for Voluntary Organizations (NCVO) also gives consideration to the matter in its publication on malpractice in fundraising (NCVO 1986), while the Woodfield (1987) report recognises that the large amounts of money and property held by the sector constitute an increasingly promising field for sharp practice.

As mentioned previously, in Ireland, public unease about possible abuses in fundraising for charitable purposes prompted the government to set up a committee, chaired by a high court judge, to review the whole area of fundraising. In its report (Report on Fundraising 1990:68) it notes:

> We have evidence that both fraud and malpractice have occurred in the past. It is difficult to ascertain precisely the present position but there is no doubt that the potential for fraud and abuse exists and is likely to be availed of in the absence of adequate statutory controls.

100

In sum, it can be stated that there is considerable concern about fraud and malpractice in the voluntary sector. This, combined with other factors about to be discussed, gives rise to demands for more accountability from voluntary bodies.

The demand for accountability

A number of other factors have contributed to the current interest in voluntary sector accountability. "The ever whirling wheels of change", to use Spencer's analogy, are turning in the voluntary sector environment. Evidence of changing patterns in voluntary organizations themselves; changes in the general economic climate in which they operate; a higher profile for the sector; different funding patterns, and more discerning donors and clients is indicative of mutations in both the "inner" and "outer" contexts (Pettigrew 1987) of voluntary sector activity. In addition, even within the sector itself, there seems to be a growing awareness of the need for greater accountability. Some of these issues are now reviewed.

Changed patterns in voluntary organizations

Traditionally many voluntary organizations operated as "closed systems" (Kast & Rosenzweig 1985), at least in terms of funding and management. Hartogs and Weber (1978:2) describe this situation: "Boards of directors were truly in charge. They gave the money, made the policies, saw to their implementation and laboured no doubts about the "righteousness" of the service".

In such circumstances accountability to outsiders did not arise, as the operation was a relatively "closed shop" in terms of external influences on funding and management. Now things are different; patterns of funding are more diverse and there is a separation between organizations and funding sources. As described in the chapter on management (chapter 5), organizations are now operating as open systems, having greater interaction with their environment (Kast & Rosenzweig 1985). In this altered situation, demands for accountability can arise from the various outside funding sources.

The general economic climate

Butt & Palmer (1986:34) present a good summary of economic reality in recent times:

The economic scene has been characterised by the recession, falling tax revenues from the private sector, the high cost of borrowing money, . . . and an increase in the need for the state to provide help to organizations and individuals in trouble due to the recession. . . . The change in economic and political conditions over the past decade has brought a transition from an expansionary period to an age of accountability.

This difficult economic climate has heralded a renewed focus on value for money (VFM), a concept outlined by Butt & Palmer (1986). Voluntary organizations are given no exemption from this overall concern for fiscal husbandry in these straitened times.

The changing role of the voluntary sector

"Whereas in the past voluntary organizations existed but were largely ignored, now they are seen as an essential element in policy and practice" (Leat 1988:6). Although it is "notoriously difficult to estimate the total revenue of the voluntary sector in Britain" (Knapp et al 1988:3), available data indicate a total figure in excess of twelve billion pounds for England and Wales in 1985 (Posnett 1987:6), accounting for over 4% of GNP. The Charities Aid Foundation estimates a level of funding of 15 billion for the sector in 1992 (CAF 1992). The sector also benefits from considerable fiscal benefits, detailed in Diamond et al (1986). All this adds up to a significant profile for the sector, in economic terms.

The situation in the US is somewhat similar as it is reckoned that "the third sector, sometimes called the "voluntary" or "independent" or "nonprofit" sector, constitutes . . . 6% of the national economy" (Van Til 1988:3). A more detailed account of the scope and dimensions of nonprofit activity in the US is provided by Rudney (1987).

In the absence of any official regulatory authority to date, reliable statistical data on funding in the Irish voluntary sector is not available, and even the government report on fundraising (1990) does not hazard a guess at the overall figure for the sector. In fact the report is bereft of statistical data. However, an estimate of 150 million pounds for charitable fundraising (McCarthy 1989) has not been disputed, so "in anyone's book, charity is big business in Ireland today" (Gibbons 1985:13), bearing in mind the small overall population of 3.5 million.

The general picture emerging is one of a higher profile for the voluntary sector in national economies. The considerable financial input involved brings with it concerns about accountability.

The inescapable fact that "even altruism resources needs to thrive" is noted by Leat et al (1986:140), while Van Til (1988:93) refers to "the mercurial financial support" that provides the necessary funds. As mentioned earlier,in times past the tendency was for a group of concerned individuals to "run the whole show" by both providing and disbursing the funds of a voluntary organization. This situation has changed considerably.

One very significant departure is the increasing reliance on government funding. In the US context, Rosenbaum (1981:82) refers to "the increasing dependence of voluntary sector institutions upon government financial support", while Kramer (1987:247) states that government support is the most important source of revenue. Salamon (1987:99) clarifies the position even further: "Government has become the single most important source of income for most types of nonprofit agencies, outdistancing private charity by roughly two to one".

State funding for voluntary organizations is likewise a key factor in the UK. Even avid supporters of welfare pluralism such as Gladstone (1979) reject private giving as an adequate resource and acknowledge the need for statutory funding. The Wolfenden Committee (1978) also notes the striking failure of private giving to keep pace with inflation and, having examined various options to compensate for this shortfall, points to greater reliance on statutory funding. According to Norton (1985), there is scarcely a government department in the UK which does not make a contribution to the voluntary sector.

The Irish situation is quite similar, with an increasing number of voluntary bodies seeking government funding to finance their operations. In a discussion document on voluntary social services in Ireland the National Social Service Board (NSSB 1982:18) states that "clearly, statutory funding figures considerably in the financing of voluntary bodies." This finding is endorsed by the more recently appointed government committee on fundraising which remarks that most voluntary bodies "now depend to a greater or lesser extent on financial support from the State" (Report on Fundraising 1990:4).

Government funding has implications for the voluntary sector in terms of accountability. Voluntary bodies must be aware that "in accepting public money they also accept the right of the elected guardians of that money to make greater demands of them" (Leat et al 1986:139). Using the term "third party government" to denote this sharing of responsibility between public and private institutions in the US, Salaman (1987:110) considers that it "involves real problems of accountability." Public funding "will usually be accompanied

103

by regulatory practices and accountability requirements" according to Knapp et al (1988:18), while Hartogs & Weber (1978:11) see accountability as "a central and permanent feature for any social agency that accepts funds from Government".

Even though the government purse is tapped for resources, voluntary organizations have always raised funds from non-government providers. Constraints in government expenditure in recent recessionary times mean that "merely to maintain a great many of the existing services greater effort at raising funds from the public has been required" (Report on Fundraising 1990:4). Some of the many fundraising methods used in Ireland are outlined in this government report on fundraising (1990:23-9). The long list indicates the tremendous scope and variety of avenues travelled to tap contributions. It is presented under the main categories of collections, lotteries, sales of goods or services, fundraising social events, sponsored fundraising and, finally, two residual categories of "other" and "newer" forms including legacies, direct mail appeals and telethons. Yet, despite its range and diversity, it is mentioned that this list is not comprehensive as

> methods are continually evolving and technological and other socio-economic changes within the State both force and enable charitable bodies to become more imaginative and innovative in appealing for funds to the public.
>
> (Report on Fundraising 1990:23)

At present in Ireland "there is no requirement for organizations which raise funds from the public for charitable purposes to account to any authority in relation to them" (Report on Fundraising 1990:33). The committee which issued this report was established by the Minister for Justice due to "a great deal of public disquiet and unease" (Report on Fundraising 1990:126). Its recommendations include a system of registration for all organizations raising funds for charitable purposes and the submission of an annual report and account to the registration authority (Report on Fundraising 1990:14).

In the UK where registration of charities is obligatory, problems still arise. Various studies, e.g., Austin & Posnett (1979), NAO (1987), have demonstrated the inability of the regulatory authority, the Charity Commissioners, to enforce the statutory requirements effectively. Irvine (1988:92) states the position in stronger terms:

> The charity's watchdog is so short of funds that it cannot afford to pay the postage to send out reminders to all registered charities, let alone monitor

whether their annual returns are filed. Criticism of the Commission has been vociferous.

This seems to indicate that legislation alone is insufficient; provision must be made also for its effective enforcement to address adequately the demand for accountability.

It is clear that patterns of funding for voluntary organizations are becoming more complex. Governments now make significant contributions to this sector and additional funds flow from other multiple streams. This complex financial web has led, in time, to demands for greater accountability.

Donors, clients and voluntary organizations

As mentioned already, one of the distinguishing characteristics of voluntary nonprofit organizations is their dual system of solicitations and services (Mason 1984) involving donors who provide resources and clients who receive services. Both donors and clients are "customers" of these organizations, but for different reasons. The issue of accountability arises for donors because, as Dubin (1977:270-1) explains, "when money is given, the donor needs to find out if it is helping to accomplish the noble objectives that the receiver of the grant so eloquently stated in its application". In marketing terms, donors are sold a "product", albeit an intangible one (Lovelock & Weinberg 1977) and, bearing in mind that "the public is demanding greater accountability from non-profit . . . organizations" (Hopkins 1980:19), it seems pragmatic to give them some feedback regarding the outcome of their "investment", in order to maintain donor allegiance.

In the UK the Goodman Committee (1976), being concerned about public accountability, stressed the need for charities to be accountable to the public and donors. A later report by the National Audit Office (NAO 1987) on the monitoring and control of charities highlighted the significant level of non-compliance with existing regulations regarding accountability.

An example cited by Rose-Ackerman (1982:193) shows how accountability to donors can be used to positive advantage, in terms of fundraising. She states that the United Way justifies its existence by noting the small proportion of its contributions used to conduct the annual campaign, thus accounting to contributors for their subscriptions and assuring them that excessive amounts are not being absorbed on administration. A similar strategy is adopted by Action Aid UK which covers its administrative expenses through tax relief on covenants from 60,000 subscribers (Irvine 1988). With this arrangement, its director, Andrew Hind explains that "one of Action Aid's most persuasive fundraising messages has been the fact that every penny donated goes directly overseas" (Irvine 1988:92). Once again, this approach acknowledges the importance of accountability to donors.

In contrast, an account by Gibbons (1985) shows how negative feedback about fundraising can cause donors to change their allegiance to competitors in the same "market" for funds. When the Chief Executive of Concern, an Irish Third World relief agency, was convicted and imprisoned for embezzling the funds of the organization, Oxfam (Dublin) got donations from people who had specifically transferred from Concern as a result of the fraud (Gibbons 1985:20). These examples illustrate donors' reactions, both positive and negative, towards the utilisation of their subscriptions. In an era of "increasingly fierce competition for funds" (Irvine 1988:92), voluntary organizations seeking contributions need to be attentive to the needs of their "customers" on the input side (Andreasen 1982). Accountability for funds is one aspect of this process.

Moving to the output side of the equation, there is now a growing recognition that voluntary sector clients also merit attention. As Leat (1988:12) explains, in an era of more critical consumerism:

> Instead of doing things for others, instead of knowing and doing what is best, many voluntary organizations have been challenged to do things with others, or even to serve others, not in the old paternalistic way but in a new relationship in which the user defines and provider provides.

The merits of user accountability are endorsed also by Hinton & Hyde (1980-81:15).

External demands for accountability from both donors and clients is now being reflected in some instances by similar demands from voluntary organizations themselves. For example, in 1988 the Chief Executive of an Irish Third World relief agency, Gorta, stated that existing legislation was "totally inadequate . . . Gorta's demands include the regulation of charities, accountability and the control of administrative costs" (Irish Times 1988). Subsequently the Irish government's committee on fundraising, which held its inaugural meeting in February 1990, also reports the keen interest of charitable organizations themselves in having the present unsatisfactory situation changed:

> We have reached the conclusion . . . that further statutory controls are necessary. These conclusions have been greatly strengthened by the opinions expressed to us by the representatives of long established and

highly regarded charitable organizations in this country. . . . We have heard very persuasive arguments from these sources . . .supporting in principle a scheme of reform which would involve the registration of organizations raising funds for charitable purposes and the establishment of a supervisory authority.

(Report on Fundraising 1990:68)

More recently, a draft charter for the sector, prepared from a voluntary sector perspective and representing the views of over sixty voluntary organizations, suggests that it should "develop its accountability to those who avail of the services provided . . . (and) to those who fund the work done"

(CWC 1992:3).

Likewise, Leat (1988:84), in her study of accountability in a UK setting, found that despite the difficulties involved, staff interviewed "mentioned the benefits of being accountable and being seen to be accountable". In another study with a group of one parent families, group members also voiced concerns about "the lack of accountability" to outsiders (Billis 1984a:13).

To summarise this sub-section, there is evidence of an acceptance among donors, clients and even voluntary bodies themselves that accountability in the voluntary sector is important. As "accountability" and "accounting" are "clearly related" (Laughlin 1990:93), and also as voluntary sector accountability has become a live issue in recent accountancy literature, the next section reviews the contribution of the accountancy profession to the topic of accountability in a nonprofit setting.

Accountants and voluntary sector accountability

Until recently, little attention has been paid to the voluntary sector in terms of accounting and reporting. Rather, as Jones & Pendlebury (1985:490) observe, "the profession of accounting has, in the UK and the US, overwhelmingly concerned itself with business." Olenick (1988:33) makes the same point, stating that "the accountancy profession has long paid little heed to the non-profit world and has only in recent years begun to struggle with its special needs".

However, some change was discernible in the 1980s. A report of a research subcommittee of the Institute of Chartered Accountants of England and Wales (ICAEW) made a key contribution to raising the profile of financial reporting by charities. Its joint authors, Bird & Morgan-Jones (1981), were asked to undertake a critical survey of the published accounts of charities and then to draft recommended principles of accounting and disclosure for charity accounting, in the light of their findings. The bulk of their research is based on a survey of the annual accounts of the larger fundraising charities in the UK. Reports and accounts were requested from 100, and 85 obliged. The analysis of the data received demonstrated immense variety in accounting practices. On a positive note, the use of diagrams in some accounts, showing a breakdown of income and expenditure, is commended by the researchers who consider them to be "often more informative to a layman than the accounts themselves"

(Bird and Morgan-Jones 1981:102).

On the negative side, a number of examples of contentious accountancy treatments is given by the authors who comment that "management is fearful that, if it reports truly and fairly, its fund-raising activities will be adversely affected" (Bird & Morgan-Jones 1981:196).

Regarding the possible use of business accounting methods by charities, the authors consider the differing goals of charities and commercial enterprises as an important factor in terms of financial reporting. Whereas a commercial enterprise might be judged in terms of profitability, a charity should be judged on the basis of the success of its efforts to achieve the objectives for which it was established. Yet, this team considers that the adoption of practices similar to those in the commercial field would improve the situation, while little attention is paid to other non-financial information.

This major study by Bird and Morgan-Jones prompted the Accounting Standards Committee (ASC) to set up a working party in 1982 to consider the matter and subsequently it published three documents on the subject of accounting by charities. This departure marks the first time that the accountancy profession had taken an official interest in the voluntary sector and its accounting needs.

The first of the three publications, a discussion document on accounting by charities, was issued in 1984 (ASC 1984). This initial momentum was maintained by the publication of an exposure draft, ED 38, the following year (ASC 1985). Finally, following extensive discussion and consultation, a statement of recommended practice, SORP 2, was issued in May 1988 to "help improve the quality of financial reporting by charities . . . provide assistance to those who are responsible for the preparation of charities" annual reports and accounts . . . assist in reducing the current diversity in accounting practice and presentation" (ASC 1988:2). Regarding the annual report, its suggested contents include legal and administrative details, a trustees" report covering a description of the charity and a commentary on the figures in the accounts, and finally the actual accounts. Overall the SORP leans heavily in the direction of technical issues related to the production of audited accounts and here again relatively little attention is paid to other information.

These ASC documents are not without their critics. Comments on the ASC discussion document (ASC 1984a) include one from Gray who, in his response, viewed financial accounts as having only a secondary role in accounting by charities, and criticised the discussion paper for "failing to explicitly recognise that financial accounts cannot show the effectiveness of a charity and are thus a quite inappropriate medium with which to attempt to discharge accountability" (ASC 1984a:281). Gray maintains this stance in another article significantly entitled "Uncharitable view of accounting" (Gray 1984). In it he argues that "to discharge accountability for actions related to social benefits given to a section of the community, it necessarily follows that the accounts must be in a form which reflects these actions (Gray 1984:84).

Another contributor to the debate, Chilvers (1987), also refers to the over emphasis on commercial accountancy practices. In keeping with this stance, Randall (1989) considers that annual reports are not just a matter of accounts - they must be qualitative as well as quantitative. This approach would certainly ease the burden of comprehension, given that many of the users of charity accounts are not in general as "sophisticated" as regular users of commercial accounts (Falk 1987). Also the narrative section of the report can be utilised to elaborate on factors not readily amenable to monetary assessment, such as the contribution of volunteer help and intangible income received.

The limitations of over-reliance on financial accounting in the case of non-profit organizations are addressed by Jones & Pendlebury (1985:494):

> The main emphasis of accounting in such organizations has traditionally been that of securing financial stewardship. . . . Such accounting, although essential in terms of financial probity, reveals very little in terms of efficiency and effectiveness.

In general it seems that the efforts of the accountancy profession to address the issue of accounting by charities go some way towards encouraging a more orderly approach to this task, and thus replace the rather liberal regime with regard to charity accounts in the past, replete with dubious practice. It can be said that SORP 2 represents an important step forward and it is to be hoped that

> all involved in the management of charities will welcome the attempt to improve the regulation of these bodies, so as to make life increasingly

difficult for the tiny minority who misuse charitable status for private profit.

(Randall 1989:71)

Yet, SORP 2 has been criticised for having an over-emphasis on financial aspects which, given the non-profit nature of voluntary organizations, is insufficient on its own to convince contributors that effectiveness and efficiency have been achieved.

Some implications of accountability

Undoubtedly life was easier in nonprofit organizations, at least in terms of accountability, when they operated largely as "closed systems" with regard to funding. Now, funding patterns have changed, bringing with them "the woes of accountability" (Hartogs & Weber 1978:6). Demands for accountability can give rise to concerns about possible threats to independence, while complying with accountability requirements has implications in terms of costs, time and skill (Hartogs & Weber 1978:13; Leat et al 1986:144).

"Organizations are naturally loath to compromise their independence and frequently resent what they regard as the intrusion of the funding agency into their affairs" (NSSB 1986:19). This perceived threat to independence seems to be associated primarily with the acceptance of statutory funding. As Gladstone (1979:88) observes, "it is necessary to face the knotty issue of how far Government funding is reconcilable with the independence essential for genuine voluntary action". Concern about independence is referred to by many writers including Knapp et al (1988), Kramer (1981), Leat et al (1981 & 1986), Leat (1988) and Mellor (1985). However, there does not appear to be any strong evidence to support the perceived concern that independence may be significantly curtailed through acceptance of State funding.

Kramer's (1981:291) study found that "voluntary agency autonomy is seldom compromised by the accountability requirements of governmental funding sources", while a later study by Kramer & Grossman (1987:42) endorsed this finding, stating that "service providers are generally able to maintain a relatively high degree of independence." The findings of Leat et al (1986:94) concur: "the most striking fact is how few organizations (at all levels of aid) mention loss of independence as a disadvantage of statutory aid." Likewise Mellor (1985:139-40) comments that "it was pleasing to be able to state that none of our sample felt that their independence was improperly jeopardised by having to account in agreed ways for government grants".

110

One way for organizations in the sector to avoid having their independence threatened is to ensure funding from a number of different sources, rather than be dependent on any one stream of supply. As Kramer (1981:161) notes, "there is considerable agreement on the importance of income diversity as a means of avoiding overdependency." Lee (1987:9) makes a similar point in relation to Irish agencies: "There is a reluctance on the part of some voluntary organizations to rely too heavily on statutory funding, as this may restrict . . . their ability to criticise their funders".

Responding to demands for accountability may involve additional work for benefitting agencies. Hartogs & Weber (1978:14) report difficulties in this regard, particularly for smaller agencies "because of the limitations of dollars, staff and expertise." Similar problems are noted by Leat (1988:57): "One of the most common and emphatic complaints of organizations receiving funding from several statutory sources was the time spent in preparing separate and different reports and accounts for each body", a point supported by Poulton (1988:15). This cost problem is often compounded by the fact that the additional costs incurred are not always taken into account by the funding agency seeking greater accountability. As Rosenbaum (1981:85) describes it: "a special irony here is that government often fails to cover the full cost of administrative work necessitated by its grants".

To summarise, the available evidence suggests that while the independence of voluntary agencies is not greatly threatened by demands for accountability, the associated costs in complying with this requirement may pose problems.

Accountability and control

The previous chapter (6) examined control in organizations which essentially is concerned with monitoring activities to ensure that they are being accomplished as planned, and correcting any significant deviations. It was established that control is important in an organization because it monitors whether objectives are being accomplished. Due to the particular characteristics of nonprofit organizations, implementing control is laced with difficulties.

These same characteristics impinge on accountability as, once again, the nonprofit nature of voluntary organizations means that fiscal information alone does not give the whole picture regarding attainment of objectives (Chilvers 1987; Gray 1984; Jones & Pendlebury 1985; Randall 1989). Yet the cumulative evidence outlined indicates that "the problem of voluntary sector accountability is not going to go away" (Leat 1988:84).

It may be asked: "What is the connection between control and accountability?" As Day & Klein (1987:227) see it, "to be fully accountable implies the ability to exercise control." A similar view is expressed by Leat et al (1986:138) when they state that "being accountable entails being prepared to submit one's work to the critical appraisal of others and that in turn implies a more self-critical approach to one's own work." In other words, unless there is a clear picture of what is going on in an organization, i.e., unless there is control, it is difficult, if not impossible to account to outside interested parties about progress. For instance how can an organization assure donors that only X% of their contribution is being spent on fundraising if X is an unknown quantity?

Therefore it seems reasonable to conclude that internal control is a prerequisite for external accountability. If an organization is itself unclear about objectives and their attainment, how can it report reliably to outsiders that these objectives have been achieved? Yet, if it does not manage to convince funders about its effectiveness in achieving objectives, how can it hope to sustain further contributions from the same source, or indeed from other donors who may need to be convinced about the effectiveness of the organization before they part with their money?

Summary

This chapter has focused on accountability in voluntary organizations. The concept of accountability was explored and its dimensions reviewed, showing how it can broaden out beyond the realm of mere fiscal concern. Then concerns about fraud and malpractice in the voluntary sector were considered. These, in turn, led to calls for greater accountability in nonprofit organizations. Adopting an "open systems" approach, the impact of various environmental influences on the voluntary sector were explored to establish how the perceived greater demand for accountability has evolved. Various factors, including the general economic climate, the overall profile of the voluntary sector in society, funding patterns and demands from both donors and clients were identified.

The deliberations of accountants on the issue of voluntary sector accountability were reviewed. A brief discussion followed about perceived threats to the independence of the sector, arising from greater accountability, together with consideration of the additional costs involved in providing more detailed accountability. Finally, the link between external accountability and internal control in voluntary organizations was explored.

To conclude this chapter, it has been established that the higher profile of the voluntary sector in society has been accompanied by a demand for greater accountability. In broad terms this entails assuring external funding and regulatory bodies and individual donors that objectives are being achieved and that financial probity is being observed in the process. Unless organizations have appropriate internal control measures to provide information on these areas, they will not be in a position to convince outsiders of their attainment. In other words, to put the argument succinctly, internal control is a prerequisite for external accountability.

The chapter also brings Part III of the study to a conclusion. The fieldwork for the research is detailed in Part IV which now follows, commencing with a short chapter on research methodology.

Part IV
THE FIELDWORK

8 Research Methodology

An overview of the research methodology is presented in this chapter. It commences by defining the terms "research" and "methodology". This is followed by a brief look at qualitative and quantitative research methods and the "best method" debate is touched on briefly. Finally, qualitative research, the chosen method for this study, is explored in some detail.

Defining terms

According to Williamson et al (1982:31-2), the purpose of research is

> to produce findings that add to our knowledge. . .Social research is a dynamic process that involves the collection and analysis of data and the formation of conclusions based on those data. Its goal is to add to knowledge through exploration, description and explanation of social reality.

Methodology, on the other hand, refers to "the way in which we approach problems and seek answers. In the social sciences the term applies to how one conducts research" (Taylor & Bogdan 1984:1).

Methodological choices available

Broadly speaking, the researcher has a choice of two paths to follow, choosing either a quantitative or a qualitative course. This choice derives from two major theoretical perspectives which have dominated social science research (Bruyn 1966; Deutscher 1973). The first of these, positivism, originated in the social sciences with the great early theorists of the nineteenth and early twentieth centuries, notably Durkheim (1938; 1951). Essentially positivists seek the facts or causes of social phenomena apart from the subjective states of individuals (Gill & Johnson 1991). In contrast, the second major theoretical perspective, described by Deutscher (1973) as phenomenological, is committed to understanding social phenomena from the actor's own perspective. Strike's (1972:28) observations are relevant here:

> Human beings can be understood in a manner that other objects of study cannot. Men have purposes and emotions, they make plans, construct cultures, and hold certain values, and their behaviour is influenced by such values, plans and purposes. In short, a human being lives in a world which has "meaning" to him, and, because his behaviour has meaning, human actions are intelligible in ways that the behaviour of nonhuman objects is not.

As positivists and phenomenologists approach problems in different ways, their research demands different methodologies. The two broad approaches used are explained by Taylor & Bogdan (1984:2):

> Adopting a natural science model of research, the positivist searches for causes through methods such as questionnaires, inventories, and demography that produce data amenable to statistical analysis. The phenomenologist seeks understanding through qualitative methods such as participant observation, in-depth interviewing and others that yield descriptive data.

In other words, positivists adopt a quantitative approach, while phenomenologists choose a qualitative course.

Selecting a research methodology

In their now classic work on the generation of "grounded theory", Glaser & Strauss (1967:15) graphically capture the tenor of the earlier methodological debate when they refer to "the clash" between advocates of quantitative and qualitative data. They go on to explain how advances in quantitative methods

> initiated the zeal to test unconfirmed theories with the "facts". Qualitative research, because of its poor showing in producing the scientifically reproducible fact . . . was relegated to preliminary, exploratory, groundbreaking work for getting surveys started. (Glaser & Strauss 1967:15)

The kernel of the debate centred on the primacy of emphasis on verification or generation of theory.

This debate has now softened and there is an acceptance of methodological diversity. In fact there seems to be a return to the position advocated by Burgess (1927:120) over sixty years ago when he reminded social scientists that qualitative and quantitative research are deserving of "equal recognition". Certainly the primacy of verification has passed and qualitative methods "now occupy a central position in both teaching and research" (Silverman 1985:ix).

The reality of the research process is captured by Patton (1987:45) when he acknowledges that

> there are no perfect research designs. There are always trade-offs. These trade-offs are necessitated by limited resources, limited time, . . . and limits in the human ability to grasp the complex nature of social reality.

Likewise, one of the major themes in Gill & Johnson's (1991:2) book on management research is that "there is no one best approach" in research methodology. McGrath (1982) aptly uses the term "dilemmatics" to describe the intricacies of selecting a research method.

Essentially, a choice between adopting a qualitative or a quantitative approach to research involves deciding between breadth or depth in a study. Choices have to be made about either (a) studying a few issues in great depth - a qualitative approach - or (b) studying more questions, but in less depth - a quantitative approach. The advantages of the latter approach is that is can measure the reactions of a great many people to a limited set of questions, thus facilitating comparison and statistical aggregation of the data. This in turn yields a broad generalizable set of findings. In contrast qualitative methods typically produce a wealth of rich data about a much smaller number of people and cases. To put it another way, qualitative data deliver depth and detail.

Given the different emphasis in each approach, when deciding on a research strategy, the issue becomes one of methodological appropriateness, i.e., selecting a method that is considered suitable to address the particular research questions under review (Downey & Ireland 1983). In some cases, both in-depth treatment and survey methods appear attractive, but limited resources do not allow for pursuing both options. For example, in one study on the effects of centrally imposed financial constraints on the management of the public sector of higher education (Gill & Pratt 1986), the research team favoured an in depth approach whereas the members of the steering group showed preference for a survey method. As the level of resources precluded the ideal strategy of doing both, the steering committee accepted the qualitative approach.

The underlying philosophical orientation of the researcher can also have a bearing on the "mode of engagement" (Burrell & Morgan 1979). As Gill & Johnson (1991:126) observe:

> If we accept the philosophical assumptions of positivism and its consequent epistemological prescriptions, we are inevitably drawn towards the exclusive utilization of nomothetic methodology. Conversely, if our philosophical orientation is interpretative, the ensuing epistemological mandate impels us towards a more ideological methodology.

In sum, methodological appropriateness, allied to philosophical orientation, are the key factors in methodological choice.

In this study, the researcher decided that the emphasis should be on the collection of qualitative data, using a limited number of information-rich case studies. Having opted for a qualitative approach, this method is now explored in some greater detail.

What is qualitative methodology?

"The phrase "qualitative methodology" refers in the broadest sense to research that produces descriptive data; people's own written or spoken words and observable behaviour" (Taylor & Bogdan 1984:5). The emphasis in qualitative methods on "depth and detail: in-depth interviews, detailed descriptions" is highlighted by Patton (1987:45). The resultant qualitative data "are attractive for many reasons: they are rich, full, earthy, holistic, "real" " (Miles 1983:117). In essence, qualitative research relies on verbal rather than numerical notations and focuses on phenomenological aspects of the research topic.

Qualitative research is inductive, as concepts and insights are developed from patterns in the data, i.e., "grounded theory" (Glaser & Strauss 1967), in contrast to the deductive approach in quantitative research of collecting data to assess preconceived hypotheses or theories. As Williamson et al (1982:25-6) describe it, the hallmark of induction is "the discovery and building of new theory as research progresses . . . induction is initially exploratory and vividly descriptive" whereas, in contrast, "deductive theory does not emerge immediately from the data; it is conceived beforehand and applied to the data."

Historical background to qualitative research

Although the strong re-emergence of qualitative data is of relatively recent origin, the approach itself is not new. In fact, according to Wax (1971), who provides a detailed history on the qualitative approach, descriptive observation, interviewing and other qualitative methods are as old as recorded history. However, it was not until the nineteenth century that qualitative methods were consciously employed in social research. A Frenchman, Frederick LePlay, whose major work *Les Ouvriers Europeens* was published in 1855, relied on participant observation, in-depth interviews and case studies in family research and he was "probably the first qualitative social researcher" (LaRosse & Wolf 1985:532). The first work to be carried out in industry in this tradition was that of Charles Booth in his study of the working people of London in the 1880s (Gill & Johnson 1991). However, qualitative research was not fully recognised until the early part of this century when Thomas & Znaniecki (1918) published their famous monograph *The Polish Peasant* which represented "a turning point in the development of social science method" (Redfield 1942:vii).

The "Chicago tradition", also in the earlier part of this century, was associated with qualitative research (Glaser & Strauss 1967; Taylor & Bogdan 1984). Then a gradual shift in emphasis towards rigorous verification of existing theories meant that interest in qualitative methods waned. As noted previously, since the 1960s there has been a re-emergence in the use of qualitative methods (Bruyn 1966; Glaser & Strauss 1967; Wax 1971). Focussing on management research, Gill & Johnson (1991) detail numerous studies which employed a qualitative methodology, ranging from Lupton's

121

(1963) study at shop floor level, to Winkler's (1987) observational research at board level. Therefore the present situation is one which offers a choice for researchers "according to whether we seek breadth or depth in our investigation" (Williamson et al 1982:419-20).

Qualitative research methods

What are the "tools" of qualitative research? "Doing description is . . . the fundamental act of data collection in a qualitative study" (Van Mannen 1983:9). This emphasis on description is echoed by Mintzberg (1983:106) who recounts that his own "direct research" in organizations has been "as purely descriptive as we have been able to make it".

Actual data collection can be approached in three ways: (i) in-depth interviewing; (ii) direct observation and (iii) written documents (Patton 1987:7). As in-depth interviewing is the major tool used in this study, it is now examined. Taylor & Bogdan (1984:77) provide details on the method, explaining that

> by in-depth qualitative interviewing we mean repeated face-to-face encounter between researchers and informants directed towards understanding informants' perspectives on their lives, experiences or situation as expressed in their own words.

The label "intensive interviewing" is used by Williamson et al (1982) to describe the same approach. It is very different from the more standardised format of structured interview used in large-scale surveys, opinion polls and questionnaires which usually entail the administration of a pre-selected set of questions and so fit diverse various opinions and experiences within a range of pre-determined responses. The relatively open-ended flexible nature of in-depth interviewing, in stark contrast, avoids the constraint of pre-determined groupings. Rather, it "permits the respondent to describe what is meaningful and salient without being pigeonholed into standardised categories" (Patton 1987:15) and so provides a rich storehouse of information.

The relative flexibility of in-depth interviewing does not release the researcher from the need to be orderly and systematic in approach. Mintzberg (1983:110) stresses the need for a well-designed focus in order "to collect specific kinds of data systematically". This process is facilitated by the use of an interview schedule or "topic outline" (Williamson et al 1982:178) which lists specific issues to be brought to an interviewee's attention. Using this tool ensures that key topics are explored with a number of informants. As Taylor & Bogdan (1984:92) explain,

> the interview guide is not a structured schedule or protocol. In the interview the researcher decides how to phrase questions and when to ask them. The interview guide serves solely to remind the interviewer to ask about certain things.

The interview schedule used for this research is detailed later in chapter 13. Due to the relatively unstructured nature of the in-depth interview, Williamson et al (1982:181) caution that "it is important for the intensive interviewer to nurture rapport with the other party, within the framework of an appropriate degree of objectivity".

Limitations of qualitative research

Despite the attractiveness of a qualitative study in terms of richness and depth of data, it does have some limitations. One common concern centres on the subjectivity of the researcher and hence the lack of objectivity in the overall qualitative research, in comparison to the perceived objectivity of quantitative research. However, whereas the sense of precision and accuracy conveyed by statistical data in quantitative studies may indicate detachment, the construction of questionnaires to produce the raw data on which the statistical calculations are based is no less open to the intrusion of bias than asking questions at an interview.

As Patton (1987:166) discerns, "numbers do not protect against bias; they sometimes merely disguise it. All statistical data are based on someone's definition of what to measure and how to measure it". To substantiate his case, he cites the example of the seemingly "objective" Consumer Price Index which, in reality, has large subjective elements in terms of deciding on what items to include in the index. So, when examined closely and stripped of impressions, quantitative methods are no more synonymous with objectivity than qualitative methods are synonymous with subjectivity.

The small sample size of qualitative studies can also give rise to concern, due to the ensuing difficulty in generalizing. In relation to this perceived shortcoming, Williamson et al (1982:422) make the relevant observation that "human beings" unparalleled capacity for adaptation . . . makes any generalizations produced by social scientists time-specific". The context-free implications of generalizations also pose problems for Guba & Lincoln

(1981:62) as they consider that "it is virtually impossible to imagine any human behaviour that is not heavily mediated by the context in which it occurs".

In organizational research, limited samples do not pose any problems for Mintzberg (1983). Commenting that "too many of the results have been significant only in the statistical sense of the word," he asks: "What, for example, is wrong with samples of one? Why should researchers have to apologise for them?"(Mintzberg 1983:107).

While qualitative studies may give rise to concerns about subjectivity, in reality such concerns may equally apply to quantitative studies, where the subjective element may not be as apparent, as it is distanced from the final statistical outcome. Qualitative studies may not lend themselves to generalizations, but as generalizations are limited in both time and context, this is not seen as a major drawback.

Summary

This chapter on research methodology includes a review of both quantitative and qualitative approaches to research, together with the underlying theoretical perspectives of each approach, and establishes how these varying perspectives give rise to the need for different methodologies. Positivists travel the broad quantitative track, using questionnaires and surveys, while phenomenologists pursue the qualitative path, relying on in-depth interviews and other methods that yield rich descriptive data.

The erstwhile strident debate on the alleged superiority of quantitative methods has now died down, being replaced by an acceptance that either method can be appropriate, depending on the context of the research and the requirements for either breadth or depth of data.

As this study is qualitative in approach, the nature of this research method was explored in some detail, tracing its origins and reviewing the "tools" used to gather the required descriptive data. In common with other research methods, qualitative research does have limitations. The main constraints were debated. These related to possible subjectivity and lack of generalizability of data.

Having completed this review of methodology, the fieldwork is now presented.

9 Preliminary Fieldwork, Case Study Selection and Interview Process

This chapter introduces the fieldwork undertaken for the study. The data collected covered two main areas, consisting of background data on the Irish voluntary sector and case-study material emanating from a series of in-depth interviews in ten Irish voluntary organizations. The background research, case study selection and the actual interview process are detailed in this chapter. Findings from the main study are presented in the following chapter (10).

Background field research

Prior to deciding on a specific focus for this research, it was considered essential to obtain a broad appreciation of how the Irish voluntary sector operated. Therefore, following on from the initial review of the general literature relating to the voluntary sector, a series of interviews was conducted with a cross-section of key informants, mainly during the latter part of 1989, in order to provide background information for the more focused part of the research on management, control and accountability.

The aims of the preliminary fieldwork were:

- To gather background information on Irish voluntary organizations so that the researcher would be equipped with a broad working knowledge of the sector in Irish society.
- To "test the water" regarding the feasibility of undertaking research relating to the management of Irish voluntary agencies

- To establish contacts with a range of voluntary organizations in order to identify possible cases for the main fieldwork planned for a later stage of the research.

Nineteen respondents from fifteen different organizations were contacted during the course of this preliminary fieldwork. These informants were selected in order to provide insights on voluntary activity in Ireland, from a range of perspectives. Included were statutory bodies whose area of operation impinged on the voluntary sector, religious organizations with an interest in voluntary action, and a cross-section of voluntary organizations. These various bodies were identified by a gradual process of "poking around" (Mintzberg 1983). Table 9.1 below provided details of those interviewed, indicating their organizational affiliation and the focus of each interview.

Table 9.1
Interviews for preliminary fieldwork

Organization	Main activity	Respondent	Focus of interview
Commrs. of Char.Dons. & Bequests	Statutory body	Information officer	Scope of work
CMRS	Umbrella grp. rel. orders	Director	Gen discussion on vol. sector
Council for Social Welfare	Church body	Council member	Vol.sector involvement
CSSC	Vol.org.	(i) S/wkr. (ii) AIDS prog. dir.	Scope of work Management of programme
FLAC	Legal Aid	Bd. member	Management
Focus Point	Homeless	Director	Management
IPA	Training	(i) Trainer (ii)Res. wkr.	Mgmt. training Research

126

Table 9.1 (Contd.)
Interviews for preliminary fieldwork

Organization	Main activity	Respondent	Focus of interview
Irish Heart Foundation	Vol. org	Director	Management
IWA	Vol. org	Acting CEO	Management
Natl.Council Blind	Vol. Org	Director	Management
NESC	Statutory body	Head of Soc. Policy	Role of Vol. orgns.
NSSB	Statutory body	(i) Dir.	Information on vol. sector
		(ii)Info. officer	Information on vol. sector
Revenue Commrs.	Gov.	Section head	Regulation of charities
St.Vincent's Trust	Vol. org	Director	Management
UVOH	Umbrella vol org	(i) late CEO	Management
		(ii)CEO	Management

This table indicates the wide spread of respondents. In addition, contact was made with the six government departments - education; the environment; health; justice; labour and social welfare - which are involved in grant aiding voluntary organizations operating in Ireland. The data provided on the Irish voluntary sector gave the researcher an opportunity to piece together various aspects of its operation, yielding a much more complete picture of the entire sector.

The interview with the spokesperson for the Commissioners for Charitable Donations and Bequests confirmed that, unlike the Charity Commissioners in the UK, this body is very limited in the scope of its operations, having only "enabling powers rather than enforcing powers". It has eleven commissioners who are appointed by the government. Dating back to the middle of the last century, this body is mainly concerned with holding funds in trust for various charities and administering small trusts, a lot of which are very old. In 1989 it had 17.5 million pounds in trust, 13 million pounds in unit trusts and 4.5 million pounds on deposit (Newman 1989). These commissioners have no overall responsibility for charities in general.

The respondent from the Revenue Commissioners clarified the position regarding registration of charities. He explained that, at present, there is no onus on them to register with any statutory authority. Those who do register are motivated mainly by self interest, their incentive being to qualify for tax exemption or to reclaim Deposit Interest Retention Tax (DIRT). For instance, this spokesman said that claims for tax repayments, which are entertained only from registered charities, shot up from about 40 per annum prior to the introduction of DIRT to over 1,000 once DIRT was introduced in the 1986 Finance Act. A second motivation for registration is to procure statutory grants which are paid only to registered charities.

This informant also stated that "accounts of charities are not scrutinised at this time", confirming the rather lax approach to overall control of charities. His personal estimate of the total annual amount collected for charities was around 200 million pounds, indicating a sizeable sum in the context of concern about accountability.

There is some legislation relevant to Irish charities which are governed by the following Acts: the Charities Act 1961; The Street and House to House Collections Act 1962; the Income Tax Act 1967, sections 333 and 334; the Charities Act 1973 and the Gaming and Lotteries Act, 1956, sections 27 and 28.

As O'Connell (1988) explains, the Charities Act, 1961, merely deals with any charitable bequest or devise and does not provide for the supervision or monitoring of the activities of charities. The Street and House to House Collection Act, 1962, deals with collection permits and is mainly concerned with illegal organizations as a permit is only refused if the collection is for unlawful purposes or purposes contrary to public morality. The Charities Act, 1973, is concerned with extending the powers of the Commissioners of Charitable Donations and Bequests and amending the 1961 Charities Act. The

Income Tax Act, 1967, in sections 333 and 334, provides for exemption from tax for a body of persons established for charitable purposes in respect of income applied to those charitable purposes. The Gaming and Lotteries Act, 1956, concerns itself with the issuing of Garda permits and court licences to hold lotteries.

Putting together the information supplied by the spokespersons for the Commissioners for Charitable Donations and Bequests and the Revenue Commissioners, together with the legislative provisions outlined above, it can be concluded that, currently in Ireland, there is relatively little statutory control exercised over the voluntary sector as a whole.

The spokesperson from the Department of Health confirmed that they receive "thousands of applications" for grant aid, so that even those whose applications are recommended by the relevant Health Board cannot all be facilitated. In cases where grants are made, a certificate of expenditure is requested which is checked by auditors from the Department to ensure that "the money is spent for the designated purpose". In other words, the focus is on fiscal accountability. A respondent on the receiving end of grant aid, the Director of St. Vincent's Trust, confirmed this approach, stating that receipts were requested to match the amount of the grant received, and that was the extent of the accountability sought. This information indicates that the accountability demanded from voluntary organizations by statutory funders tends to be confined to the fiscal area.

The total amount of statutory funding provided to voluntary organizations operating in Ireland amounts to over 200 million pounds, as detailed in Appendix I. This confirms the importance of this source of funding for the voluntary sector.

Moving to the arena of social policy, in 1989, the Head of Social Policy in the National Economic and Social Council (NESC), described the voluntary sector to this researcher as being an "unploughed furrow" in terms of social policy. However, the proposed White Paper and Charter on the sector, as part of the government's Programme for Economic and Social Progress (PESP 1991) suggests that change may now occur.

Management

Turning to management in voluntary agencies, respondents from the voluntary bodies indicated a need for input in this area and, in addition, were very supportive and enthusiastic about the proposed research being undertaken. Perceived shortcomings in management, both at an organizational and sectoral level, were highlighted by the various respondents. The CEO of the National

Council for the Blind commented that voluntary organizations, unlike commercial undertakings, "can be as inefficient as possible in the service they provide and yet stay in business, as their inefficiencies are not tested". He considered that older organizations, in particular, can have problems as "the starters [founding members] are dead and therefore the fanaticism is gone". In the case of his own organization, with roots going back to the end of the last century, it was in the process of going through a period of fundamental change and consolidation with a view to improving its overall performance. Managerial problems cited included the lack of a proper organizational structure, under utilisation of its 600 volunteers due to a lack of co-ordination, and the need for specific training for both volunteers and professional staff.

One of the earliest interviews was with the late Paddy Byrne, then CEO of The Union of Voluntary Organizations for the Handicapped (UVOH), who had worked previously in the Irish Wheelchair Association (IWA) and so had a wide understanding of the voluntary sector at both a specific and more general level. He expressed great concern about management in voluntary agencies and was particularly enthusiastic about any research being undertaken which might lead to an improvement in this area. Sadly, his untimely death put an end to his personal involvement in promoting this cause.

Roger Acton, his successor in UVOH, also rated management as being a "significant problem" in the sector. In his experience, gleaned from dealing with a broad range of organizations, "a lot of voluntary organizations are managed by people motivated by an interest in helping, befriending, counselling and everything except management!" He explained that this came about because many of those operating in the sector became involved in reaction to a personal trauma in their lives, citing examples such as an organization for polio sufferers which was set up by a man whose son had contracted polio and the Cystic Fibrosis Association being managed by a mother who had lost two children to the disease. In other words, it was suggested that personal interest was the prime motivating force in many instances.

Three of the CEOs interviewed confirmed this inferred lack of management in the sector. While all three were actively managing their respective agencies on a day-to-day basis, they were very vague and tentative when this researcher asked them in a discussion about their overall approach to management at a more theoretical level, indicating little appreciation or understanding of the actual management process.

The acting CEO of another organization, who shall remain anonymous in deference to the nature of some of his adverse comments about this organization, was in broad agreement with Roger Acton of UVOH. As he perceived the situation in his organization, "there was a lack of a structured management approach to the operation of the business" and so "performance was not all it should be." He felt that, with an annual budget in excess of 1 million pounds, "the operation is now big business, yet very few adopt a business-like approach." As an example, he stated that until the mid 1980s the organization had never dismissed any staff for poor performance, resulting in "a lot of passengers" being carried. Regarding the proposed research, he welcomed it as, in his view, managerial input "was badly needed."

On the training front, a trainer with the Institute of Public Administration (IPA),a statutory body, felt that voluntary agencies "are all engaged in management, at some level, and so should apply some principles of management". However, he confirmed that, to date, very little had been provided by way of formal management training specifically geared to the voluntary sector.

In general, the interviews which focused on management in the voluntary sector highlighted some of the attendant problems in this area. Also, respondents were supportive of the proposed research. This endorsement from practitioners in the field encouraged the researcher to proceed with the main fieldwork.

Establishing research contacts

During the course of the initial fieldwork this researcher always had an eye to the future, bearing in mind the need to identify a specific set of case-study organizations for the planned study on management, control and accountability. It was felt that the positive response received during the initial fieldwork augured well for further investigation in the field. The researcher was able to establish an "open door" in the various organizations contacted as a first step to further exploration.

As mentioned previously, it was decided to do a qualitative study, confined to a limited number of in-depth case studies, rather than a more broadly based quantitative study. The general plan for the focused study was to undertake this research in ten voluntary organizations. Bearing in mind Gill & Johnson's (1991:13) cautionary note that "students often start with ideas for projects where accessibility will clearly prove difficult", the necessity to tread carefully in the area of case selection was appreciated.

Having considered various possibilities, it was finally decided to pursue a generous offer of support from the CEO of the Union of Voluntary Organizations (UVOH) and select the sample from its affiliated organizations as it was considered that having the backing of the CEO of the individual

131

organizations' umbrella body, UVOH, would be very advantageous in gaining access to individual organizations. This was confirmed subsequently in the course of the fieldwork, as it smoothed the path of entry into all ten selected organizations and helped to allay any reservations that might have arisen if an unknown researcher had presented herself "cold", seeking specific and, at times, sensitive information.

While access is obviously a vital consideration, the quality of the sample is of equal import. Here again UVOH measured up to requirements, as it is the umbrella organization for 44 of Ireland's leading service providers to people with physical disability, sensory disability, invisible disability and mental handicap. (See Appendix II for a list of affiliated organizations.) A measure of its overall impact and significance can be gained from the following global statistics. Collectively, the organizations affiliated to UVOH have a payroll of over 5,000 employees and a combined gross income of approximately 50 million pounds per annum, while an estimated 50,000 clients are in receipt of services from the affiliated organizations at any one time (Acton 1991). Therefore UVOH as a whole is representative of a broad spectrum of voluntary action in Ireland. So the study sample chosen from UVOH, while not representative in the statistical sense, is nonetheless representative of a significant part of the sector in terms of financial importance and clients served.

At this stage, the preliminary fieldwork had progressed to the point of obtaining pertinent background information on the Irish voluntary sector, verifying the usefulness and feasibility of undertaking research focused on the management of voluntary agencies, and establishing contacts in order to progress to a more focused study.

Case site selection

This section introduces the host organizations selected for the main fieldwork. The selection of the ten agencies is described, together with a brief background sketch on each one. The actual selection process aimed at including a cross-section of organizations in terms of five key variables, as follows:

- size: large/small client base
- age: long established/new
- staff: use of paid staff/volunteers
- scope of operation: local/national
- funding source: statutory/mixed/ non-statutory.

These key variables were chosen in order to examine what influence, if any, they might have on management, control and accountability in the participating organizations.

Once these selection criteria had been established, a meeting was arranged with the CEO of UVOH, seeking his assistance in identifying organizations from among the UVOH membership which matched these requirements. He clarified the characteristics of the affiliated organizations in terms of the established criteria and also provided a list of CEOs for each organization. When this information had been obtained, the researcher was then in a position to select ten case study organizations which fitted the overall selection brief. A number of additional organizations were identified also at this stage, as an "emergency bank" in case of not being able to gain access to all the organizations selected initially. However, the need to call on this reserve group did not arise as full co-operation was negotiated and, in turn, received from the first ten agencies selected.

Details of each organization are itemised in the next chapter which presents an analysis of the fieldwork. At this stage, an introductory vignette of each agency is provided, in order to give an overview of the scope of their combined activities. All the participating organizations were guaranteed anonymity at the outset of the fieldwork. This was done in order to elicit open and unguarded responses to the questions asked in the course of the individual interviews which it was felt might not have been obtained if organizations and respondents were to be individually identified.

In order not to betray the research bargain made with each respondent, the ten organizations have been given pseudonyms to protect the identity of individuals and context. As Taylor & Bogdan (1984:87) note, "there are few legitimate research interests served by publishing people's names. The risks are substantial". Also other researchers, e.g., Leat et al (1986) adopt a similar anonymous approach in their reporting. In this study it was decided to "rechristen" the various organizations with names of various Irish trees, as a means of identifying them individually. Each one, in turn, is now examined briefly, the order being determined by the alphabetical order of their real names.

The Ash organization is one of the newer agencies in the study group, being founded in 1983, as its PR leaflet describes it, "out of desperation by dedicated relatives and friends' of victims of the degenerative disease which is its focus. Its current chairperson and development officer both lost relatives to this disease which affects an estimated 20,000 people in Ireland. The organization progressed slowly until 1989 when it became a registered charity and a new full-time CEO was appointed. Early in 1991 two development officers were employed. Currently they are active in establishing a network of branches throughout the country. At present the Ash has a client base of 1,100 and it is almost entirely dependent on voluntary fundraising.

In contrast with the Ash, the Beech agency is part of an international network with roots going back to the middle of the last century when it was first established in the UK. However, the Irish branch is of recent origin being only established here in 1989 to provide a range of community-based specialist services in co-operation with statutory authorities and other voluntary groups and agencies. Although it receives some statutory subvention for the services it provides, at present its main source of funding is the UK parent body. Future plans envisage tapping more Irish sources of funding in order to move away from its present heavy reliance on the UK source.

Unlike either of the two previous undertakings, the Chestnut organization is entirely dependent on voluntary effort in providing a range of social events for both physically and mentally handicapped people. Its main aim is to develop friendship between the handicapped and helpers through the various activities it organises. The Chestnut has 23 branches spread throughout the country, serving a total of 600 clients, and depends exclusively on its own fundraising efforts to finance its operations, receiving no statutory support.

The beginnings of the Elm agency are similar to that of the Ash organization, as it was started by its present CEO in the early 1960s when she, together with a small group of concerned colleagues, got together to address the needs arising from an inherited life-threatening disease which is still without a cure today, 30 years later. The organization is now established throughout the country, having about 30 branches nationwide. It has a small paid staff at headquarters and is otherwise dependent on voluntary input which focuses mainly on fundraising for the overall operation which caters for about 800 clients. Once again, statutory funding is minimal.

The Fir organization fares no better in terms of statutory funding, as it too has to depend on fundraising to fuel its coffers. Founded in 1980, it is one of the smallest organizations in the sample, catering for a rare genetic disease of the central nervous system. A measure of the disease's obscurity, even in medical circles, can be gathered from the fact that the founder's son was diagnosed by a doctor as suffering from flat feet! The founder, now its CEO, contacted a similar organization in the UK and was asked to start up the association in Ireland. Now this Irish organization provides information and support to sufferers and their families, in addition to arranging holidays with the twin purpose of giving victims a treat while their carers get a break from the onerous duties which the disease imposes.

In contrast with the Fir's narrow client base, last year the Larch organization provided information, advice and counselling to over 7,000 clients. It has 5 regional offices spread throughout the country, in addition to its Dublin headquarters and also arranges periodic meetings at other venues nationwide. An estimated 20,000 people in Ireland suffer from the disease on which it is focused, but, unlike some of the preceding organizations, the severity of the disease can vary tremendously and sufferers do not have the same need for on-going assistance on a day-to-day basis. In addition to assisting sufferers, the Larch also focuses on improving public understanding of the ailment through its educational and research programmes. Although it receives grants for its training activities, it is still heavily dependent on fundraising to support its wide agenda of activities.

Fundraising is a perennial problem also for the Oak agency as its numerous pleas for statutory support so far have fallen on deaf ears. The Oak has a profile similar to that of the Fir agency as it caters for a small group of just over 100 clients who suffer from a harrowing degenerative disease with a life expectancy of only 1 to 5 years after onset. A measure of the severity of the disease can be gained from the fact that, in 1991 alone, 30 of its clients died. The association had an inauspicious start in a suburban kitchen back in 1985 when three ladies, who had been personally touched by the disease, planned a public meeting to see if anything could be done to help the distraught families of the victims. Sixty-two turned up at this inaugural gathering and the association took off from there. The present CEO, a teacher by profession, lost her husband to the disease and there was a similar personal dimension to the involvement of many others in this organization.

Although the Poplar was started also by a small group who had personal experience of the needs of its present clients, its roots go back over 30 years and it has now grown into a large organization, serving over 3,500 clients nationwide through a network of 4 regional offices and 53 branches. Its primary aim is to achieve the complete social and economic reintegration of its members into their local communities. At present a wide range of services is provided for clients by a full time staff of 55, augmented by 150 paid part-timers and a very large group of about 1,500 volunteers spread throughout its branches. Unlike many of the previous organizations, it receives considerable statutory funding which accounts for over 40% of its total annual budget. When its long-serving CEO, with over 25 years service, retired in 1987, the Poplar became virtually rudderless for a few years and incurred very large debts of over half a million pounds in the process. Just very recently it has appointed a new CEO who is now struggling to get the organization back on track. The debt has been reduced to 300,000 pounds, but still stands as a major constraint. In the immediate future the organization is faced with a period of fundamental change as the new CEO strives to regain control over the operation.

Statutory funding is the only source of supply for the Rowan organization which provides a range of services for the mentally handicapped. This agency is unique also among the case-study group as it relies totally on paid staff to provide services for its 320 clients. Its "voluntary" label goes back a long way as its interesting historical roots were set in 1872 when it was started by a titled lady in gratitude to God for her rescue from a shipwreck! However, it underwent fundamental changes in 1977 when the present CEO took the helm and the Department of Health was persuaded to fund the operation.

The tenth and last organization, the Sycamore, was set up in 1983 by its present chairperson and two interested colleagues. She was a relatively young victim of the malady from which clients suffer and, appreciating the need to provide some services for other victims, was helped to get operational by a similar UK based organization which gave a generous start-up grant. At present the agency is Dublin-based only, providing a range of services for about 300 clients, with the assistance of two supervisors who are funded by the local Health Board. Some additional funding is generated by a fundraising committee in order to augment the Health Board subvention and cover other running costs.

These brief background sketches show the varied scope of services provided by the ten case-study organizations, both in numerical terms and diversity of activity. The selection criteria itemised at the outset of this section are now examined to see how the study sample measures up in terms of variation in size, age, staffing, scope of operations and funding patterns. Starting with size and using number of clients served as a measure, the study cohort showed considerable variety; the Fir and Oak organizations, both of which focused on rare disabilities, had only a few hundred clients between them whereas, at the other end of the spectrum, the Larch agency interacted with an estimated 7,000 clients. In fact, five organizations numbered clients in hundreds, while the remaining five had four-figure client bases.

A similar divide is discernible in terms of organizational age. In the first group of five, two agencies have roots going back to the middle of the last century, although their present format is of more recent origin. A third, the Poplar, celebrated its 30th anniversary during the course of this fieldwork and two others (the Elm and the Larch) were established also in the 1960s. The remaining five were newer organizations, all dating from 1980 onwards.

Staffing patterns in the host organizations also indicated considerable variety. The sample included the Chestnut which was entirely dependent on voluntary effort while the Rowan represented an organization which was in marked contrast, as it had no voluntary input other than on its governing board. Further details on the voluntary/paid staffing mix are provided in the next chapter.

While a majority of the organizations, seven in all, operated at a national level, in the case of the remaining three their scope of service was confined to one area, i.e., they were localised in their activities.

Patterns of funding also showed considerable diversity. At one extreme, the Rowan agency was completely dependent on the statutory purse. Other agencies such as the Poplar, Larch, Beech and Sycamore, received a significant percentage of their funds from statutory sources. In contrast, the remaining five agencies were heavily dependent on fundraising to finance their activities.

Research interviews

Once the case study organizations had been identified, the next step in the fieldwork was to interview a number of respondents in each one, to get information on management, control and accountability in the ten organizations. Details of the interview schedule are described in the next chapter, together with the research findings.

The plan for this stage of the research was to conduct an in-depth interview with four respondents in each agency - the chief executive, the accountant (or person dealing with accounts), a member of the Board and a voluntary worker. This total of 40 respondents was in keeping numerically with the general trend in an in-depth study, as Williamson et al (1982:184) note that "the typical intensive interview study is based on fewer than fifty respondents".

Regarding the actual interviews, the first step was to contact the CEO in each of the selected organizations in order to explain briefly the purpose of the research and outline how it was endorsed by the umbrella organization, UVOH. Then the co-operation of each agency was sought in undertaking the proposed series of interviews.

In all cases the response was positive and a first interview was arranged, in most cases with the CEO. This initial interview was considered crucial to the overall success of the project as it decided whether or not permission would be given to see other members of that agency. Therefore at these initial interviews, before embarking on collecting the specific data sought, the researcher's interest and previous experience in the voluntary sector were explained and an assurance of confidentiality was given regarding information disclosed in the course of the individual interviews. This opening pattern was used subsequently when interviewing other respondents. After the introduction and before proceeding with the main part of the interview, each respondent was invited to seek further clarification on aspects of the project that might be of concern to him/her.

This approach helped to establish rapport with individual respondents, in line with the guidance given by Williamson et al (1982:181) who stress that "it is important for the intensive interviewer to nurture rapport with the other party within the framework of an appropriate degree of objectivity". In turn, the rapport established cleared the path for the full and open discussion on the specific research areas, as detailed later in the research findings.

Regarding the actual recording of the interview details, after careful consideration of the possibility of using a tape recorder to gather the data, finally it was decided to opt for manual recording. This option was chosen for two reasons. Firstly it was anticipated that some respondents might be unhappy, if not altogether unwilling to have their interview material taped. Secondly, armed with considerable interviewing experience gained in the course of her work as a management consultant, the researcher was confident that she could handle the task of manual recording adequately, and was also comfortable with this method of approach. To ensure accuracy and comprehension of the interview data at the analysis stage, immediately following each interview and before any further fieldwork was undertaken which could cloud recollection, the relevant interview notes were read over and abbreviations were filled out.

In the course of the initial interviews in each host organization, background information (detailed in chapter 10), together with relevant documentation, e.g., annual reports, policy documents, organizational literature, were made available to the researcher. Another task undertaken during the first interview in each organization was to identify the remaining respondents and negotiate a seal of approval to continue with the research project by establishing contact with them. This did not present any major difficulties as, once the first respondent was comfortable with the project, s/he was agreeable to have other organizational colleagues interviewed.

In due course contact was made with these other respondents, interview dates were arranged and interviews were duly completed, yielding a final total of forty, in line with the planned complement. In the interests of courtesy, all respondents were sent a personal letter thanking them for their co-operation with the research project.

Returning to the individual interviews, in all cases respondents were open and co-operative. Individual interviews were quite long, mostly varying from

1.5 to 2 hours, with a few lasting up to 3 hours. A measure of the overall success of the fieldwork, in terms of establishing rapport and goodwill, was that in all organizations the researcher left with an offer of future access, should any follow-up information be required.

Regarding the designation of respondents, in some cases there was a slight deviation from the planned quartet of CEO, accounts person, chairperson and volunteer. This arose due to the fact that, in a few agencies, the staffing arrangements did not quite match these preselected designations. For instance, in two organizations, the Ash and the Poplar, the CEO also handled the accounting function. However, both agencies had a development officer who was interviewed and provided a worthwhile fourth respondent in each case. The Larch development officer was interviewed also as she offered to substitute for the CEO who was unavailable at the time of initial contact. (He was interviewed also at a later date.) Finally, as the Rowan organization it did not have any voluntary input (apart from the board members), only 9 volunteers in total - one from each of the other agencies - were interviewed. Therefore, while incorporating these minor variations on the original schedule of respondents, the total still amounted to 40 interviews, corresponding with the initial target. Although there was a higher female representation in the overall complement - 24, with 16 males - both males and females were represented in each respondent category, i.e., CEO, accounts person, board member and volunteer.

Summary

This chapter began by describing the preliminary fieldwork which provided background information on the Irish voluntary sector and also confirmed the usefulness of the proposed research. The main fieldwork was then introduced, describing the ten organizations selected for the study. Finally, an account of the actual interview process was presented.

10 Research Findings

The findings from the main field research are presented in this chapter. The data is prefaced by a description of the interview schedule used in gathering the information, in keeping with the general approach to the study (as outlined in the chapter (11) on methodology) which was based on in-depth qualitative research.

The actual data which emerged from the forty interviews are grouped into four main areas, covering:

- characteristics of the ten case-study organizations
- an analysis of some aspects of management in theseorganizations, including profiles of the CEO and accounting personnel and the boards of management
- approaches to control
- perceptions on and responses to accountability.

Interview schedule

The broad aim of this study was to explore aspects of management and approaches to control and accountability in Irish voluntary organizations by means of an in-depth interview with 40 respondents chosen from a sample of ten organizations. To facilitate the actual interview process, an interview schedule was drawn up. Its main purpose was to provide a framework for each interview and thereby ensure overall comparability in data collection, rather than serve as a rigid, fixed questionnaire. A copy of the research instrument is provided in Appendix III which also indicates the specific purpose of the individual items listed. Its content is now explained in more detail.

Data collected

To begin, the background characteristics of each undertaking were established in terms of age, services, spread of operation and client population together with particulars of staffing, both paid and voluntary. Details on income were sought in order to establish the pattern of funding, i.e., statutory, voluntary or a mixture of both sources. This information was necessary to ascertain whether different sources of funding gave rise to differing demands for accountability.

Profiles of the CEO and accountant (or person responsible for accounts) were prepared in order to establish how relevant their educational background and experience were to their work in the organizations.Particulars were obtained on the boards of management, again to find out the occupational background of members, the turnover of board membership, client and funder representation on the board, and patterns of board meetings and attendance. Information was sought also on the selection criteria and training for board members. It was considered that all of these items could have a bearing on how the various boards actually managed each organization.

The themes of control and accountability incorporated into the interview schedule reflect issues arising in the academic literature, together with those raised in the course of the preliminary fieldwork. Regarding control, the first task was to ascertain the overall approach to control in each organization, as perceived by individual respondents. Information was requested on organizational objectives, to see if they were clearly established and to find out how their achievement was judged.Next, information was sought about specific aspects of control in the following areas: personnel; finance; operations and information requirements. Finally, possible dysfunctional aspects of control were explored.

In the area of accountability, respondents' views on external accountability were sought. This was followed by probing for perceived advantages and disadvantages of accountability, and information was requested also about its impact on the independence of the organization. Respondents were then asked to identify the bodies to whom they saw themselves as being accountable and differences in accountability to different agencies were explored. A question was included about why accountability was seen to be necessary, in order to find out if respondents had a proactive or a reactive approach to it. In order to establish the scope of accountability from the perspective of respondents, each was asked to itemise the areas for which accountability arose.

Next, the interview proceeded to check out the response to accountability in each agency, both for funds received and services provided. In the case of services, financial aspects and also issues of standards and appropriateness were taken into the reckoning. The publication of an Annual Report constitutes one method of making information available to outsiders. Therefore details were requested about the preparation, content and circulation of annual reports by the participating organizations.

At the conclusion of each interview, in an effort to establish how familiar respondents were regarding broader aspects of accountability in the voluntary sector, they were questioned about their familiarity with two relevant publications - the Statement of Recommended Practice (SORP 2 - ASC 1988) on charity reporting and the recently published (1990) Irish government report on fundraising.

The foregoing outlines the content of the actual interview schedule used in the course of the fieldwork. The final schedule was formulated after pre-testing and refining the initial schedule prepared. This piloting process is now described.

Pilot testing

When the first interview outline had been drawn up a pilot test was undertaken using respondents from two voluntary organizations outside the sample frame. One respondent was a treasurer in a voluntary women's welfare agency and was also both a qualified accountant and an academic researcher. Therefore she was ideally suited to judge the interview content from a number of perspectives and had some valuable comments to offer. It was considered important also to check out the interview with a respondent from a non-academic background, to ensure that it "made sense" to a person who was more representative of the proposed respondents in the field. Accordingly, a second pilot interviewee was identified, the CEO of a voluntary overseas development agency. Previously she had worked in another voluntary agency dealing with travellers and so her knowledge of the sector was not confined to one agency.

The final research instrument incorporated suggestions arising from this pilot stage which was useful also in confirming the suitability of the schedule in terms of general comprehension, i.e., establishing that it was appropriate at an operational level. Once the interview schedule had been drafted, tested and finalised, it was used in the course of the fieldwork to gather the required data. Before presenting the actual findings, the method of analysis is described.

The data gathered in the course of the fieldwork fell into two broad categories yielding information on (a) characteristics of the ten study organizations, and (b) approaches to control and accountability in these organizations. The analysis of the data relating to organizational characteristics involved aggregating the information on the individual agencies in order to present an overall profile of the study sample. This part of the analysis progressed smoothly, using individual analysis sheets for the various aspects under review and recording the relevant facts in a systematic manner.

However, the data relating to control and accountability did not yield to mere systematization. Referring back to the chapter on methodology, it was established that one of the merits of qualitative research is its capacity to provide information-rich data. While the actual interviews confirmed this attribute, yielding an impressive array of data, handling this open-ended flow of information was not a straightforward task. Rather it had to be coaxed into coherence by adopting a two-pronged approach.

To facilitate the task, a very large analysis grid was prepared, with respondents on the horizontal axis and the ten agencies on the vertical axis, giving a total of 40 "boxes". Numerous photocopies were made of this basic analytical "tool". Then, using the various themes on control and accountability in the interview schedule as a guideline, the individual responses for each theme were extracted from the individual interview records and mapped into the appropriate "box" in the master analysis sheet for that particular theme. This procedure provided a "raw" analysis of the data, by theme. The next process was to focus on these individual master sheets and examine each one in further detail in order to draw out the broad findings in relation to each topic. Even though this overall process was time-consuming, it did ensure an orderly review of the data obtained during the individual interviews.

Now that the content of the interview schedule and thee method of analysis have been described, the emerging data are reviewed.

Characteristics of case-study organizations

Whereas outline sketches of the individual organizations were presented in chapter 9 by way of introduction, this section reviews some of these characteristics in a more systematic manner.

Table 10.1, overleaf, in which organizations are ranked according to client numbers, also provides details of the founding dates and geographical spread of the ten case-study organizations.

Table 10.1
Client base, founding date and geographical
spread of case study organizations

Organization	Founded	No. Clients*	Geog. spread
Larch	1967	7000	national
Beech	1989(Irl) 1866(UK)	4000	local
Poplar	1960	3500	national
Elm	1962	1400	national
Ash	1983	1100	national
Chestnut	1980	600	national
Rowan	1872	320	local
Sycamore	1983	300	local
Fir	1980	250	national
Oak	1985	103	national
Total		18573	

* The number of people to whom service was provided in 1990

This table shows that, cumulatively, the ten organizations have a substantial client base, catering for over 18,000 clients. In the case of individual agencies, client numbers vary from 7,000 in the largest, the Larch, to just over 100 in the smallest, the Oak which caters for victims of a rare but very debilitating disease which creates heavy demands for ongoing services. In fact half of the ten organizations have in excess of 1,000 clients while the remaining five could be rated as relatively small, with downwards of 600 clients. The overall data on clients served establish the significance of the study sample in terms of numbers of clients served.

Likewise the ten organizations are varied in terms of age. While five were established in the 1980s, the other five are older with two having their roots in the last century.

The majority of organizations (seven) provide services at a national level, while the operations of the remaining three are locally based, showing how the sample as a whole incorporates agencies operating at both levels.

Affiliations to outside bodies

As mentioned previously in the literature review, organizations are open systems, interacting with their environment (Kast & Rosenzweig 1985). Bearing this in mind, respondents were asked about their formal links with outside bodies, as this was seen as one indicator of how actively "closed" or "open" they were at an operational level. As the sample was chosen from UVOH affiliated agencies, all ten organizations had connections with this umbrella body and, in the case of two (the Chestnut and the Poplar), this was their only formal link with an outside agency. The remaining eight agencies had forged multiple links with outside undertakings. Of these, five had an association with the corresponding UK organization in their particular field of operation. Six were affiliated to a relevant international body and one of this group had hosted an international conference in 1989 while another was in the advanced stages of planning the 1992 international conference of its affiliated group.

The general picture indicates that most organizations made a positive effort to move their contacts beyond the Irish context regarding their specialism. However there was a noticeable lack of interest in areas such as management/administration, with only one agency mentioning such a link with the Irish Management Institute.

Income - size and sources

The relevant data on income and funding sources are outlined in table 10.2, overleaf, in order of income size. It differs markedly from the order by number of clients served, e.g., the Rowan, which ranks seventh in terms of client numbers, is second in income terms. This is explained by the fact that its

146

clients require an ongoing intensive level of service which is provided solely by paid staff.

Table 10.2
Income and funding patterns

Organization	Income 1990 '000 IR pounds	Source Statutory %	Other %
Beech	2927	10	90
Rowan	1431	100	-
Poplar	1189	42	58
Larch	393	12	88
Elm	350	-	100
Chestnut	181	-	100
Oak	131	-	100
Ash	101	-	100
Fir	23	-	100
Sycamore	21	56	44
Total	6747		

As can be seen from this table, the combined income of the ten organizations amounted to almost 7 million pounds in 1990. Once again, considerable variation is apparent in size of income, with the largest (the Beech) having almost 3 million pounds and the two smallest (the Fir and Sycamore) relying on a very modest budget of just over 20,000 pounds to fund their operations. Turning to the sources of funding, there is an even divide between those agencies which receive some statutory support and those which have to depend on fundraising. While five receive some public money, their success in tapping this source is varied. At one extreme, the Rowan gets full statutory funding, while at the other extreme the Beech and Larch receive only 10% and 12% respectively from the State coffers. The remaining two organizations in this group (the Poplar and Sycamore) have a significant statutory input at a level of 42% and 56% respectively, even though in the case of the Sycamore, the actual amount is small. At present, the other five agencies in the study group receive no statutory support for their endeavours. The overall funding data show that the study sample is varied in terms of both income size and sources.

Staffing patterns

While the ten organizations had a combined workforce of just over 5,000, over 90% of this input was provided by unpaid volunteers. Staffing numbers in individual organizations are detailed in table 10.3.

Table 10.3
Staffing patterns in the study sample

Organization	Paid staff			Volunteers
	Full time	*Part time*	*Total*	
Poplar	55	150	205	1500
Beech	68	47	115	150
Rowan	58	42	100	-
Larch	12	5	17	1000
Elm	4	1	5	600
Ash	5	-	5	600
Oak	1	2	3	50
Sycamore	-	2	2	90
Chestnut	-	1	1	600
Fir	-	-	-	53
Total	203	250	453	4643

The data in Table 10.3 show that the total paid employment provided in the ten case study agencies amounted to 453, with slightly under half of these (44.7%) being employed on a full-time basis, while the remainder worked only part-time. As might be expected, the three organizations with the highest incomes (the Poplar, Beech and Rowan) also had the greatest number of paid staff. In six of the remaining agencies, paid staff were scarce, while the seventh had to rely totally on voluntary effort.

In contrast to the modest numbers of paid staff, volunteers were a major source of input in all but one organization (the Rowan). The Rowan CEO explained that "we back away from volunteers because of the big management problems in terms of discipline, training and control when trying to run a sophisticated service." However, his organization was in the relatively advantageous position of being in receipt of statutory funding to meet the cost of paid staff.

The estimated total of over 4,600 volunteers serving in the remaining nine organizations was more than ten times the total in paid employment (453), thus indicating the heavy reliance on voluntary input in these nine organizations.

So far it has been established that the ten study organizations, with a combined income approaching 7 million pounds, cater between them for a total of over 18,000 clients, with the assistance of about 5,000 staff, 90% of whom work in a voluntary capacity.

Management profiles

Profiles of the CEOs, accountants (or accounts person) and boards of management were prepared for each undertaking. This section commences with a background review of the CEOs.

CEO profiles

Particulars regarding age, education and management training, in relation to the ten respondents who headed up the various agencies, are given in Table 10.4. overleaf.

Table 10.4
Profiles of CEOs in the study sample

Organization	Age group	Education	Mgmt. train.	Bus.Exper.
Ash	50 +	ACA	courses	30 years
Beech	31-40	CQSW	courses	-
Chestnut	31-40	B.Sc.	-	-
Elm	50 +	L/Cert.	-	-
Fir	50 +	L/Cert	-	-
Larch	41-50	L/Cert	-	-
Oak	41-50	B.A.	-	-
Poplar	41-50	B.Eng.	courses	10 years
Rowan	50 +	Dip.Eng.	-	8 years
Sycamore	50 +	L/Cert	-	-

Commencing with the age of respondents, it can be seen from this table that half of the CEOs were over 50 and a further three over 40, leaving two in the 31-40 age bracket. Regarding educational achievements, although six of the ten CEOs had availed of some 3rd level education, most of the qualifications received were not directly relevant to the field of management, apart from the accountancy qualification held by the CEO of the Ash agency. The remaining four respondents had completed their formal education at secondary level, obtaining a leaving certificate.

Evidence of formal management training was scant: only three of those interviewed had attended short management courses, while the remaining seven had not received any formal input in this area. Managerial experience in areas other than the voluntary sector was also in short supply as seven of the ten CEOs had no previous experience at managerial level outside the voluntary sector. From gleanings gathered in the course of the individual interviews, it became apparent to the researcher that in the majority of cases their primary motivation stemmed from a personal vocation and inner belief in the espoused cause of their organization.

Staff in the accounting area

Background details on the personnel dealing with the accounting function in each of the ten participating organizations is given in Table 10.5.

Table 10.5
Profiles of accounting personnel interviewed

Organization	Age	Employm't	B'ground	Mgmt. Tr.	Bus. exper.
Ash *	50 +	f/time	ACA	courses	30 years
Beech	31-40	f/time	b'keeper	-	-
Chestnut	41-50	vol.	b'keeper	-	-
Elm	50 +	p/time	b'keeper	-	-
Fir	50 +	vol.	ACWA	-	16 years
Larch	31/40	f/time	secret'l	-	-
Oak	41/50	p/time	secret'l	-	-
Poplar *	41-50	f/time	B.Eng	courses	10 years
Rowan	21-30	f/time	BBS	courses	-
Sycamore	50 +	vol.	b'keeper	-	-

* Note: In these two organizations, the CEO also attended to the accounts.

This table shows how the accounting input was dependent on a mixture of full-time, part-time and voluntary effort in the various organizations. Age wise, the spread was fairly similar to that of the CEO group. Regarding educational background, only two of the ten had a professional accounting qualification while a third (in the Rowan) had a degree with relevant

151

accounting input. Of the remaining seven, four were dependent on bookkeeping skills and two had a secretarial background, while the remaining one (who was also a CEO) had an engineering degree. On the management front, only three of the ten had received any structured input, and only one (in the Fir) had previous commercial experience, apart from the two "dual" CEO/accounting people already covered in the CEO profiles.

Generally speaking, there was not a high level of professional training in evidence. Once again, as was the case with CEOs, a strong sense of interest in the particular cause was discernible among the majority of those interviewed. For example, the accounts person in the Oak, who had a secretarial background, gave the following explanation of her initial involvement with accounts: "They were desperate when I joined. Two people were doing the accounts and it was very difficult. So I tried for a year and it worked out OK."

Composition of boards of management

The ten host organizations had a total of 103 on their boards of management, with individual boards ranging in size from six to nineteen members. A breakdown of membership is given in Table 10.6, (overleaf). Housewives headed the list, accounting for almost 20% of the total. The first three categories - housewife/medical/retired - between them accounted for just over 50% of the combined membership. In contrast, people with a business background accounted for only 5.9% of the total.

Table 10.6
Composition of boards of management

Category	No.
Housewife	20
Medical/para medical	18
Retired	15
Education	12
Clerical	7
Financial	7
Business	6
Other	18
Total	103

Information was sought about provisions for rotation of membership on individual boards. Of the nine organizations in existence in Ireland for over three years, only three had more than one new face in this period. Two of the ten (the Ash and Beech) had built in mechanisms for ensuring rotation in board membership. Another three (the Elm, Poplar and Sycamore) had procedures for election of board members. Despite this arrangement, the CEO of the Elm said that members "are all here for years" and the Sycamore had the same members since its inception in 1985. This indicates that an election procedure, on its own, does not automatically ensure rotation of membership and an injection of new "blood", i.e., the same members can be re-elected from year to year.

Apart from the exceptions outlined above, the approach to board membership seemed somewhat unstructured and could be summed up by the comment of one respondent (the development officer in the Larch) who described it in the following terms: "It's all very informal." Yet again, it was indicated to the researcher that an interest in the particular "cause" of an association was an over-riding factor in many cases, rather than the particular occupational background of a member.

Training of board members was another area reviewed. Only two of the ten agencies (the Beech and Rowan) had anything by way of formal induction for board members. The Beech agency held briefing sessions for new board members which included visits to their various operations, and also provided training in the required areas, while the Rowan also had a two-day induction process. The remaining eight organizations provided no training whatsoever for board members.

It was suggested in the literature that the level of attendance at meetings, and their frequency are other indicators of board involvement. There was a pattern of monthly board meetings in most organizations. The data provided also indicated an overall high level of attendance, with only one agency reporting a turnout of under 75% at meetings, while 6 recorded an attendance of over 90%. The regularity of meetings, combined with a satisfactory overall attendance, endorsed the high level of commitment on the part of board members.

Approaches to control

This section contains an analysis of the views of the forty respondents in the study regarding control in their respective organizations. The data are presented under various themes, corresponding to the ground covered in the interview schedule. In the course of discussing each theme, sample comments from the actual interviews are included, as appropriate, to augment the analysis and "let the data speak". The source of each quotation is identified by using the following abbreviations:

CEO = chief executive officer/administrator
A/c = accountant/accounts person
Bd = board member
Vol = volunteer
Dev = development officer

The name of the relevant organization is also cited. To begin, views on and approaches to control in the case study organizations are presented.

General views on control

As outlined previously, the section of the interview which focused on control commenced by explaining the concept to each respondent, to ensure that the context of the ensuing questions was understood. The next step was to ascertain the general approach to control in each of the ten organizations. The overall response was very positive as informants indicated a - strong appreciation of the need for control. Only one of the forty interviewed, a volunteer in the Poplar agency, had no view, explaining that she merely did her own job where she had "a free hand and no one interferes". Twenty of the remaining respondents considered control to be vital, while the other nineteen saw it as being either very necessary (8) or necessary (11). Some sample responses which endorsed its importance were:

You have to control all the time - it's absolutely necessary. If you don't, you don't know what's going to happen. (Dev / Ash)

Everybody right through the organization is aware of control. (A/c/Beech)

The group would not be successful unless standards were set and maintained. (Vol / Chestnut)

Control is vital - otherwise you'd never get anywhere. (CEO / Elm)

Having established that respondents considered control to be important in their respective organizations, the next question sought to explore the reasons underpinning this stance.

154

Why is control important?

Half of the respondents (20), from nine different organizations, linked the importance of control to financial considerations, e.g.,

It's nice to know where the money is going.   (Vol / Ash)

You could get overdrawn so quickly.   (A/c / Elm)

You could very quickly run out of money if you had no control over it.
                    (Bd / Fir)

It's important to have control to analyse and evaluate where the money comes from.   (CEO /Larch)

A further 13 placed the need for control in the broader context of ensuring that (i) standards are maintained; (ii) aims and objectives are achieved; (iii) feedback on activities is provided. Control was viewed as a basic requirement for any organization by another six respondents. This was exemplified by remarks which indicated that, without control,

. . . the whole organization would fall apart.   (A/c /Rowan)

. . . you're going to have chaos.   (Vol/Sycamore)

As mentioned in the previous section, the fortieth respondent expressed no views on control.

Therefore, while financial considerations predominated, the need for control was associated also with the requirements of ensuring the achievement of objectives, standards and feedback, and as a basic requirement for an organization.

Difficulties associated with control

Respondents were asked to identify any perceived difficulties associated with implementing control. Just under half (18) of those interviewed had some comments to offer, but most of these (15) related to the human factor in control and are dealt with later under this label. Of the remaining three, all from different organizations, the difficulties raised were of the "once-off" variety. The Board representative from the Elm felt that tensions can arise in

155

relation to control between headquarters staff and local branches, as overall organizational priorities do not always mesh in neatly with local needs. The cost factor in control was highlighted by the CEO in the Larch agency who substantiated his claim by referring to a computer programme installed to monitor fundraising which cost over 10,000 pounds. In the case of the Oak organization which, in growth terms, was "spiralling very fast" as the volunteer described it, this rapid expansion, in her opinion, "makes control harder".

To summarise, the main difficulties associated with implementing control were seen to be "people-centred" and are discussed later under the "human factor" label.

Perceived formality of control

When asked to evaluate the overall approach to control in their organizations, in terms of its formality, results showed some variations in approach among the study sample. Six of the organizations (The Ash, Beech, Chestnut, Elm, Rowan and Sycamore) considered that control was implemented in a formal manner, e.g.,

Formal - it must be run like a business if you're going to get anywhere.

(Bd /Ash)

We have procedures and everyone is aware of these procedures.

(A/c/Beech)

A further two (the Larch and Oak) reported a mixed approach. In the case of the Larch, while financial control was very formalised, otherwise, according to its development officer, the approach was "very informal, in my opinion." A formal report was prepared for the monthly meetings held by the Oak agency, but apart from this the approach to control was rated as being fairly informal. One relatively small body, the Fir, considered its approach to be informal. Finally, regarding control, the Poplar was in the process of "trying to formalise partially" according to its CEO, while the chairman of the Board admitted that "it hadn't happened in the past."

Organizational objectives

The literature review on control indicated that, in essence, control is concerned with finding out whether or not organizational objectives have been achieved.

To undertake this exercise necessitates having objectives set out which are clear and, ideally, quantifiable, to facilitate measurement. Yet the findings in the literature established that, in the case of service provision as opposed to physical goods, there can be difficulties in this regard.

Information was sought on the particular objectives of the case-study organizations. Whereas all ten indicated that they had written overall objectives, none had departmental objectives set out. One, the Ash, had a clear mission statement with seven specific aims centred on three main areas: improving information and awareness of the particular disease; providing support and assistance; supporting research into the disease. This mission statement was translated into eleven operating goals which spelled out how the aims were to be achieved, thus providing a working list against which to measure actual achievements.

In contrast, the objectives of the remaining nine organizations were very general in nature. For example, the objectives of the Poplar included the following: "To achieve social and economic integration and rehabilitation of participant members into the community and all work undertaken by the Association shall at all times and in all situations be so directed." Whereas this may be a laudable overall objective towards which to aspire, it does not provide a good basis for measuring actual achievements. In fact the CEO of this organization recognised this limitation as he rated the objectives as being "very general"; the CEO of the Beech agency described its overall objectives in similar terms.

Apart from the Ash agency, none of the other nine CEOs was very forthcoming about overall objectives. Any information given was couched in very general terms and centred on helping the particular client group which was of concern to that agency. Therefore the Ash stood apart from the others in terms of having definite, clear objectives which were translated into operating goals. This went someway towards providing a base against which to assess actual achievements. The remaining nine agencies had nothing to resemble this clarity of objectives and operating goals and seemed to have little by way of a firm basis against which to measure performance.

Long-term planning

In an effort to ascertain the future direction envisaged by respondents for their respective organizations, they were asked about long-term planning. In fact, none of the ten organizations had a long-term plan. Only two (the Beech and Poplar) had even aspirations in that direction. The CEO in the Beech reported that "they were working on a four-year rolling plan", while the new CEO in the Poplar saw it as a priority for the new regional directors whom he hoped to appoint soon. The other eight organizations seemed to work on a year-to-year basis. As the Rowan CEO described it, the approach in his organization was "crisis management all the time", while the Board member in the Elm mentioned how "it was difficult to plan in an uncertain financial environment". So, long-term planning was not, as yet, a reality for any of the organizations studied.

Measuring achievement of overall objectives

It was established in the literature review that the lack of a profit yardstick in voluntary nonprofit organizations leaves them with no overall comparable "tool" for measuring performance. So, how do they satisfy themselves that they are achieving their overall objectives? Apart from three volunteers (in the Beech, Elm and Larch) who saw their commitment in terms of their particular task and had not reflected on wider organizational issues, the remaining 37 respondents had views to offer.

First of all the data are examined by organization. Four organizations (the Ash, Beech, Chestnut and Rowan) indicated that they had some method of gauging the achievement of overall objectives. As mentioned already in the section on setting objectives, the Ash, which was at a stage of fairly rapid development, had a list of 11 specific operating goals which was made available to the researcher, together with a list of achievements indicating progress in terms of facilities provided to date and branches established. This showed a systematic approach to setting objectives and monitoring progress.

A "built-in process" had been established in the Beech agency which reviewed actual projects undertaken against pre-set project objectives. As the chairman of its board explained:

> It [the work] is divided into projects. Each keeps the director informed and he reports to Board meetings and gives a picture of what's being achieved and what's being done and then it's open to discussion.

The primary objective of the Chestnut association focused on the relationship between individual clients and volunteers. It had in place an ongoing system of regular meetings and reviews to ensure that this objective was achieved and maintained.

The CEO of the Rowan, the only organization in the study group entirely dependent on statutory funding, saw achievement of objectives in financial terms. He felt that, once the yearly budget was struck, "our business is to run according to budget" and he received monthly information from the accountant to indicate how effectively this was being achieved. Of course financial compliance does not necessarily give any indication of the level and quality of service provided.

Apart from these four organizations, none of the other six indicated that they had any comparable systematic approaches to measuring overall achievements.

An analysis of the individual responses received indicates a reliance on feedback from clients and/or their carers (where appropriate) as the major source of information regarding the achievement of objectives. Twenty-eight interviewees, spread throughout the ten organizations, mentioned feedback as a way of monitoring progress. Some sample responses are:

The profit is seeing people who need the help getting it - if they're not happy we're going to know.   (Vol / Fir)

Success is gauged on clients' reactions to what we're doing. (A/c/Chestnut)

. . . good vibes from the families   (Bd / Oak)
. . . when you look around at the faces and see how happy they are.
                                                    (CEO / Sycamore)

Several of those interviewed mentioned more than one approach to assessing the achievement of objectives. One source of information, mentioned by seven individuals (from five different organizations), flowed from periodic reports and meetings, reviews and inspections. A further five respondents considered that the growth in numbers of clients augured well for achievement of objectives. Financial indicators were used as a yardstick by four informants. Finally, two board chairmen (from the Fir and the Poplar) indicated that they relied on "personal knowledge" to be satisfied that achievements were in line with goals.

The general impression gained from the interviews was that, in the majority of cases, there was a lack of a systematic approach to monitoring the achievement of objectives. In its place there was a very definite reliance on receiving voluntary feedback from clients as an assurance that the mission of the organization was being met at an operational level. In other words, client feedback was a major source of organizational information.

Setting standards

It was established in the literature that the basic control model operates by setting standards against which to measure actual performance. This approach

159

is facilitated when standards are easily quantifiable and can be set objectively, e.g., if 10% return on investment is the set level of performance it is possible to calculate whether or not it has been achieved. Endorsing the difficulties raised in the literature in relation to setting standards in service-based organizations (Hofstede 1981), the interview data indicated that, in the case of voluntary organizations, the exercise is not so easy to carry out.

Quite a number of respondents commented on the inherent difficulties in setting standards in a service-based operation. As the board chairman in the Poplar saw it, "we're basically a service industry and therefore almost impossible to quantify". Another informant cited two contrasting situations in making a similar point. She put forward an example of selling jumpers where, if you have six to sell and achieve your target, "you know you're doing OK," whereas, on the other hand, for the service she was providing, "it's very hard to judge it because you can't quantify it" (CEO / Sycamore). The chairperson of the same organization endorsed this view, explaining that the unpredictable nature of progress with the particular disability does not facilitate the setting of specific times regarding achievements. To endorse her view, she gave examples of two clients, one of whom regained his former level of ability within eight months, while the second, while receiving broadly the same type of input, needed it for six years before regaining the same level of ability.

The comment of a Fir volunteer, in relation to his clients, summed up the quantification difficulty: "You can't put it in statistical terms, only smiles - to see someone totally happy." Two further constraints mentioned in relation to establishing standards centred on not having "the capacity to analyse to that extent" (CEO / Fir) and , in the case of the Poplar, on its cultural norms whereby "there's very, very strong resistance because the culture is that you don't ask questions" (Bd / Poplar).

Against this background of perceived difficulties, how did organizations go about setting standards? Various approaches were presented. First of all, responses are looked at in five agencies which indicated a specific awareness of the need for standards. The Rowan was able to come up with a cost per place statistic for its services. Unlike any of the other case-study organizations which provided a distinct service, there were organizations comparable to the Rowan operating in other catchment areas, so it was able to use their costs for comparative purposes. Once again, it must be noted that this cost standard was not useful as an indicator of the quality of the service provided.

The CEO in the Beech agency saw the need to establish realistic objectives that can be measured - "that's the way it's got to go," he commented. Yet he did register dissatisfaction with the present modus operandi:"I'm not altogether happy with how we do it, the way we're approaching it, it's always going to indicate a positive outcome." This said little for the objectivity of measurement!

Similar concern regarding the present system in the Poplar was voiced by its CEO who conceded that, up until recently, standards were based on the maxim: "Do the best you can." To shift from this situation, currently the association was in the process of trying to implement formal reports for service staff, setting out the number of calls made by each member. Although experiencing some resistance to this move, nevertheless he felt that in the future "a service audit was on the cards".

A fourth agency, the Chestnut, which relied totally on voluntary input, conveyed great concern about standards of performance. It had prepared a two-page working document setting out eight guidelines for maintenance of its standards which stressed, inter alia, the need to be selective in only choosing volunteers who accepted these standards and the need to reinforce the importance of these standards on a regular basis. In addition it noted the possibility of having to make unpopular decisions at times, in order to uphold these standards. Respondents from this organization indicated to the researcher that the achievement of these standards was monitored consistently through meetings, discussions and regular reporting.

The CEO of the fifth organization, the Oak, stated that a deliberate policy of setting high standards of service was adopted when the agency was set up in 1985. In practice, it is based on putting the patient first and its achievement is measured by feedback from a letter sent to individual clients every two months to enquire if s/he requires any assistance or equipments.

Apart from these five organizations, respondents in the remaining five did not give the impression that they had put much thought into setting objective standards. In the case of the four organizations (the Ash, Elm, Fir and Sycamore), which interacted with their clients on an ongoing basis, there appeared to be a reliance on feedback from these clients as assurance that service standards were acceptable, respondents in all four mentioning this source when asked about standards. In addition personal monitoring was mentioned in the Ash and Sycamore as a means of ensuring acceptable levels of service.

Finally, the CEO of the Larch, which served a large number of clients on a less frequent basis, said that he relied on "professional guidance and advice" as a measure of ensuring the provision of acceptable service standards. The chairman of its Board considered that while achievements were "not strictly measurable, an approximate measure of success" could be gathered from the "high profile people in the business and social world" that support them as, if the service were not good, he felt that "reasonable and responsible people of this nature would not be involved." This appears to be in the nature of an "arms length" standard.

To summarise, the data emerging from the interviews in relation to setting of standards against which to measure actual achievement indicates that, in practice, this is not an easy exercise to implement in a non-profit setting. It confirmed the difficulties raised in the literature. While half of the ten organizations showed an awareness of the need to have standards and were moving or had moved some way in that direction, the remaining five veered more towards relying on client feedback to keep them "on their toes" in terms of service provision.

Personnel control

Personnel is one of the areas where control can be exercised. It is of particular importance in voluntary organizations which, in the main, provide services rather than a tangible product and so the service provided by staff is, in fact, the "product". Respondents were asked about their approach to monitoring the performance of both paid staff and volunteers. The general impression gained by the researcher was one of a very relaxed, informal approach to personnel matters, both in the area of performance appraisal and training.

An analysis of the interview data shows that only one agency (the Beech) from the group of ten agencies, had a formal approach to monitoring paid staff. The Beech had delineated clear organizational relationships and prepared detailed job descriptions for all paid staff. Underpinned by this clarity of relationships, supervisors or project managers, as appropriate, were able to exercise day-to-day control over staff reporting to them. In addition, there was an annual formal appraisal system in operation, based on a two-way process between supervisor and subordinate, where areas such as achievement, strengths and weaknesses, training needs and goals were appraised. Positive reinforcement was implemented by working out a plan to address areas identified in the assessment as being in need of improvement, and ensuring progress was monitored in a month's time.

In the area of staff training, the approach in the Beech was formal also, with a specific training and development budget and a joint management/staff training committee which made recommendations to management regarding training priorities. Identified training needs were met either by in-house courses, or by giving financial support to staff who undertook external courses.

Volunteers in the Beech agency also reported to a specific manager. The CEO indicated that provision was made for induction courses. However, the volunteer respondent in this study stated that "there was talk about a course, but it never came to anything", indicating that the system in practice did not quite measure up to the theory. In fact she said that she learned through the "sitting by Nellie" system which "works if you're told by someone good at what they're doing." Yet the overall approach in the Beech could be rated as indicating a positive approach to staff control and appraisal.

This organization proved to be the exception to a more general laissez faire approach in the remaining nine. The CEO of the Larch agency stated that he held an informal session with each staff member annually, "with no questionnaire." He admitted to shortcomings in this process, stating that: "It's extremely difficult for me to evaluate the quality of service of a social worker" and posed the question :"How can I measure counselling skills? A third agency, the Rowan, reported trying to start a performance appraisal scheme earlier in 1991 but its accountant commented that "it didn't seem to work out in practice".

These were the only indications of any attempts at formality of approach towards control in the personnel area. So how are paid staff controlled in the remaining organizations? Some informal approaches were mentioned during the interviews. For instance, the Ash chairman said that while there was no formal appraisal of staff, "if they fall down I tell them".

In the Elm, its CEO reported that while she liked to have a weekly meeting of staff, "it falls apart because of pressure." The Board respondent for the Elm endorsed the view that they relied on an informal approach, due to the small number of paid staff, but were able to identify a staff member with unsatisfactory performance who was let go as a result. Another dismissal was described by the Chairperson of the Sycamore who heard of the "dossing" (involving fabrication of visits) through a report from a referral agency.

These two cases of dismissal contrasted with the views expressed by the Chairman of the Poplar who said it was "almost impossible to get rid of staff", citing the case of an employee who reported for work in an inebriated state and yet had his appeal against dismissal upheld on the grounds that the proper procedures had not been followed. Finally he had to be paid to leave the organization.

Regarding staff training, the picture emerging from the data was one of minimal input. Apart from the Beech agency which, as mentioned already, had a formalised approach to training, none of the other nine had anything comparable to report. In the case of paid staff, three agencies, the Larch, Poplar and Sycamore, had minimal training. Last year the Larch held one training workshop. The new CEO in the Poplar, being aware of the need for staff training, had made a start by organising two three-day management courses for fifteen staff members - the first attempt ever to do so in this organization. Finally, the field supervisor in the Sycamore was sent on a three-day course to the UK association working in the same field. The remaining six organizations had no formal training schemes in operation.

Volunteers did not fare too well either in terms of training. Of the nine interviewed - (the Rowan had no volunteers) - only one, from the Sycamore, reported receiving minimal training. As she described it, "we had a variety of lectures, which gave me confidence." The Chairperson of the same agency conceded that training was "not ideal" but said it was difficult to get volunteers to attend training sessions.

Two other agencies, the Oak and the Poplar, identified a definite need for training of volunteers. In the case of the Oak, it planned to extend its service to cover home visits but, appreciating that this venture would require considerable sensitivity in view of the nature of the disability, is not prepared to proceed with the project until volunteers have been trained appropriately. The CEO in the Poplar felt that volunteers in branches "need training very badly" and now a start is planned by setting up pilot training projects in two regions. Apart from the Beech agency which, as indicated earlier had some provision for volunteer training, the other five organizations reported nothing by way of systematic training for volunteers.

In sum, in the personnel area there was very little evidence of formal control of either paid or voluntary staff. In the area of training, the general norm in the case-study organizations seemed to be that described by one CEO: "They learn as they go . . . they pick it up" (CEO / Elm).

Financial control

The combined income of the ten case study organizations, which was in the region of 7 million pounds in 1990, suggests the need for financial control. All ten had annual audited accounts prepared by professional auditors. However, when it came to budgeting, the score was not so high.

In the course of preparing the original interview schedule, the section on financial control envisaged organizations having a reasonably sophisticated budgetary system and the two pilot case study agencies complied in this regard. The reality proved otherwise in the majority of the case study organizations as only three, the Beech, Larch and Rowan, (which were first, fourth and third respectively in terms of overall income), had formalised budgetary systems firmly in place. These had annual budgets, broken down by projects or cost centres as appropriate, into monthly reporting periods. This facilitated a monthly formal financial reporting system with which to measure actual against budgeted performance. These periodic financial reports were sent to the relevant line staff and any variances were sorted out with the staff member concerned. The CEO in the Beech agency admitted considerable dependence on its UK parent body in this area, stating that, without this input, "I'd see us as being weak in the financial area".

As indicated previously, the Poplar, which ranked third largest in the study sample in income terms, was in the process of recovering from a very difficult financial period, resulting in a debt in excess of half a million pounds. Now the Poplar is planning to install a budgetary control system with five different cost centres, to enable discrepancies to be pinpointed. This contrasts with the situation in the past when, according to its chairman, it was "all mixed up together". Unlike the previous incumbent who never consulted staff, the new CEO believes in participation from the regional managers and fundraisers, when setting budgets.

The approach to financial control in the remaining six organizations did not measure up to that in the foregoing four agencies. An overall annual income and expenditure budget was prepared by the Ash and the Elm. There was no formal financial reporting system in the Ash and the impression gained by the researcher was that the CEO, a qualified accountant who also looked after financial matters, just kept an overall eye on the agency's purse. The CEO and Hon. Treasurer in the Elm, neither of whom had an accounting background, looked after the overall income and expenditure budget. Branches were given targets for fundraising and the resulting income raised was monitored on a monthly basis by the accounts person, a bookkeeper. She explained that expenditure was controlled as follows: "We don't buy unnecessarily and we don't waste." Overall expenditure was decided by the CEO who reported to the board on a monthly basis.

The remaining four agencies, the Chestnut, Fir, Oak and Sycamore, had no formal budgetary system in place and their handling of financial matters indicated little by way of planning. In the case of the Chestnut, the CEO reported that "we just aim to break even". There was some control over financial affairs as each affiliated group prepared an annual financial report, backed up by a bank statement. Also financial reports were prepared following major events. The chairman of the board explained the approach to money as follows: "There is tight control on money, but money is not the big factor." He added that groups help out one another, in cases where one has a deficit and another had a surplus of funds.

In the Fir, Oak and Sycamore agencies, expenditure seemed to be dictated to a considerable extent by income received, e.g.,

Expenditure is controlled by the amount of money raised. (A/c / Fir)

Up to now, if the money was there we just spent it. (A/c / Oak)

We work on what we have and what we get in we decide what to do with it when we have it. We don't spend in advance. (Bd / Sycamore)

Efforts to generate income seemed equally unstructured, with no specific targets set. The CEO in the Oak described it as being "very loose", while the accounts person in the same organization explained that "we put a spurt on if reserves are low and come up with an idea to bring in a quick thousand or two".

All three agencies said that monthly financial statements were prepared for board meetings, indicating that whereas the approach to money matters was fairly basic, none the less they all tried to ensure that their organizations were solvent and that in the end, as one CEO described it, "things even out" (CEO/Oak).

So far in this discussion on financial control the involvement of volunteers has not been mentioned. Of the nine volunteers interviewed, none was involved in the overall control of financial affairs in his/her organization. Two (from the Chestnut and Larch) did have some experience in the fundraising area. The Chestnut volunteer, a branch member of the organization, explained that "raising money was part of the group's work". Yearly requirements for activities arranged by her particular branch were estimated to be about 8,000 pounds, so plans had to be made to raise the necessary revenue. She reported that the actual collection was totally "based on trust, but we know that they [collectors] are trustworthy." Then the leader of the branch made monthly returns to the core group of the organization.

The Larch agency ran a school-based fundraising programme in which the volunteer respondent was involved. She reported being "left very much to her own devices" and felt that the operation was run "very much on trust", based on making a judgement about collectors. The same volunteer was involved also in the major fundraising drive of this organization when flowers were sold at one pound per bloom. However, despite the strict computerised control outlined by the CEO, she felt that there was still some room for fraud, as generous people donated five or ten pounds per flower, and so the "surplus" could be creamed off.

The volunteer in the Poplar reported that she "had nothing to do with the money area" and this reflected the views of the remaining six volunteers.

Therefore the majority of volunteers had no direct involvement in the financial affairs of their respective organizations.

Control of operations

When asked specifically about how operations were controlled, the vast majority of respondents referred back to comments made earlier in the interview relating to the achievement of overall objectives and indicated that they had nothing further to add. Therefore the few additional comments received have been incorporated into the earlier section, as they do not merit separate mention.

Control of information

Informants were asked about what information they required to help them run their organizations and how they went about procuring it. The general impression gained was that, although information relating to the particular concerns was far from complete, many were so busy trying to cope with current clients that they were not overly concerned about this lack of fuller information. Some sample comments endorse this point:

There are more clients than we can take.   (Dev / Ash)

There's no shortage of needs - we could go anywhere and justify our existence.   (CEO/ Beech)

Every group has a long waiting list.   (A/c / Chestnut)

All the organizations had built up referral systems through which clients were put in touch with them. These were mainly medically based and included specialists, public health nurses, social workers and direct hospital links, as appropriate to the particular disability. Two organizations, the Fir and Oak, which catered for relatively rare medical conditions, mentioned difficulties in getting co-operation from some of the relevant medical specialists, regarding referrals, while another (the Elm) indicated that referrals from hospitals were problematic in some cases. Only one organization, the Poplar, mentioned that it had plans to develop a major data base as a foundation for future planning.

Therefore comprehensive information on the overall extent of the various disabilities catered for was in short supply. Established referral systems ensured a steady stream of clients for all the case study organizations. Yet this limited information base did not serve as a good foundation on which to base future plans.

The human factor in control

This sub-section looks at the reactions of members in the various case-study organizations to control. As, in the final analysis, control is dependent on human beings for its implementation, not surprisingly, it was indicated earlier in this section that most of the difficulties raised in relation to control were people-centred, so they are included here. Two specific areas were explored - perceived resistance to control and manipulation of data. First of all, the resistance factor is examined.

Twelve respondents, from seven different organizations, discerned a certain amount of resistance to control in their respective agencies. In one of these, the Poplar, the problem seemed to permeate the whole organization. This arose because "staff hadn't been controlled for years", according to the newly appointed CEO and so they were now "suspicious of new initiatives" relating to control, a point endorsed by the chairman of this agency. In the remaining six organizations, the resistance encountered did not appear to be endemic. Rather pockets of non-compliance were reported, e.g.,

Some people can't follow rules.   (Vol / Beech)

Sometimes you get resistance from people who think that there's too much control.   (Bd / Chestnut)

People don't always comply with the system.   (A/c / Larch)

Oh yes, there are some people who don't think that way at all - they just spend money as if it's going out of fashion.   (A/c / Rowan)

Two respondents specifically mentioned professional resistance to control. In the experience of the first, the chairman of the Beech agency who also sat on a number of other voluntary boards, professionals "don't like being queried regarding skills or performance" and so he suggested that "you need people of professional standing on the board to counter the allegation: "What do you, as a lay person, know about what I am doing?"." The CEO of the same agency felt that its organizational culture helped to counter this resistance. He explained that "control is seen as part and parcel of this organization. Therefore if people want the job they accept it and run with it".

168

The second comment on professional resistance came from the CEO of the Poplar association where, as explained already, the organizational climate had not been supportive of control in the past. Although he was now trying to remedy this deficiency and establish control, one of the obstacles he mentioned was that "it's not easy to monitor the work of paramedics - they don't take kindly to being monitored closely". Apart from the situation in the Poplar, resistance to control did not appear to pose major problems for the case-study sample.

Manipulation of data was another area of investigation. Once again, it did not present a significant problem for the group as a whole. Four organizations (the Ash, Chestnut, Poplar and Sycamore) recalled examples of malpractice in the past. Two of these related directly to misappropriation of money while the other two concerned falsification of reports. In all cases they have since taken appropriate steps to prevent a reoccurrence of the problems. However, to quote the chairman of the Chestnut, "you can never be 100% sure" as, even though the remaining six organizations were not aware of any malpractice, this does not necessarily mean that none exists. In fact, respondents from the Ash, Larch and Oak agencies admitted that, especially in the area of collections, there is a considerable element of trust involved.

Therefore, although both resistance to control and manipulation have been encountered, they are not seen by respondents to be major concerns in their respective organizations. Of course this finding must be put in the context of the general pattern of fairly limited control in the participant organizations.

Control - summary of findings

The findings in relation to control have been presented in this section. To begin, it was established that control is perceived to be important in all ten case-study agencies. While associated primarily with financial considerations, control is seen also as a basic requirement for any organization and useful in ensuring the achievement of objectives and making feedback available.

In all but one organization, objectives tended to be stated in very general terms. Not surprisingly therefore, information on measuring the achievement of objectives indicated the lack of an overall systematic approach to undertaking this task in the majority of the organizations under review. Likewise setting standards was identified as an area fraught with difficulties.

Moving from general to more specific aspects of control, in the personnel field it was largely informal and also there was little evidence of systematic training. While financial control varied considerably, from a system of formal budgetary control in some agencies to rather basic approaches in others, none

169

the less all ten organizations showed an appreciation of the basic requirement to remain solvent.

Although comprehensive control on information requirements was scarce, all organizations had built up some information links to facilitate client referral. Finally, a review of the human factor in control provided some evidence of both resistance and manipulation but, congruent with the overall less than stringent approach to control, these did not present a major problem in the study sample.

Control is concerned with the internal workings of an organization. But, in keeping with its standing as an open system, interacting with its environment, an organization has to relate to key players in that environment. This leads on to the subject of accountability, the next topic for review.

Accountability in the case study organizations

As open systems, interacting with their environment, organizations receive inputs from this environment and produce outputs to satisfy the perceived needs of customers (Kast & Rosenzweig 1988; Daft 1986). In the case of voluntary organizations involved in service provision, the inputs consist of funding from outside sources, while service supply features on the output side of the equation. Accountability arises on both sides, as organizations need to be accountable both for incoming funds and the ensuing services provided.

This section focuses on how this need for accountability is addressed in the ten organizations in the study sample. To begin, respondents' general approach to "giving an account of one's stewardship" are explored.

General approach to accountability

The section of the interview dealing with accountability commenced on a general note, by trying to ascertain respondents' broad approach to the subject. This was considered necessary as it was felt that their basic approach would colour responses to the more detailed implementation of accountability. For instance, if accountability to outsiders were seen to be unimportant, then one could not expect any great efforts on the part of organizations to address the issue with any marked degree of enthusiasm, if at all.

In fact, when asked about their general approach to accountability, an analysis of the responses received indicates an overwhelmingly positive response. Only three informants - two volunteers (from the Fir and Poplar) and an accounts person from the Elm who functioned as a bookkeeper, indicated that they had not really considered the question of accountability. The response of the volunteer in the Poplar - "I've never thought about it to tell you the truth" - sums up their stance. Apart from these three, the remaining 37 respondents were all in favour of being accountable to outsiders. Many of these considered it to be such a basic requirement that it could almost be taken for granted. A sample of responses, from a CEO, an accounts person, a Board member and a volunteer, shows that this perception was not confined to any one sub-group of respondents, but rather spread across the range of informants.

Of course naturally there should be accountability. Every organization in receipt of voluntary and public money should be accountable. (CEO / Larch)

There's no two ways about it - it's only right that we should be accountable. (A/c / Rowan)

It's essential - you have to be accountable because you're talking about other people's money. (Bd / Elm)

If you're not accountable, you're not going to get anywhere. (Vol / Ash)

Others saw accountability in terms of not being a problem to their organization, e.g., We're totally accountable - we've nothing to be ashamed of. (CEO / Ash)

I think we shouldn't mind having accountability to outsiders. We can stand up to any scrutiny. (A/c / Beech)

The general response indicates a high awareness of a need for accountability to outsiders. This view was shared by all respondents, irrespective of their position in an organization, apart from the three who had not reflected on the matter.

Having outlined the basic stance of respondents regarding accountability, some of the reasons underpinning this perceived accountability requirement are now explored.

Why be accountable?

Respondents were asked to reflect on why this need for accountability arose. Once again, the majority had some thoughts to offer, as only five did not express views on the matter. Reasons put forward by the remaining 35 as to

171

why accountability arises can be grouped as follows, in descending order of frequency of mention.

Reason	Frequency of mention
Fundamental requirement	11
Donor considerations	8
Legal requirements	6
Charitable status	4
Safeguard for the organization	3
Client considerations	2
Social responsibility	1

The largest category of "fundamental requirement" includes respondents who saw accountability as a basic requirement, e.g.,

Everyone should be accountable. (A/c / Beech)

We all need to be accountable for what we do. (CEO / Larch)

If you have a conscience, you have to be accountable if someone gives you money. (Bd / Oak)

It's only morally right that if someone gives you money you should tell that person what it was used for. (Vol / Sycamore)

Donor considerations were seen by eight respondents as giving rise to accountability. These felt that contributors to their organizations were either entitled to know, needed to be informed, or wanted to know about their contributions, e.g.,

People might get fed up donating if they don't know where the money is going. (Vol / Elm)

It's good to let people see where the money is going - people want to know. (Vol / Ash)

Six of those interviewed referred to the legal requirement to be accountable, arising from being a registered charity. This charitable status of the organizations seemed particularly significant to four respondents, in terms of the need for accountability. Three of this latter group referred to the vulnerability of charities to fundraising abuses. As the chairman of the Board in the Beech agency explained: "Because fundraising is subject to criminal abuse you have to have financial accountability - otherwise you'd have abuse and misuse of funds." Another alluded to what he termed "the suspicion of charities" (Bd / Fir), while a third noted that in the fundraising arena, "so many scams have occurred" (Vol / Oak).

Phrases such as "safeguard" and "self-protection" indicated the importance of accountability in terms of the organization's own status. Only two informants saw accountability as playing an important role in ensuring that services are, in fact, provided as claimed. Finally, one CEO (in the Beech agency) felt that the need for accountability stemmed from a need for social responsibility as "we don't operate in a vacuum and what we do impinges on other players."

To summarise, the need for accountability is seen to stem from a variety of specific considerations, chief among them being donor and legal requirements, underpinned by a perceived need for accountability to be a basic need in any organization.

Next, the focus turns to the advantages and disadvantages of accountability, from the perspective of respondents.

Perceived advantages of accountability

In keeping with the positive views expressed on accountability, the vast majority of respondents saw advantages arising from being accountable. Once again, there were exceptions. For instance, the volunteer in the Fir admitted that : it's something I've never thought about", while the accounts person in the Oak expressed doubt about any possible advantages, commenting that: "because we're so small and insignificant in numbers I'm not sure if it makes any difference at the end of the day".

Returning to the majority view, the perceived advantages itemised can be grouped into four areas relating to:

- the image of the organization
- funding
- information to donors
- internal effects.

Each one is now reviewed in turn. The public image of an organization is obviously important, as a negative image could be particularly damaging to a voluntary organization which is dependent, often totally and nearly always to some extent, on donor funding. Being accountable was seen as contributing towards the formation of a good image, and so became a useful tool in the public relations arena. As respondents themselves explained:

It shows that you're doing a great job on a limited budget.   (CEO / Ash)

It reflects well on the organization. It's the reverse of misuse of money and the public perception that we're lining our own pockets.   (CEO / Beech)

People may become aware of and interested in the Society.   (CEO / Fir)
It proves you're honest and above board and have nothing to hide.

(Bd / Sycamore)

Funding is perceived as a perennial problem in the voluntary sector. The case-study group was no exception to this general rule. Not surprisingly therefore, the practical advantage of accountability in assisting the flow of funds was highlighted. The volunteer in the Ash agency stated it in blunt terms: "To get more funding". Other comments in the same vein were:

If a person gives a subscription and sees what is being done, they might subscribe again next time around.   (A/c / Sycamore)

It's something to show, especially the following year when you're looking for more money.   (Vol / Sycamore)
If people are aware that you are accountable they are more likely to support you again.   (Bd / Oak)

The advantage of accountability in providing information to donors also received frequent mention. Sample comments included:

People like to hear what the money is used for.   (Vol / Elm)

It tells people what we do with the money.   (Bd / Fir)

Being accountable to outsiders can have implications for the internal workings of an organization and influence the internal organizational climate. As the Board member from the Elm explained, if people in the organization see you want to be accountable, "there's a lesser chance of money being misappropriated." Another opined that without accountability "we ourselves could become complacent" (Bd / Larch). On the other hand, as the volunteer

174

from the Oak explained, "if you're accountable it will follow that you'll keep a tight rein on things and spend money more wisely." An additional perceived advantage of accountability in relation to the internal workings of an organization was that "it keeps you open and stops you becoming a secret society" (A/c / Chestnut).

To conclude, accountability was viewed as being advantageous in helping the image of the organization, in fundraising, in providing information to donors and finally, in having a positive impact on the internal operations of the voluntary agencies studied.

Perceived disadvantages of accountability

In marked contrast to the outpouring of views on the advantages of accountability, over half of those interviewed did not articulate any corresponding disadvantages. In response to the query about perceived disadvantages, replies such as: "No, I can't see any" (Dev / Ash); "I wouldn't see any" (Bd / Poplar), were quite typical of the group as a whole.

Of the fourteen who did identify some disadvantages, eight of these related to the possibility of interference from outsiders. As one Board member expressed it: "There's always a disadvantage that if you make the organization too accessible to the public that they'll start interfering" (Bd / Beech). In similar vein, another voiced resentment about "people not involved telling us what to do" (A/c / Chestnut) which, in her view, can arise when the organization functions as "an open book".

Four other informants made a negative connection between accountability and state funding. One of these considered that "you have to have a poor mouth when dealing with the state" (CEO / Ash) and he felt that buoyant accounts might jeopardise this stance. The accountant in another organization (the Larch) expressed similar sentiments: "If the figures are good, it can put you in a bad light for getting grants".

Internal disadvantages of accountability were mentioned by three respondents. Two of these (CEO / Elm and Bd / Fir) considered it to be demanding in terms of time while a third noted the difficulties of getting staff to comply with necessary procedures, observing that "some people take exception to the fact of being asked to fill in forms - sometimes you're beating your head against a stone wall, but we try" (Bd / Elm).

Finally, the disadvantage of having to share information with competitors by being accountable, was mentioned by the CEO of the Beech agency.

In sum, the majority of those interviewed did not see disadvantages in being accountable to outsiders. Among the group of fourteen who did identify drawbacks, interference from outsiders was the main concern, while a few balked at the effort involved in being accountable. However, the overall tenor of responses to this question indicated that disadvantages arising from accountability were not seen as a major constraint.

Another concern identified in the literature in relation to accountability is its possible impact on the independence of the recipient agency (Leat et al 1986; Leat 1988). This aspect is now examined in the case-study group.

Accountability and independence

Threats to their independence did not loom large in any of the case-study organizations. This is not surprising, as encroachment on independence usually arises in the context of state funding, and only three of the case study group (the Poplar, Rowan and Sycamore) were dependent on the public purse to a significant extent. Respondents from this sub-group did not perceive their independence to be eroded to any great degree. The Chairman of the Poplar commented: "I don't see any major problems", while the accountant in the Rowan gauged the impact of State funding to be "marginal." Although the third agency, the Sycamore, was over 50% dependent on statutory funding, the actual sum involved was modest. Its chairperson had no complaints about undue interference, but she did indicate compliance with the funder's requirements.

None of the remaining seven organizations expressed concerns about their independence being eroded by accountability. The opinion expressed by the Beech CEO that "it's still possible to retain autonomy while embracing the principle of accountability", seemed to reflect the generally held view in these organizations.

Interestingly, five organizations associated their independence with their non-reliance on statutory funding, e.g., "We don't get much from the Health Board, therefore it doesn't arise" (Vol / Ash).

It was quite evident too from some of the responses that organizations valued their independence, e.g.,

There's nothing to be gained from becoming an arm of the Health Board. If there is virtue in voluntary organizations then there is virtue in voluntary organizations retaining their independence.   (CEO / Beech)

We would resist any buy-out of our independence by government money and only accept it on a partnership basis.   (Bd / Larch)

176

Our desire for independence prevents us from getting money from the Health Board - they would give you money with strings attached.

(A/c / Chestnut)

The evidence from these case studies indicates that their independence is a valued prize and that accountability does not undermine it to any uncomfortable degree, even in the case of organizations receiving significant public funding.

Accountable to whom?

The question considered in this sub-section is: "To whom do you see the organization as being accountable?" Apart from two volunteers (in the Fir and Poplar) and the bookkeeper in the Elm who admitted that they had not thought about this aspect of accountability, the remaining 37 respondents all identified funders as a group to whom they were accountable. Eight of these distinguished between statutory and non-statutory funders, while a further three considered that the main emphasis should be on donors of large amounts, defined by the volunteer in the Sycamore as "amounts of over one thousand pounds".

Clients were identified by twenty informants as another group to whom the organization should be accountable. However, only eight of these gave first mention to clients. Other recipients of accountability mentioned by two respondents (from the Larch and the Sycamore) were the personnel who referred clients to them.

Therefore, to put it succinctly, funders were identified by all organizations and nearly all respondents as a focus of accountability, while clients were the other main group mentioned.

Variations in accountability

In the course of the preliminary fieldwork undertaken early on in the study, the researcher learned that accountability can vary, depending on the source of funding. Bearing this in mind, respondents were asked about their experience in this regard.

As the Rowan agency was entirely dependent on statutory funding, this variation did not arise. In seven of the other nine organizations, some variations were reported. The four agencies which received significant statutory funding (the Beech, Larch, Poplar and Sycamore) all identified this as a special case in the context of accountability. The Poplar, which was given money from the European Social Fund, described accountability requirements as being "quite fussy" (Bd / Rowan). An agreement had to be signed which was open to monitoring and inspection. Another agency, the Larch, which received funds from FAS (the Statutory Training Authority) reported that accounting for it "was not difficult but involves a bit more paperwork" (A/c / Larch). Both the Beech and the Sycamore were in receipt of Health Board funds and their experience was that once reports, as specified, were furnished for the money received, no difficulties arose.

Three organizations, the Ash, Chestnut and Oak, distinguished between large and small donations. The CEO of the Ash explained that, in the case of larger donations, they "try to personalise information directly." He cited the example of a golf club funding venture where he made a point of going out himself to collect the proceeds and took the opportunity of thanking the members and explaining how the money raised would be used. His eloquence was rewarded by a promise of a similar fundraising event the following year. In contrast, more modest contributions to this organization from individual donors are acknowledged, accompanied by a copy of their newsletter.

The Chestnut and Oak organizations both reported receipt of large amounts where the donor in question requested specific information on how the money was spent, and both organizations were happy to accede to this request. In contrast, smaller donations were accounted for in the general audit.

The case study material endorsed the earlier finding that accountability can vary, depending on the source and size of the subscription. Statutory requirements tend to be specifically laid down by the funding source. In the case of non-statutory money, understandably, larger amounts can merit different treatment from more modest mites. Therefore it can be concluded that accountability is tailored to meet the expectations of the particular donor.

For what are organizations accountable?

In posing the question: "For what do you see the organization as being accountable?", the aim was to ascertain whether respondents viewed accountability in strictly financial terms, or considered it to have a wider focus.

An analysis of the data shows that, apart from two informants (A/c / Elm and Vol / Poplar) who "didn't think about that", the remaining 38 all mentioned money. However, in addition, the 38 also articulated the need to be accountable for services to clients. A sample of responses shows how they appreciated this latter need:

The services we provide have to be the right kind, fulfilling the needs of the
people there.   (A/c / Beech)

I see it as part of my job to see that they [clients] are getting what they
request.   (CEO / Elm)

We pride ourselves in offering a service to a client group and take ourselves
to task if something goes awry.   (Bd / Rowan)

Thus money and service were identified as the main foci of accountability,
apart from two contributors (Dev / Ash and Bd / Fir) who, in addition, raised
the need to keep up to date with research and information in their particular
field of activity, and a third, the chairman of the Poplar, who stressed the need
to highlight the issues associated with the broad range of disabilities for which
his organization catered.

So far in this examination of accountability the focus has been on mapping
respondents' views regarding various facets of this subject. However, being
aware of the need for accountability and taking action to address this need are
quite separate matters. So, how did the case study sample tackle the latter task?
This question is now addressed, beginning by examining how the participant
organizations accounted for funds received.

Accountability on the input side

The general impression gained from responses to the question about
accountability for incoming funds was that all the host organizations had a
healthy appreciation of the need to be accountable for funds received, together
with an awareness of the need to be seen to respond to this demand. For
instance, all ten agencies had audited accounts prepared by professional
auditors. The chairperson of one, who asked specifically not to be identified on
this score, recounted how problems had arisen in the past when audited
accounts had not been prepared. These difficulties were of such magnitude that
salaried staff could not be remunerated for a six-month period. Therefore, as
one of her prerequisites before taking up office, she stipulated that audited
accounts had to be prepared.

As the Rowan agency received all its funding from the Health Board,
financial accountability was fairly straightforward, based on monthly returns,
in line with pre-set budgets. Fundraising was a reality for the remaining nine
bodies, making accountability more problematic. Respondents in all nine were
able to elaborate on systems of recording and receipting money, once it had

been received at headquarters. Some sample responses indicate their concern in this regard:

All donations are acknowledged with a personal response directly to the donor.   (CEO / Ash)

Every penny received is receipted - I feel very strongly that everything should be receipted.   (A/c / Oak)

We receipt all [donations] - we're very fussy about it.   (Bd / Elm)

Three organizations (the Beech, Elm and Oak) had a system whereby one person opened the post and recorded any money sent, while a second sent out the actual receipt. This minimised the chance of dishonesty which could arise with only one involved in the total process, enabling "shrinkage" to arise between amounts receipted and amounts recorded, as there are no invoices against which to check donations. This loophole was at the nub of a major scandal some years ago when the CEO of a major Irish third world agency was found guilty of pocketing large amounts of donated money, while the innocent donors got receipts for the full amount donated (Gibbons 1985). The "dual" arrangement also makes life more comfortable for the personnel involved. As the accounts person in the Oak reported: "The secretary controls the receipts and they have to balance with my lodgements - that eases my conscience".

Despite these precautions, problems can arise at an earlier stage in the donation process. For instance, the auditors' report for one organization included the following:

The Association, in common with many others of similar size and organization, derives a substantial portion of its income from voluntary donations which cannot be fully controlled until they are entered into the accounting records and are not susceptible to independent audit verification.

Such a qualification is common in charity accounts and arises due to the difficulty in accounting for fundraising money at the stage before it reaches the headquarters of the organization in question. One chairman, who understandably did not wish to be identified on this count, reported that the credibility of his organization had been damaged in the past when it was alleged that the proceeds of a "bucket" collection for the association, which took place in a public house, were used to finance a round of drinks in situ. The CEO of the same agency admitted that this aspect was "very difficult" with "quite a lot of looseness", as he termed it. One approach taken by him was to monitor receipts from various functions by comparing them with the previous year's take, and then seek an explanation for any marked discrepancies.

Another agency which also relied to some extent on "bucket" collections had a policy of engaging only families and friends of clients, e.g., known collectors, with a view to avoiding misappropriation of money. However, as one volunteer involved in fundraising commented, the reality is that "there's no foolproof method - we rely on the goodwill of collectors".

The major fundraising drive for the Larch agency, as mentioned already, consisted of selling flowers at one pound per bloom. This facilitated accountability to some extent as, unlike a "bucket" collection where contributions vary greatly and there is no exchange involved, both the flowers and the pounds could be counted. It is recalled that an elaborate computerised system had been installed to compare the numbers of flowers distributed against actual funds received in return. This system cost about ten thousand pounds, so could only be justified when large amounts are at stake. Yet, as indicated earlier, even such a system cannot accommodate fluctuations that arise when a generous donor contributes in excess of the pound per bloom stipulated. The same organization also raised additional funds by means of collection boxes left in shops and, according to its CEO, had to rely on "watching trends" in order to monitor donations, i.e., the trustworthiness of the collectors was an important factor.

The Sycamore had a system whereby two members attended each fundraising event, in addition to the organiser. Its chairperson reported that this procedure was adopted in order to avoid accusations of personal gain on the part of the organiser which could arise if the event were run single-handed.

The broad situation regarding accountability for incoming funds in the case study organizations is that they did respond to the need in so far as they were able, by having routines in place to acknowledge donations received at headquarters. Yet, in the final analysis, total accountability was less tight, due to the lack of control at the fundraising stage prior to funds being delivered to the officials in each organization.

This sub-section has reviewed provisions for funds received by the various agencies. Accountability is concerned also with showing how these funds were used. The approach adopted by the case study organizations in coping with this aspect of accountability is now explored.

Once again, all ten organizations mentioned audited accounts as a vehicle of accountability on the output side. Undoubtedly these accounts showed how the money was spent. However, as highlighted earlier in the literature review, mere financial accountability for services has considerable limitations. Even when every penny is accounted for, this in itself does not indicate that it has been spent in a constructive manner. In addition to financial accountability, it is suggested that there is a need to be accountable in terms of achieving organizational objectives and in meeting accepted standards of service (Leat 1988). Another significant aspect of accountability relates to the appropriateness of the services offered (Leat 1988). All three areas are concerned with the non-financial aspects of accountability.

Findings in relation to these areas are connected with the findings on control, where the difficulties in establishing standards were noted already. Obviously when problems are encountered in establishing working objectives and standards internally, this does not facilitate reporting to outsiders on achievements in these areas.

In fact, data for individual organizations showed that the main vehicle of accountability was seen to be the audited accounts. In addition, seven organizations, (the Ash, Elm, Fir, Larch, Oak, Poplar and Sycamore), issued periodic newsletters as another mode of giving non-financial accountability for their activities. However, the content of these periodicals tended to give general information on the work of each organization rather than structured information which would account specifically for achievement of objectives and standards of service. Yet these seven organizations did go some way towards providing non-financial information on their activities, albeit at a rather general level.

Published annual reports constitute another method of conveying non-financial achievements to outsiders, as well as financial data. The use of this information channel is now reviewed.

Annual reports

Only three of the case study organizations (the Beech, Larch and Poplar) prepared published annual reports. These were among the largest organizations in terms of income, ranking first, second and fourth in order of income size. An analysis of these published reports shows that the broad areas covered are:

- chairman's report

- broadly based reports on the year's activities
- fundraising report
- highlights from annual income and expenditure report.

These were circulated to significant supporters, relevant statutory bodies and government departments. Only one organization, the Beech, reported getting additional requests for copies of its annual report. An estimated sixty requests per year are received, primarily by phone.

A further five agencies (the Chestnut, Elm, Fir, Oak and Sycamore) indicated that they prepared annual reports for their AGM. In the case of one of these, the Oak, outsiders, e.g., Health Board and medical/para-medical representatives were invited to the AGM. In the four other instances the AGM was an "internal" affair. Of the two remaining agencies, the Ash relied on "on-going progress reports" (CEO / Ash), while the Rowan prepared annual accounts for its statutory funders.

Therefore, among the organizations studied, published annual reports did not play a major role in the process of being accountable to outsiders.

Yet another method of ensuring accountability is to give a place on the board to outside funders and/or clients. The use of this method by the study cohort is now examined.

Board representation for funders and clients

Respondents were asked whether they had funders and/or clients represented on their boards. Regarding funders, the aim was to ascertain if any major funders sat on the board specifically to monitor how their contribution was being spent. For instance, it is not unusual for statutory funders to have representation on the boards of funded organizations.

In the study sample, three organizations (the Poplar, Rowan and Sycamore) received a significant percentage of their total income from statutory sources. Yet only one of these, the Rowan, had representatives from the funding Health Board on its board. In the case of the Sycamore the actual amount of money involved was small and so it was understandable that the Health Board was satisfied with regular reports on its usage and did not find it necessary to have board representation. The chairman of the remaining association, the Poplar, said that it did not have a statutory representative on its board "because independence comes into play there".

The other seven organizations were not dependent on statutory funding to any great extent. Whereas none had a member who was responsible specifically for funding, they reported that many of the board members rowed in to help keep each organization financially afloat.

Client representation on boards of management is another option. Voluntary agencies are set up to meet client needs. Faughnan (1977:10) suggests that "a guiding principle for service agencies must be need as defined by the recipient." This approach ensures congruence between services and client needs, i.e., it is a check on the appropriateness of services offered. According to Faughnan (1977:10), practice does not always measure up to this ideal as "frequently . . . even where there is planning to meet needs, this is based on existing services rather than on the real needs of individuals or groups".

One way of ensuring that clients have a say in the type of service provided is to give them a place on the relevant board. However, it was quickly realised that, in the case study organizations, personal client representation is not always feasible in practice, due to the age of the client and/or the nature of certain disabilities. For instance, three of the ten agencies in the sample catered for clients whose disability precluded them from acting as representatives. In the case of a further three, representation was problematic, again due to the nature of their disability. In the past, one of these had a client on its board who died from the disability while serving, and the other had a former client. Of the remaining four, three had client representatives on their present boards and the fourth did have a client member in the past, together with provision for possible re-election in the future.

To summarise, having funder and/or client representative on boards was not a widespread practice in the cluster of organizations studied. Whereas client representation may seem desirable, data on the study group showed that this is not always possible.

Finally, this section on accountability concludes by examining how attuned respondents were to some general developments in the field of voluntary sector accountability. Informants were asked about their familiarity with and views on two documents, the Statement of Recommended Practice (SORP 2) relating to charity accounting (ASC 1988) and the recently published Irish government report on fundraising (1990).

SORP 2 and government report on fundraising

When asked about the ASC's (1988) SORP 2, responses pointed to an almost complete lack of knowledge about this document. With one exception, no one was even aware of its existence. Even the one respondent who was aware of it, the chairman of the Poplar, did not appear to be very knowledgeable about its contents, as he offered just the bland comment that "it was badly needed" and he did not elaborate further. Therefore it can be safely concluded that, among the study sample, familiarity with the ASC's SORP 2 was non-existent.

Respondents were asked also about the recent Irish government report on fundraising (1990). Nine of the ten case study group were engaged in considerable fundraising from the public. Therefore it seemed reasonable to assume that they might have some interest in and be familiar with this relevant government report. Results from the interviews indicated otherwise.

Relatively few of the respondents (twelve) had even looked at this report. The remaining 28 had not read it, and of these only four seemed to know of its existence, judging by remarks such as: "I got it but I didn't read it" (A/c / Chestnut). Of the minority who said that they had looked at the report, eight of them appeared to be rather vague about its contents, e.g., "I read it without digesting it" (Bd / Sycamore); "there was a lot of it that I couldn't follow" (CEO / Oak). This left only four respondents who appeared to have any appreciable knowledge of the report's contents. All four, representing the views of only two organizations (the Beech and Larch) accepted the broad thrust of the report which fitted in with their philosophy on fundraising, e.g.,

> We support it entirely as an organization and there was no significant point of difference. There is a need for control over fundraising because in the past there was a great deal of fraud and it was wide open to abuse.
>
> (Bd / Beech)
>
> I'm very happy to see it coming through because we're strong advocates of cleaning up the fundraising area. (A/c / Larch)

To summarise, while the government report on fundraising (1990) seems to have generated very little interest among respondents in general, the reactions of the four who had reflected on it were positive.

Findings on accountability - summary

To conclude this section on accountability, the main findings are recalled briefly. The first step was to explore respondents' views on accountability and the data showed that it was considered to be of importance in all ten case-study organizations. This need for accountability was seen by over a quarter of informants as a fundamental requirement, while others saw its significance in terms of satisfying donor and legal requirements. The perceived advantages and disadvantages of accountability were next for review. Findings here indicated that advantages outweighed disadvantages. Accountability was not seen as a major intrusion on the independence of agencies. Further probing identified funders and clients as being the main foci of accountability, with some variation in approach being reported to take account of the requirements of different funding sources. Money and services were highlighted as the two areas requiring accountability.

Next, actual responses to the need to be accountable were examined and findings suggested a definite emphasis on financial accountability both for funds received and services provided. Only three organizations published annual reports and Board representation for clients and funders was not widely used. Finally, in an effort to capture respondents' broader interests in accountability, they were queried about their familiarity with SORP 2 (ASC 1988) and the recent Irish government report on fundraising (1990). The response on both fronts pointed to a low level of knowledge in relation to these publications.

Summary

This chapter reported on the findings emerging from the main research. It began by explaining the content of the interview schedule used to gather the data. The pilot testing process was then described as was the method of data analysis. The report on the interview data began by outlining the characteristics of the ten case study organizations, establishing how they varied in terms of age, client population, funding sources, staffing patterns and geographical spread of operations. Affiliations to outside bodies, by and large, were connected to each organization's own particular service specialism.

When viewed as a group, the case study organizations made a significant contribution to the Irish voluntary sector as they had a combined income approaching 7 million pounds and catered between them for a total of over 18,000 clients, with the assistance of about 5,000 staff, 90% of whom worked in a voluntary capacity.

With background details on the ten organizations in place, profiles of management were next for review. Findings in relation to CEOs indicated a strong orientation towards the particular "cause" of individual organizations and there was no strong evidence of formal management training. In the accounting area, once again a high level of commitment was apparent but only two of the ten incumbents had a professional accounting qualification. Turning to the boards of management, their composition also seemed to reflect a strong interest in the concern of each particular agency.

Findings in relation to control indicated an appreciation of the need for control in organizations, particularly in the financial area but also as a means of ensuring the achievement of organizational objectives. However, at an operational level, objectives tended to be stated in only very general terms and this did not facilitate the implementation of control. The review also considered control in the areas of personnel, finance and information provision. Finally, the human factor in control was explored.

Accountability was another major concern in the research. As was the case with control, views on the need for accountability were very positive, with advantages being seen to outweigh disadvantages and little threat to independence being perceived. Responses to accountability were mainly financial, both for funds received and services provided. Generally speaking, informants indicated no great awareness of the wider debate on accountability in the voluntary sector.

These were the main findings emerging from the fieldwork.

11   Discussion on Findings

This chapter discusses the preliminary fieldwork and background information relating to the Irish voluntary sector, together with the findings from the case study interviews, taking a more holistic view of the data (Robson & Foster 1989). Using an open systems organizational model (Daft 1986; Kast & Rosenzweig 1985), the environmental characteristics that impact on Irish voluntary organizations are reviewed. This is followed by a discussion on organizational characteristics. Then the findings arising from the fieldwork in relation to management, control and accountability are interpreted.

Environmental characteristics

An earlier chapter (4), dealing with the scope of voluntary activity in the past, established that historically, given the limited extent of government provision, voluntary organizations played a significant role in the provision of social welfare. Therefore there is a strong tradition of voluntary action in Ireland. Whereas Billis (1992:227) reports that, in the UK, "the sector, like some remote tribe, has been "discovered" (or more accurately rediscovered") in recent years", Irish voluntary action has been a continuous feature in the overall provision of social services (Curry 1980). This indicates a generally supportive environment for voluntary organizations which depend, either directly, or indirectly through taxation, on support from the public.

The positive reaction to the recent famine in Somalia (Rocke 1992) is instructive. Just one of the many fundraising ventures - Messiah for Somalia - doubled its initial target of 100,000 pounds when even the choir members paid for their tickets as did many people who could not attend but yet wished to support the cause (Waters 1992; Sheehan 1992). The world premier of Handel's Messiah, performed in Dublin 250 years ago, was also a fundraising event. Although relegated to "a club for fiddlers in Fishamble Street" by the then Dean of St. Patrick's, Jonathan Swift, its packed audience contributed greatly to the three benefitting charities - Mercer's Hospital, the Charitable Infirmary and the Charitable Musical Society for the Relief of Imprisoned Debtors (Boydell 1992).

This long unbroken tradition of Irish voluntary action is one factor in the public support now given to the sector. As referred to previously, the Charter and a White Paper on the voluntary sector, currently being prepared by the government as part of its Programme for Economic and Social Progress (PESP 1991), are indicative of the sector's heightened profile in Irish society in recent times.

Evidence gathered in the preliminary fieldwork (chapter 9) shows that the present regulatory climate for Irish nonprofit organizations is fairly lax. However, if the recommendations put forward in the government's Report on Fundraising (1990) are implemented, this is set to change. The Report came about as a result of concerns regarding accountability in the sector, particularly in relation to money collected for voluntary organizations.

The earlier review of the general literature indicated an era of increasing competitiveness for voluntary sector funds (Butler & Wilson 1990; Kramer 1990). This situation also obtains in the Irish voluntary arena where "fund raising is becoming riskier, more time consuming and frequently less rewarding than heretofore" (UVOH 1991:7).

One recent event in Irish society, the advent of the National Lottery, has had a major impact on the voluntary sector. This lottery was set up under the National Lottery Act 1986 and launched in March 1987. The extent of its popularity can be gauged from the fact that, in its first year, sales forecast at 20 million pounds actually achieved over 100 million. By 1990 this figure had soared to 170 million pounds (UVOH 1991). So "the National Lottery has changed the face of fund raising. It has removed millions of pounds of discretionary income from circulation. This income has not made its way back to the voluntary organizations" (UVOH 1991:1).

Although surpluses arising from the lottery are transferred to a National Lottery Beneficiary Fund, voluntary organizations have not benefitted greatly. For instance, while the Department of Health received 10.6 million pounds of "lottery money" in 1990, less than one third of it was passed on to voluntary organizations (O'Morain 1991). In an effort to capture some of this discretionary income, Rehab Lotteries was set up in October 1987 by a group of charities. However, its operation is regulated by the Gaming and Lotteries Act 1956 which sets a maximum prize limit of 10,000 pounds. In comparison, the National Lottery has had prizes of up to two million pounds and has no upper limit. Not surprisingly, therefore, Mr John Maguire, CEO of Rehab Lotteries, calling for changes in the 1956 relevant legislation, said that "the current restrictions place charitable lotteries at a very severe disadvantage compared with the National Lottery" (Kilfeather 1992). He estimated that, at present, charities are losing 15 to 20 million pounds per year to the National Lottery (Kilfeather 1992). So, competition for funds is a reality in the Irish voluntary sector, as elsewhere (Kramer 1990).

Another way of encouraging people to donate to voluntary organizations is by giving tax relief on donations (Anthony & Young 1988; Rayney 1988). At present in Ireland such tax benefits are very limited, being restricted to deeds of covenant applicable only to charities providing an educational or research function in Ireland. Recently the Irish Charities' Tax Reform Group (ICTRG), representing sixteen charities, was set up to seek wider tax benefits on donations to charities. This group wants the tax benefits in Ireland brought into line with concessions in the UK (McKevitt 1992). Gift Aid is another measure sought by the ICTRG whereby a donation of 400 pounds upwards after tax is made to a charity which can then collect back the tax paid (McKevitt 1992).

The requests of the ICTRG confirm the rather restricted nature of current tax provisions as a means of encouraging donations to the voluntary sector. This contrasts with the more favourable tax provisions available to voluntary organizations in the UK and the US (Knapp et al 1988; Kramer 1981; Simon 1987).

Although the relief on donations might motivate taxpayers to consider donating to a voluntary organization of their choice, it is of little interest to those unemployed in Ireland, now numbering almost 300,000, who are outside the tax net. In fact, as was shown earlier in section 3.2, the major unemployment problem in the Irish economy can create additional demands for voluntary organizations, while those now unemployed are no longer likely to be potential contributors to the sector. This very high level of unemployment also places a drain on the Exchequer and, coupled with the large national debt (see section 4.2), leaves less money available for other areas, including funding for the voluntary sector. Of course cutbacks in public expenditure and their impact on voluntary organizations are not unique to Ireland. Similar trends are in evidence in the UK and the US (Knapp et al 1988; Salamon 1987).

It is suggested in the literature (Kramer 1987; Leat 1988) that consumerism is another facet which now needs to be taken into account by voluntary sector

191

organizations. Ireland is no exception to this general trend. For example, the Rt. Hon. Earl of Dunraven, outgoing president of the Irish Wheelchair Association (IWA) and himself confined to a wheelchair, sharing some of his views on changes towards the disabled over the years, notes:

> Attitudes (too) have changed. In the old days disability was looked on slightly as a sin - you have sinned and this is what has happened. . . . Nowadays a disabled person does not sit around - they want to go out and get jobs. In the old days they were happy to stay at home and go to lovely IWA parties of tea and buns . . . Nowadays they want more. They are younger - they do not want to spend the rest of their lives just sitting around in a wheelchair at home. (IWA 1991:22)

These changes over time record the move of disabled people from spectator roles to being actively involved in their future so that voluntary organizations providing services now need to do things "with others" rather than "for others" (Leat 1988:12).

As mentioned earlier, the major policy issues which surround participation, including its promotion in the voluntary sector, were discussed at a recent conference organised by the Conference of Major Religious Superiors (CMRS 1992) in response to the perceived need for greater participation in society of which voluntary organizations are a part. The launching of a Charter of Rights for Hospital Patients by the Minister for Health in September 1992, as part of the government's Programme for Economic and Social Progress (PESP 1991), is another example of increased consumer involvement in the health area. Therefore consumerism and participation are topics of current relevance both in the Irish voluntary sector and Irish society in general, thus endorsing the findings in the general literature (Leat 1988).

To summarise this section which looks at some of the environmental factors impacting on Irish voluntary organizations, the long unbroken tradition of voluntary action in the country creates a generally supportive climate for the current operation of the voluntary sector. While regulation of voluntary activity is fairly lax at present, indications are that this situation could change if the proposals of the relevant government committee are implemented (see Report on Fundraising 1990). Competition for funding in the voluntary sector is a reality in Ireland and efforts in this area have been adversely affected by the advent of the National Lottery in 1987. In addition, present tax relief on donations to voluntary organizations in Ireland is very limited in scope. Likewise the present major economic problems of unemployment and a large national debt have negative effects on the overall Irish economy and, in turn, on the voluntary sector. Finally, an increased interest in consumerism is also discernible.

Organizational characteristics

When choosing the ten case study organizations, certain key variables were identified including organizational size and age, staffing patterns, geographical spread and sources of funding. Findings in relation to these variables are now discussed.

The ten organizations in the fieldwork were ranked by size, as determined by the number of clients served (see Table 10.1). As can be seen from this table, client numbers varied greatly from 7,000 in the Larch to just over 100 in the Oak. In fact, five had over 1,000 clients each, while the remaining five numbered their clients in hundreds. How did this variation in terms of client numbers impact on the participating organizations?

Regarding service provision, obviously it is easier to keep in contact with a smaller client population and this can impact on control of services provided. For instance the Oak agency, with just over 100 clients, was able to check on the suitability and appropriateness of its services by sending a letter to each client every two months to check if his/her needs were being met. Likewise the Sycamore, with about 300 clients, had a control system whereby its Chairperson "does a round once per year and visits every patient on the books" in addition to having monthly reports on clients submitted by its two supervisors. In the Rowan, its Board chairman said that the Director of the referring agency knew all of its 300 clients personally so that if concern is voiced about anyone, "action is taken".

Another small association, the Fir, with 250 clients, was described by its CEO as being "very close to members". Having visited most of them in their houses, she "knows the situation of each one" and therefore can respond easily to needs. Although the Chestnut had 600 clients, its main mission was to have one-to-one contact between each helper and a handicapped person. This facilitated the provision of appropriate services to clients.

It can be seen from the foregoing that, in the case of smaller organizations, it is possible to maintain contact with individual clients as a means of receiving feedback on services provided, and thus serving as a method of control. In contrast, the large numbers of clients in organizations such as the Larch did not facilitate this method of control. Rather the Larch relied on reactions from the public to the various services it offered, according to its CEO and Development Officer, while its Board chairman felt that the support offered by "high profile people" indicated "in an indirect way" that it was achieving its objectives. The four remaining organizations with client numbers in excess of a thousand - the Beech, Poplar, Elm and Ash - also mentioned relying on clients to indicate achievement of their objectives. In addition, the Ash had a development officer operating in the field as a means of keeping in touch with clients, while the Beech broke down its operations into specific projects and set objectives for each one against which to measure achievements.

Therefore it can be concluded that organizational size in terms of clients served did impact on control, as smaller numbers facilitated on-going interaction with clients, whereas those with a large client base had to rely on other methods, including client feedback, as a way of ensuring that clients' needs were being met.

Reviewing the study sample in terms of age (Table 10.1), five were relatively new organizations, being established in the 1980s while the other five varied from 25 to over 100 years. The one organization that stands out in relation to having a major problem with control in the financial area is the Poplar. Set up just 30 years ago, it has grown from a small Dublin-based agency to a large national body during that period. As explained previously, in recent years the organization encountered major financial difficulties, resulting in a debt of over half a million pounds. The same CEO had been in charge for 25 years from 1964 and "ran the show his own way", using "dictatorship management", according to the present CEO who added that "there was little or no control right across the board". Against this background of lax control, both the current CEO and Board chairman reported that efforts to introduce control are meeting with strong resistance from staff. This confirms Handy's (1988:95) view that "organizations are to some extent stuck with their past".

The situation in the Poplar contrasts with that in the Beech where, according to the CEO, control "is seen as part and parcel of the organization, therefore if people want a job here they accept it and run along with it", a view endorsed by the accounts person who saw it as being "part of the culture so you just accept it". These two contrasting examples suggest that organizational practice over time, rather than its age, can be an influencing factor in the acceptance of control in an organization.

With regard to staffing patterns in the study sample, it can be seen from Table 10.3 that nine organizations availed of the services of volunteers. (The tenth agency, the Rowan, did not use volunteers for service provision.) Of the remaining nine, apart from the Beech agency, volunteers greatly outnumbered paid staff. Therefore there was a heavy dependence on voluntary input in eight of the ten study cohort which between them had 238 paid staff and 4,493 volunteers.

Of the nine volunteers interviewed, only one from the Sycamore had attended "a variety of lectures" as a means of training. The remaining eight had received no training. Rather, the experience of the Fir volunteer of being "put in at the deep end" seemed to reflect the general approach towards volunteers. Respondents at management level in four agencies - the Beech, Larch, Oak and Poplar - acknowledged the need for training in this area. According to the Board chairman in the Poplar, his organization "was trying to initiate a period of change. . . to get more from voluntary people" and was preparing some training programmes to achieve this objective.

At a more general level there was little evidence to suggest a systematic approach to training of volunteers. This did not seem congruent with the high level of dependence on voluntary input in all but one of these nine organizations. In relation to control, how do organizations ensure that standards of service are maintained when volunteers may not even be aware of these standards? In fact the CEO of the Rowan said that his organization "backed away" from using volunteers "because of the big management problems in training and control", a point endorsed by Sherrott (1983).

To summarise, the evidence suggests that availing of the services of volunteers can add a layer of complexity to management in the voluntary sector (Gerard 1983; Handy 1988; Mason 1984; Murray 1987) and that the training of volunteers needs to be addressed.

Spread of operations was another variable taken into consideration in the fieldwork. Seven of the organizations studied operated at a national level while the remaining three confined their services to a local area (see Table 10.1). The experience in the Poplar where, according to its Board chairman, branches operated "almost like a banana republic", indicates how control in an organization can be difficult when it is geographically dispersed. The CEO of the Larch also admitted to difficulties regarding control of services. Having "no one to supervise the overall service which people receive", he felt that the level of service throughout the country "largely rests on my shoulders". The Elm had a network of regional and local branches and representatives from the former came to its regular National Executive meetings, which went some way towards ensuring a good level of contact throughout the organization. Also its total number of clients was only one fifth of that in the Larch and just over a third of the number served by the Poplar, thus making contact easier. Likewise in the remaining agencies operating at national level - the Chestnut, Fir and Oak - the relatively small client population in each facilitated contact and feedback and so, in turn, facilitated control.

In sum, whereas geographical spread can create additional difficulties in the control area, this tends to be associated more with those organizations which have a large client base.

The fieldwork data on funding sources (see Table 10.2) showed that half of the study sample received at least some money from statutory bodies, while the remaining five had to rely on other sources to finance their operations. Had these variations in funding sources any impact on management, control and accountability?

In relation to funding, the Rowan was at one extreme in the sample as it received all its income from statutory bodies, 70% of it coming from the Eastern Health Board (EHB) to cover the costs of residential accommodation and staffing, and the remainder from the European Social Fund (ESF) to meet the costs of running training workshops and programmes. The CEO of this agency explained that annual budgets for the next calendar year are negotiated with the EHB in the previous October and then "once struck, our business is to run according to budget". This makes financial control and accountability very important.

Regarding the ESF funding for training, up to two years ago it was based on the cost per centre. Then it changed to cost per place, which "reduced the level of funding by 30%" (A/c / Rowan). In addition, the CEO said that cash-flow problems can arise with ESF funding. For example, recently it was fourteen months late and the organization incurred interest charges of 38,000 pounds in 1991 as a result and is relying on a "half-baked promise" from the EHB to meet these costs (CEO / Rowan).

The conclusion that can be drawn from this example is that, in relation to financial control, the receipt of statutory finance can reduce financial uncertainty for a voluntary agency as it has a pre-set annual budgeted income, in comparison to being dependent on less certain sources from fundraising. Yet, some uncertainty can arise due to (a) changes in the operating rules of the funding source (in this case the ESF) and (b) delays in payment of these funds, leading to cash-flow problems. Similar difficulties in relation to statutory funding are reported by Leat et al (1986).

In general, statutory funding seemed to put a strong emphasis on financial control and accountability in the Rowan agency. This situation was evident also in the Poplar organization. Its Board chairman rated ESF requirements for accountability as being "quite fussy" while its Development Officer felt that they are "pretty stringent" in the financial area, but "they don't have service standards". For example, if money is allocated to "hire a title, it's OK if you show that you hired that person" (Dev / Poplar). The CEO of this agency also emphasised the practical importance of accountability to statutory funders because "the money won't come next year if you don't send a report" as "their monitoring is quite tight". He contrasted this approach to that used when dealing with "the ordinary Joe Public - we might not come out so well in that area".

Although the Beech also received some funding from the EHB, as it accounted for only 10% of its total income it was not as significant in terms of overall funding. A specific report had to be provided, showing how this EHB money was spent (A/c / Beech). The Sycamore and Larch also received some statutory finance and in both cases the actual amount had to be accounted for by periodic reports. This emphasis on financial accountability is in contrast with findings reported by Leat 1988:42) regarding UK statutory funders where "the focus of accountability was not so much on the money delegated as on the services provided with that money".

The remaining five organizations were totally dependent on non- statutory sources of funding. In practice this meant that they had to organize fundraising in order to generate resources with which to pay for service provision, as had the Larch, Poplar and Sycamore which were only partly funded from statutory sources and, unlike the Beech, had no "parent" body to provide resources. Dependence on fundraising can create uncertainties for an organization. Examples such as that of the Irish Heart Foundation quoted earlier, where the fundraising target was not met (Holmquist 1990), can have repercussions for service provision if the required money is not available. In the study sample, the Board member of the Elm mentioned how "it is difficult to plan in an uncertain financial environment" while a respondent in the Oak said that they had to come up with an idea to bring in "a quick 1,000/2,000 pounds" if reserves were low. She also said that "if the money was there we just spent it", showing how financial availability rather than need may dictate the level of service provided.

In the area of fundraising generally, it was seen that not having a yardstick (koontz & Weihrich 1988) against which to measure inflows can create difficulties in control of fundraising. Even the sophisticated computerised system set up by the Larch to monitor its "Rose" fundraising event was shown to have limitations. Firstly, it was costly (over 10,000 pounds) and so could only be justified for a large fundraising event. Secondly, it did not accommodate situations where subscribers had given more than the requested one pound donation which, according to the volunteer respondent, happened quite frequently.

To conclude, the evidence from the study suggests that different funding sources can impact on voluntary organizations. While statutory funding can reduce uncertainty for management regarding having money to meet the cost of service provision, it too may have shortcomings, as seen in the case of the Rowan. Nonetheless, it is a more definite source on which to plan, in comparison to relying on fundraising from the general public. However, it creates specific demands for accountability to the funding source and this involves internal control of the money received by the organization.

Effective fundraising has to be organised by agencies dependent on it. Control of this fundraising is more difficult, owing to the uncertain nature of this flow of resources. Attempts at sophisticated control can be costly, as seen in the Larch example. Also the uncertainly of this form of funding can create difficulties in planning service provision. The case study material showed that accountability can vary, depending on the size of the subscription.

The findings can be summarized as showing that different sources of funding do impact on management, control and accountability in voluntary organizations, in keeping with the findings in the literature (Hopkins 1980; Leat et al 1986; Mason 1984).

Drawing together the information relating to variables of size, age, staffing patterns, geographical spread and funding sources, there is evidence from the study data to suggest that size, staffing patterns, geographical spread of operations and funding patterns can impact on management, control and, in turn, accountability in voluntary organizations. Whereas there was no strong evidence in the organizations surveyed to indicate that age, in itself, was an issue, organization practice, as developed over time, was seen to influence the implementation of control in different ways, in two of the longer established agencies.

In addition to the foregoing variables, other organizational characteristics of nonprofit organizations were identified earlier from the literature (see section 5.4) including the nonprofit and service nature of their operations and their dual management systems. These characteristics also applied to and impacted on management, control and accountability in all ten case study organizations.

The interview data endorsed the problems highlighted in the literature regarding setting standards against which to measure performance, in the absence of a profit yardstick (Anthony & Young 1988; Kanter & Summers 1987; Lovelock & Wineberg 1977; Ryan 1980). Findings showed also how the service nature of voluntary organizations adds to this difficulty, again agreeing with the relevant literature (Gerard 1983; Handy 1981; McLaughlin 1986; Newman & Wallender 1978; Ryan 1980). Even in the Rowan, which was funded totally from the statutory purse, the "dual management" characteristic (Mason 1984) applied to a certain extent. As its CEO explained: "ethics demand that we don't turn people away". Therefore, in reality, services

198

provided varied from the forecast level set in annual budgets prepared three months in advance of an operating period.

So far this chapter has looked at both environmental and organizational characteristics that can impact on Irish voluntary organizations. The emerging picture is complex. Yet it is the reality which faces management in these organizations. Management in the case study cohort is now discussed.

Management in the study sample

The general picture emerging from profiles of the ten CEOs in the study sample confirmed Mason's (1984:9) view that nonprofit mmanagers have "little formal education in management". In most cases, this absence of educational input does not appear to have been compensated for by management training or previous experience. Rather, the majority of CEO respondents seemed to operate from a base of undoubted commitment to the "cause" of their individual organizations, stemming from a deep personal vocation and innate belief in the particular concern. In fact, one CEO, himself a professional accountant and not personally touched by the ailment catered for by his organization, commented wryly that "you're not considered totally "in" if you haven't had someone who has had X [the ailment] - you can be put down by an "expert" volunteer."

This was indicative of a perception that personal involvement with a cause secured a far higher accolade and was seen to take precedence over any relevant professional qualification. Such a "product champion" (Barney & Griffin 1992:299) can be very beneficial to an organization. It is particularly useful in facilitating integration towards the achievement of overall organizational goals (Lawrence & Lorsch 1967). However, the observations of Daft (1986:32) regarding the shortcomings of exclusive dependence on trial and error, contrasted with the need for organizational understanding, are pertinent:

> Organization theory provides a set of concepts and models that inform the way a person thinks about organizations. Many of these concepts and models are not obvious and will not be learned through trial and error. . . . Organization theory enables managers to understand their organizational situation, which is the first step toward effective management and control.

This suggests that specific knowledge and understanding are required in addition to commitment. In turn, it indicates the usefulness of being equipped with a range of management "tools" which would facilitate the management of voluntary agencies in undertaking their complex task (Drucker 1989; Mason 1984).

The present operational situation in relation to management in many of the study group is somewhat reminiscent of Drucker's (1989:89) description of US voluntary organizations some twenty years ago when "management was a dirty word for those involved in nonprofit organizations. It meant business and nonprofits prided themselves on being free of the taint of commercialism". For instance, the Beech was the only agency with an established staff training and development system and the Poplar had recently made a first effort in this regard by running two short courses for management staff.

It is noted also that the affiliations of the case study organizations to outside bodies, with one exception, were all connected with the particular "cause", to the exclusion of any management/administrative bodies. So, once again, the "cause" seemed to be to the fore and to take precedence over management considerations.

Profiles were prepared also on personnel dealing with financial matters in the various agencies. Here again there was no strong evidence of professional accounting expertise. Only two of the ten incumbents had a formal accountancy qualification and one of these worked only in a voluntary capacity, having a full-time position elsewhere. The majority of those responsible for financial matters depended on bookkeeping or secretarial skills which enabled them to "keep the score" in terms of accounting for monies received and spent. Yet the CEO in the Beech agency, which had a bookkeeper, considered that if they had not got assistance in accounting matters from their UK parent body, "I'd see us as weak in the financial area".

Another difficulty on the accounting side related to the level of input provided; only five of the accounting staff were full-time, while the other half worked either part-time or in a voluntary capacity.

In the review of the literature relating to the governance of voluntary organizations (section 5.4) the lack of managerial ability was noted. Murray (1987) connected this with a combination of poor selection processes and inadequate training. So, how did the boards of management in the case study sample measure up? An analysis of the overall membership showed that over 50% was accounted for by three categories - housewives, medical personnel and retired people, while the commercial side had less than a 6% representation among the combined membership of the ten Boards. In most cases the selection process seemed to operate in an unstructured way. From information given in the course of the interviews, the researcher got the distinct impression that identification with the particular interest of the various organizations was a guiding principle in the selection process, rather than concern with the particular background of a member.

There were some exceptions. For instance, the CEO in the Ash said that each board member was selected carefully with a special role in mind and replacements were decided on to match the "lost" role. Also the Beech board selected representatives which it considered could contribute to various facets of its work, e.g., financial/legal/educational/ social work. These two approaches were in line with the "specialised skills" suggested by Mullin (1980:16) for voluntary boards.

The very good attendance record at meetings endorsed the high level of commitment of board members in all ten case study organizations. It was even higher than that recorded by Mellor (1985) in his UK based study.

Rotation of membership was another area checked out, to ascertain how organizations ensured that some "fresh blood" was injected into its board, as suggested by Mellor (1985). The data here pointed towards a lack of fresh faces and only two agencies had any formal procedure installed to ensure some rotation of membership. It is suggested in the literature (McLaughlin 1986) that training for board members can be helpful. Accordingly, provision for such training in the study sample was reviewed and results showed that eight of the ten bodies had no formal procedures either for induction of new members or for on-going development of existing members.

The overall composition of the boards of management in the study group indicated that a typical board was composed of committed long-standing members, from various non-commercial backgrounds, who received no training for their task. This profile, while endorsing findings in the literature (Drucker 1990; Middleton 1987) did not seem appropriate for the task of providing overall direction to the staff under the stewardship of these boards of management.

The overriding consideration of the need for members to identify closely with the key interest of a particular agency tended to contribute to a "closed" approach (Daft 1986) in terms of organizational thinking. An example cited by one board chairman, himself an executive in an advertising agency, shows how connections with other organizations can be beneficial at a practical level. It concerned a vital piece of equipment which was needed urgently by the voluntary agency in question. Yet this agency was told that it would take six weeks to procure the required spare parts to fix the equipment. However, this chairman, through connections in his "day" job, was able to expedite the process by short-circuiting the order process and having the necessary parts delivered by courier within a matter of days. In another instance he was able to link up a client's advertising needs with the voluntary agency's need to publish information, by getting his client to agree to sponsor the required publication under its name. These examples endorse the usefulness of links between individual voluntary agencies and organizations in other sectors. Yet they apply to only one agency and the general pattern of operation at board level did not appear to replicate this experience.

To draw together this section on managerial background in the host organizations, the combined data suggests that while there was a high level of commitment, there appeared to be limitations in formal management education and training among both key operational staff and board members. This was the managerial backdrop for the implementation of control and accountability in these organizations.

Control

The section of the interview schedule which focused on control began by seeking the broad views of respondents regarding control in their respective organizations. Results indicated general assent that control was important, showing that the "mental programming" (Hofstede 1981) in these organizations, at least at a theoretical level, accepted the value of control. Further probing revealed an emphasis on financial control, while the value of control in establishing the achievement of objectives and as a means of providing feedback was also mentioned.

Referring back to the literature on control, the first step in the basic control model involves setting standards (Gray & Smeltzer 1989). It was established that these standards, in turn, are derived from the objectives of an organization (Koontz & Weihrich 1988). Therefore clarity of objectives is a prerequisite for setting precise standards, because if objectives are vague or ill-defined, no system can measure their attainment (Sizer 1977). So, how did the study sample measure up in terms of clarity of objectives? An analysis of the information provided showed that, on the whole, objectives tended to be stated in very general terms. Therefore when it came to measuring their achievement, difficulties arose and the lack of an overall systematic approach to undertaking this task became apparent.

Findings also endorsed the difficulties outlined in the literature in relation to establishing standards in areas not easily yielding to quantification (Hofstede 1981; Newman & Wallender 1978). On the output side, in the study group, instead of the individual organizations being in control and setting standards of performance, in many cases the onus was passed over to clients who were relied on to indicate whether or not objectives were being met. There was an

202

underlying assumption in this approach that clients would provide negative feedback, if warranted. Yet this did not seem to be a very reasonable assumption to make in a situation where clients were dependent on a specific organization to meet their needs and had no comparable alternative agency to which they could transfer their "custom". To use Hirschman's (1970) label, they did not have the "exit" option. This dependent "no choice" position did not provide an ideal base for clients from which to voice strong negative feedback. Thus the reliability of feedback generated in these circumstances must be regarded at minimum with some measure of reservation. In some of the smaller agencies, e.g., the Chestnut, Fir, Oak and Sycamore, their proactive approach in contacting clients, as described earlier in section 14.2, probably facilitated getting more "honest" feedback. However, as noted already, the large client numbers in the bigger agencies did not facilitate using this approach.

Turning to more specific aspects of control, in the personnel area informality was the prevailing norm in the majority of organizations, with only one agency reporting a systematic approach to staff training and appraisal, in the case of paid employees. As might be expected, volunteers fared no better; while actual training provision for them was minimal, there was a recognition in some organizations that it was desirable. As mentioned previously in section 11.2, there was a high dependency on voluntary input in eight of the ten host organizations which seemed to be under utilised through lack of appropriate training, a view endorsed by three of the agencies themselves.

The pattern of financial control varied considerably among the ten agencies. A formalised budgetary system (Anthony & Young 1988; Hofstede 1981) was in place in three of the largest organizations, when ranked by level of income. A fourth was in the process of implementing a similar system, having the legacy of a huge debt of over half a million pounds as a reminder of what can occur in the absence of tight budgetary control. In contrast, four other organizations had no formal budgetary control system, but adopted a basic bookkeeping approach to financial matters. This arrangement, while going some way towards ensuring financial probity, provided little by way of financial standards against which to measure actual results (Koontz & Weihrich 1988). Rather, their approach seemed to be to react to whatever money became available, and make sure that tabs were kept on it, to ensure overall solvency in their respective organizations, i.e., they were income driven rather than expenditure driven.

The fact that all organizations prepared annual audited accounts verified their interest in being seen to be "above board" in the financial area. The evidence from the case studies in relation to financial matters indicated that while basic control on the purse strings was adequate, at least half of the organizations had shortcomings in the area of financial planning. This is not entirely surprising when the lack of professional accounting input in the group as a whole is taken into the reckoning. In fact, when the profiles of those responsible for the accounting function is recalled, it would be unrealistic to expect any level of financial sophistication other than keeping financial affairs in basic order.

In most cases, control of operations was seen to be tied in with the achievement of overall objectives. Therefore the difficulties encountered in trying to measure achievement, in the absence of specified standards having been set (Anthony & Young 1984; Sizer 1977), were highlighted once again.

Regarding control of information, while the participating organizations had established sufficient outside contacts to ensure a steady supply of clients, in all cases the "total picture" in relation to their particular areas of interest was somewhat incomplete. Only one agency had embryonic plans to remedy this defect, realising that comprehensive information was necessary for effective long-term planning. The others seemed quite content to proceed as at present, confident that "customers" would continue coming. This finding is in keeping with the fact that none of the ten organizations currently undertake long-term planning (Koontz & Weihrich 1988). Yet if they do not extend their organizational vision beyond day-to-day operations, how can they be confident that it is heading broadly in the right direction? The availability of more comprehensive information would provide a basis for future long-term planning which is necessary to ensure that organizations have a view of where they are heading in the medium to long term (Koontz & Weihrich 1988).

A more complete global picture of the area of operation also assists in prioritising goals (Daft 1986). In its absence, an organization can only deal with the part of the picture known to it. As one respondent, a development officer who appreciated the lack of complete information, commented in relation to his own agency: "We're totally demand led, more and more." In contrast, if a solid data base became available he felt that the organization could then operate from a needs-based development model (Faughnan 1977). At present, the norm for the study group of organizations, working from a base of incomplete information, was to operate as best they could on the basis of the limited information available.

One of the concerns raised in the literature in relation to control is that human beings do not always take kindly to being controlled (Anthony & Young 1988; Child 1984; Hampton 1986; Hofstede 1967). This can give rise to resistance and manipulation (Cammann & Nadler 1976). The human factor in control was investigated in the study. Resistance to control did not prove to be an invasive factor, although some was encountered. Of course, bearing in mind that overall standards of control were not too stringent, this is not surprising. Two informants, from different agencies, mentioned professional resistance to control. However, as mentioned earlier in section 14.2, one of these organizations seemed to have countered this resistance by creating a climate where control was the norm, while the second agency was meeting with resistance when trying to turn around its established lax climate in relation to control.

While some instances of manipulation were cited, once again, it was not seen as a significant problem. However, the prevailing climate of relaxed controls was neither likely to provoke the need for more wide-spread manipulation nor uncover additional manipulation that may be occurring but going unnoticed.

To conclude this section, the interview data from the ten agencies indicated general support for the concept of control. In contrast, when it came to its implementation, the results were not commensurate with this positive stance at a theoretical level. The failure among the agencies to establish clear objectives led to a situation where there was no sound basis for establishing standards against which to measure actual performance. In the absence of standards, organizations had to rely on feedback from clients as an indicator of their overall effectiveness. While financial control was implemented to varying degrees, control in the area of personnel and information proved less satisfactory. In sum, the theoretical support for control did not appear to be effectively operationalised in all areas.

Accountability

Findings relating to accountability can be divided into two broad areas covering views of respondents on various aspects of accountability and actual responses to meeting needs for accountability.

Commencing with views on accountability, the interview data established that, like control, it was seen in a positive light by informants, in line with the findings of Leat (1988). Accordingly, there was no problem in principle about being accountable to outsiders. This positive stance was further endorsed by the perception that the advantages of accountability outweighed any disadvantages. Neither was accountability perceived as intruding on the independence of individual agencies, thus endorsing the findings in the literature (Kramer 1981; Kramer & Grossman 1987: Leat et al 1986; Mellor 1985). Funders and clients were identified as being the main recipients of accountability, while money and services constituted the two important areas in relation to being accountable.

Next, focusing on responses to accountability, a heavy reliance on financial aspects emerged. In the course of the interviews, there was a strong inference that once the organizations published audited accounts, basically this exonerated them in terms of being accountable. Yet Gray et al (1987:17) remind us that "financial accountability discharges only a small proportion of an organization's accountability", a view shared by Jones & Pendlebury 1985 and Randall (1989).

For example, some years ago, one of the case study organizations decided to employ a social worker to visit clients. In a recent review of this position, it was discovered that this social worker was not touching even a half per cent of the organization's clients, due to the limitations of what one person, no matter how qualified, can do. Also many of the visits made by her were to meet the client's basic need for social contact which did not require professional social work skills. Therefore, while this social worker's salary could be fully accounted for in terms of fiscal accountability, the job was not fulfilling its objective of visiting all clients, making the quality of service non-existent for most of them. In other words, the position was inappropriate in meeting perceived client needs.

Reviewing the situation, the agency has now decided to replace the social worker with a community development officer who can work with the pool of local volunteers and increase their expertise, enabling them to provide services for a much larger segment of clients in a locality, due to being numerically stronger. While the fiscal implications for the agency should not change greatly as only one salary is still needed, the non-financial aspects, in terms of greater client contact facilitated by a more appropriate staff member, should be enhanced.

The CEO of an organization in the preliminary fieldwork provided another example involving the employment of social workers who, despite their professional social work expertise, did not have the know-how to train clients in the necessary practical coping skills required. So, using their professional skills, they created a dependency relationship with clients whose real needs were to learn how to become independent! Thus the input from social workers on this occasion was not appropriate in meeting client needs.

These two examples show the importance of factoring in the issue of appropriateness of service provided, as well as taking the financial implications into account (Leat 1988; Randall 1989). At the extreme, an organization could control every pound it spent, while having spent it on the provision of inappropriate services or services of a very poor quality. So, financial accountability on its own, as emphasised in the literature (Gray 1984; Jones & Pendlebury 1985), can mask a large part of the picture. Yet many of the participating organizations seemed to miss this point, appearing very content with the fact that financial accountability was in place. So, once again, the practice did not match up with the theory in the arena of accountability.

While funders were identified as being important in terms of accountability, only three of the ten organizations published annual reports as a means of conveying accountability to this group. However, the publication of newsletters by seven of the study group did provide funders with some information on activities undertaken by these organizations.

Clients constituted the other main group identified as meriting accountability, but in most cases there was no strong evidence of positive action to fulfil this perceived need. While the preparation of audited accounts served to account for money received, there was less evidence of a systematic approach to accounting for services. This did not seem to match the needs of consumers, as highlighted in the literature (Leat 1988; Kramer 1987).

Of course it must be acknowledged that there is a connection between the lack of non-financial accountability and the approach to internal control in the study group. It was established in the previous section on control that there was a lack of clarity in relation to overall objectives which, in turn led to difficulties in establishing standards for control (Anthony & Young 1984). Given this situation internally, it made it very difficult for agencies to be accountable to outsiders regarding the achievements of specific objectives when they had not clarified these for their own internal control purposes.

Other ways of fulfilling accountability requirements include having client and/or funder representatives on the board of management (Leat 1988). While this option was not widely availed of in the study sample, the interview data did highlight that, in the case of clients, this is not always a feasible option, due to the debilitating nature of some ailments.

Moving outwards from immediate concerns about accountability, respondents were asked about their familiarity with some relevant current literature, in order to ascertain how "clued in" they were to the more general debate on this topic. Once again, the fact that the majority was unfamiliar with both the ASC's (1988) SORP on charity accounting and the recent Irish government report on fundraising (1990), suggested that their horizons did not extend to considerations of more general interest in the field of accountability in the voluntary sector.

To conclude this section on accountability, a certain mismatch was discerned between what respondents identified as being important in the area and their practical responses to these various demands arising from the need to be accountable. Once again, the predominance of a financial focus was apparent, the main aim of accountability, in practice, being interpreted as the need to establish that agencies were "above board" in the financial arena.

Summary

Using an open systems approach to organizations (Daft 1986), this chapter commenced by discussing some of the environmental and organizational characteristics which impact on agencies operating in the Irish voluntary sector, drawing on the preliminary and main fieldwork, together with relevant background information. Regarding environmental characteristics, there is evidence of an underlying supportive climate for voluntary action in Ireland. While the present regulatory climate is not very strict, there are indications that this may be about to change. Competition for funds and unsupportive tax provisions, together with difficulties in the wider economy, are other factors which affect the voluntary sector. A heightened interest in participation is also apparent.

Evidence from the main fieldwork suggests that variables such as size, staffing patterns, geographical spread and funding sources are relevant organizational characteristics that need to be taken into account in managing voluntary organizations, in addition to more general characteristics identified in the literature, including the nonprofit and service nature of their operations and their dual management systems.

Next, a discussion followed on the findings from the fieldwork in relation to management, control and accountability. The general picture emerging in relation to management showed a very high level of commitment to the concerns of individual organizations. The evidence relating to formal management education and training suggested limitations in this regard, thus endorsing the views expressed by respondents in the preliminary fieldwork.

While views on both control and accountability were very positive, their translation into practice confirmed difficulties highlighted in the literature, and there was considerable emphasis on financial aspects of control and accountability.

Apart from a few respondents who considered that there was a need for some change, the prevailing attitude that came across to the researcher was one of organizations being so busy dealing with day-to-day operations that little time was left to consider broader aspects of control and accountability. In fact, most of the informants did not appear to appreciate the mismatch between their aspirations in the areas of control and accountability and their responses on the ground to meeting these ideals.

Following this discussion on the research findings, the concluding chapter of the study is now presented.

12 Synthesis and Conclusions

This concluding chapter draws together the main strands of the complete study. It begins with a brief overview of the total project, followed by a synthesis of the findings emerging from the fieldwork. An outline model emerging from the research is then described. Next, some recommendations for the Irish voluntary sector are presented and possible areas for future research are outlined, with a view to stimulating interest among scholars in exploring further dimensions of voluntary action, particularly in an Irish context. The study then concludes with some final reflections.

Study overview

The structure of the study was designed with a view to presenting the major fieldwork against a background depicting voluntary action from a broader perspective. The thesis was divided into four main parts, as follows. Part I provided general background information on the nonprofit sector while the Irish dimension of the study was introduced in Part II. The more focused aspects of the research were covered in Parts III and IV.

Recalling the content in a little more detail, the opening chapter established the current importance of the nonprofit sector, at an international level, for both academics and practitioners in the field. Also the need for research in an Irish context was explained. In chapter two, some of the parameters of the voluntary sector were identified in terms of definitions, typologies, theories and roles.

Ireland is no exception to this perceptible trend of increased interest in voluntary sector activity. In keeping with the Irish context of the fieldwork, Part II of the study provided an overview of the wider socio-economic environment in which the Irish voluntary sector operates, in addition to historical data on the contribution of Irish voluntary organizations in the past. Finally, the contemporary position in relation to the Irish voluntary sector was described.

As a prelude to the data gathering process, the relevant literature on management, control and accountability was reviewed in Part III. The particular environmental and organizational characteristics that apply to nonprofit management were highlighted, indicating how it can differ from management in other contexts. In addition, the need for both control and accountability in voluntary organizations was established.

The fieldwork was detailed in Part IV of the study which commenced with a chapter on research methodology. An account of preliminary fieldwork was provided. Coverage of the main research followed, describing, in turn, case site selection and access, followed by an account of the actual interview process. Finally, the analysis and interpretation of the principal findings emerging from the data were presented.

Synthesis of findings and conclusions

This section reviews the research findings in the context of the earlier literature review. To begin, the background information on the Irish voluntary sector is considered in the broad setting of voluntary organizations in society. Before proceeding with this discussion, it is noted that the "terminological tempest" (Anheier & Knapp 1990) surrounding the sector in the international literature does not feature in an Irish setting where the term "voluntary" is the most common label used.

It was established in the literature that voluntary organizations are seen as one strand in the wider provisions for meeting the social needs of society (Wolfenden 1978). The Irish situation reflects this general pattern of provision from a range of sources including voluntary, statutory, commercial and informal input (Wolfenden 1978). However, unlike the situation in the UK where a more prominent role for the voluntary sector is only re-emerging in recent years (Billis 1992; Brenton 1985; Gladstone 1979), in Ireland this sector has contributed continuously over time to meeting social needs. The brief historical overview of Irish voluntary action established its importance in earlier times. Then in more recent years, as Curry (1980:13) observes, "despite the improvements in the provision of statutory social services, the role of voluntary organizations . . . has not diminished". The CSSC (1988:11) endorse this view, noting that "the State has always depended on the voluntary sector . . . to do a whole range of activities".

This position is explained in part by the fact that Ireland is not a rich country, by European standards (see section 3.2) and therefore there are economic constraints on the development of statutory provisions. In more recent times, the dual economic burden of severe unemployment and a huge national debt (see section 3.2) has necessitated stringent pruning of government expenditure and consequent reductions in some statutory provisions. In turn, this development has placed further demands on voluntary organizations who are called on to fill the gaps arising from government cutbacks and also to address some of the many problems associated with unemployment.

Therefore, it can be stated that, in Ireland, voluntary organizations feature continuously over time as an important component in meeting the needs of society. Given the unhealthy state of public finances, their role is unlikely to diminish. Yet, as detailed in section 4.6, despite this consistent input from Irish voluntary organizations over time, an overall operational framework for the sector as a whole has never been developed, leading Butler (1981:16) to observe that "the voluntary sector, in the sense of an identifiable and quantifiable entity, can scarely be said to exist". Although recent developments such as the proposed White Paper and charter for the sector (PESP 1991), if progressed, should facilitate shaping the contributions of voluntary effort into an identifiable sector, currently no such entity exists. It is suggested that this factor has contributed to the fragmented nature of Irish voluntary action to date. (Possible remedies are provided in the next section.)

Regarding classification of voluntary organizations, the difficulties in devising typologies for organizations in general, as highlighted in the literature (Carper & Snizek 1980; McKelvey 1975; Mills & Margulies 1980) were seen to apply also to organizations operating in the nonprofit field (Brenton 1985; Handy 1988; Hatch 1980; Mason 1984; Mawby & Gill 1987; Wolfenden 1978). In view of the problems encountered by these other writers, it is not surprising that devising a single typology for Irish voluntary organizations also proved elusive. However, the dual classificiation presented (section 4.3) captures both the wide range of activities (Brenton 1985; Handy 1988) and the organizationsl diversity (Johnson 1978) of Irish voluntary bodies and is also in keeping with Wolfenden's (1978) suggestion of having different classifications for different purposes, i.e., to indicate both activities and organizational types.

Various theories explaining the existence of the voluntary sector were explored. Relating these to the Irish situation, Weisbrod's (1975; 1977; 1988)

213

"public goods" theory, which views voluntary organizations as meeting the residual unsatisfied demand beyond the median demand satisfied by government provision, seems to have some relevance as Irish voluntary bodies, by augmenting government provision, cater for both residual demand and also diverse demands (CSSC 1988; Curry 1980).

Salamon's (1987) focus on government support for the nonprofit sector is also a factor in the Irish context where government funding to the sector, at over 200 million pounds (see Appendix 1), indicates the considerable reliance by many voluntary agencies on this source of revenue. Likewise, Salamon's (1987) "third party government" is applicable to some parts of the Irish sector. For example, one of the case-study organizations, the Rowan, which operates in the field of mental handicap, receives full statutory funding, as do similar organizations serving other catchment areas.

On the supply side, James (1987) notes the dominance of religious groups in the foundation of nonprofit service institutions, as they have objectives other than the maximisation of profit. This phenomenon is certainly evident in an Irish setting. The brief historical overview in section 4.1 endorses the prominent role of religious groups in the past in voluntary action. Currently, the considerable religious influence in this sector is still in evidence in both clerical and lay religious organizations, e.g., the Conference of Major Religious Superiors (CMRS); the Catholic Social Service Conference (CSSC); the Society of St Vincent de Paul; the Legion of Mary. In addition, it is considered that the strong adherence to the Catholic Church among the overall population (Inglis 1987) which continues the Judeo-Christian emphasis on charity (Gladstone 1982), is instrumental in shaping the generally supportive climate among the Irish public for voluntary action.

A broad appraisal of Irish voluntary endeavour supports the fact that no one theory suffices to explain the existence of voluntary organizations. However, certain theories have been shown to be of particular relevance in an Irish context.

Voluntary bodies are credited with fulfilling specific roles in society. How do the Irish institutions measure up in this regard? The earlier general literature review in chapter 2 identified the following roles: consumer choice, specialisation, cost effectiveness, flexibility, innovation, advocacy and participation. These are now examined in relation to Irish voluntary action.

Gerard (1983:29) highlights the tendency of statutory provision "to reduce variety in the system" in its efforts to meet the needs of a wide population. In contrast, voluntary agencies, through specialiisation, have the capacity to introduce variety into the system. Irish institutions are no exception as they "cater for the needs of particular groups" (CSSC 1988:11) and are adept at

214

identifying individual needs and offering appropriate means of meeting them (NSSB 1986). All of the organizations in the field study sample endorse these attributes as they focus on particular ailments or disabilities and address the attendant needs in a holistic and specific way that the wide embrace of statutory services could not emulate. In doing so, they add a layer of variety to basic statutory provisions through their "particularistic and selective" (Kramer 1987:250) provisions.

But it is suggested also by various commentators that there is another side to this specialisation, namely that it can lead to uneven coverage (Leat et al 1981; Mawby & Gill 1987; Salamon 1987; Wolfenden 1978). Some Irish studies have endorsed this problem, particularly in relation to uneven provision of services, as indicated earlier in section 4.4 (NESC 1989; Power 1980; Whelan & Vaughan 1982).

In the absence of any relevant research, the question of cost effectiveness is difficult to evaluate in relation to Irish voluntary agencies. However, based on the study by Hatch & Moycroft (1979) which showed that the use of volunteers can reduce costs, it is suggested that the large numbers of volunteers in Irish voluntary organizations, who offer their services without payment, would indicate savings in staff costs. For example, if the CMAC had to pay its 1,327 counsellors (CMAC 1987), it would face a considerable increase in running costs.

Of course many voluntary organizations employ paid staff. As indicated in section 2.4, in the US voluntary sector a study by Preston (1990) showed that wages in nonprofits were lower than those in comparable commercial employment. To date, no similar studies have been undetaken in Ireland. However, as outlined in section 5.4, the experience surrounding special employment schemes (SES), which facilitated certain voluntary organizations in getting staff, has not been altogether positive. These SESs, being of limited duration for individual staff members, have been shown to impact negatively on both continuity of service and on security of employment. Therefore this example shows how "cheaper alternatives", while reducing staff costs, are not conducive to the provision of on-going service or staff development.

The voluntary sector is credited also with being flexible and innovative (Douglas 1987; Filer Commission 1983; Gladstone 1979; Johnson 1981; Leat et al 1981; Nielsen 1983; Richardson & Goodman 1983). When viewed in an Irish setting, there is some evidence to support these attributes, as indicated by examples cited already in section 4.4 (CSSC 1988; Cummins 1989; O Morain 1989a; Power 1980; St. Vincent de Paul 1987) and endorsed by Curry (1980) and the NSSB (1986).

A word of caution is introduced by writers such as Gladstone (1982), Eisenberg 1983 and Wolfenden 1978 who highlight the fact that innovativeness can diminish over time in some organizations. The NSSB (1982;17) observes that the innovative thrust in some Irish voluntary bodies can likewise wane over time as they "become institutionalised . . . and lose the ability to took critically at themselves". One of the CEO respondents in the preliminary fieldwork confirmed this tendency which he considered particulaly relevant in situations where the original founders are dead and "the fanaticism is gone". This suggests that the Irish context reflects the wider situation which is that while voluntary bodies may have the ability to innovate, being unrestricted by bureaucratic constraints, not all of them exercise this option unremittingly over time.

Advocacy is another important role ascribed to the voluntary sector (Jordan 1983; Kramer 1981; O'Connell 1983). Unless voluntary bodies articulate the interests of the population they serve, there is a danger that they may serve only as a "band-aid dispenser" (Jordan 1983:403). Irish voluntary organizations are aware of the need for advocacy and their important role here is noted by Curry (1980). For instance, major bodies such as the Society of St. Vincent de Paul and the CSSC present annual pre-budget submissions to the government in order to raise the level of public awareness on issues of poverty and unemployment (section 4.4). The umbrella group for the disabled, UVOH, prepares a similar document to highlight the needs of its constituent members. Therefore it is evident that the advocacy role is well established in the Irish voluntary sector.

Finally, in their use of volunteers, nonprofit organizations are seen as offering a means of exercising what Nielsen (1983:366) describes as the "universal impulse to altruism". Writers such as Gartner & Riessman (1977), Handy (1988), Hatch (1983), Richardson & Goodman (1983) and Sherrott (1983) have shown how volunteering can be of benefit both to volunteers themselves and to those whom they assist. There are plenty of opportunities in Irish society to become a volunteer. The field study cohort of only ten organizations availed of the services of almost 5000 volunteers (see Table 10.3). Two major lay religious groups - the Society of St. Vincent de Paul and the Legion of Mary - are estimated to have 20,000 volunteers between them (Inglis 1987). The level of voluntary input in religious voluntary organizations generally, at 8% of the Irish population in comparison to 6% on an European average (Fogarty et al 1984), is in line with the very high level of adherence to the Catholic Church (Inglis 1987) and makes Ireland different from other European countries in this regard.

To draw together this section which compares the experiences of the Irish voluntary sector with the broader picture as revealed in the literature, it is evident that the Irish sector is similar in many respects. The continuing input from Irish voluntary organizations over time, despite improvements in statutory provision, makes it a long standing feature of Irish society. Yet, despite this continual input by numerous voluntary organizations, the presence of an identifiable sector, representing the overall interests of voluntary bodies as an identifiable group in Irish society, is not in evidence to date. A discernible religious influence is noticeable also in many Irish nonprofit groups, in keeping with the high level of adherence to the Catholic Church in Ireland.

Having sited some of the more general aspects of Irish voluntary action in the context of the relevant literature, the more focused aspects of the research, relating to management, control and accountability, are now considered.

The opening discussion on management in chapter 5 established how it is an inherent process in all organizations (Gray & Smeltzer 1987; Baird et al 1989). Also it validated the open systems nature of organizations (Daft 1986) which necessitates the management process being carried out within the context of the operating environment (Daft 1986; Kast & Rosenzweig 1985). This calls for a contingency approach in order to determine which management practices and techniques are applicable in specific situations (Kreitner 1989; Lawrence & Lorsch 1967). These overall guidelines apply to the specific focus of the research on management, control and accountability in voluntary organizations which have to be viewed in their particular environmental context.

The earlier review of management showed that the private sector model dominated thinking until recent times (Stewart & Ranson 1985). A similar orientation was seen to apply to much of the writing on control (Anthony & Young 1988; Hofstede 1981), while accountants likewise were "overwhelmingly concerned" with accountability in relation to business (Jones & Pendlebury 1985).

More recently, some change in this pattern is discernible as the need for management in the voluntary sector has been articulated by many commentators, including Billis (1984), Gerard (1983), Knight (1984), Landry et al (1985) and there is a growing literature focused on management in a nonprofit context (e.g., Borst & Montana 1987; Butler & Wilson 1990; Mason 1984; McLaughlin 1986). These contributors have focused on voluntary organizations operating in the UK and the US.

But what is the situation with regard to Irish voluntary bodies? This generally increased interest in voluntary sector management confirms the need for research in an Irish setting where, despite the important contribution of voluntary organizations to Irish society over times, relevant research is virtually non-existent (Faughnan & Kelleher 1991). Key informants in the preliminary fieldwork (chapter 9) also voiced their concerns about management in Irish voluntary organizations and endorsed the need for research with a management focus.

Therefore, although the need for relevant research in Ireland has been identified, to date, no action has been taken in response. By addressing this need, the present research breaks new ground and represents a timely contribution to the broader debate on voluntary action in Ireland. The final model emerging from the research provides an overall framework which maps out the particular organizational and environmental characteristics that impact on the management of Irish nonprofit institutions.

Control was selected as another central theme of the research as it is one of the basic functions of management (Baird et al 1990; Gray & Smeltzer 1989; Koontz & Weihrich 1988; Kreitner 1989; Robbins 1988). In addition, control is closely linked with accountability as, without regulation, "organizations have no indication of how well they perform in relation to their goals" (Barney & Griffin 1992:379) and so are not in a position to report fully to external constituents about achieving their objectives, as demanded by accountablity. This is particularly significant in a nonprofit context where fiscal accountability is only part of the overall process, by itself revealing little in terms of efficiency and effectiveness (Gray 1984; Jones & Pendlebury 1985; Randall 1989).

The distinguishing feature of the present research is its integrative nature in linking the themes of management, control and accountability in a voluntary sector setting. It links the two processes of control and accountability, highlighting the interconnectedness between them, rather than treating them in isolation. In addition, the study incorporates an examination of management in the sample of voluntary organizations under review, thus acknowledging the reality that implementation of control and accountability in any organization is ultimately dependent on the people who run the organization, i.e., management.

The discussion on management (chapter 5) explored the particular set of characteristics that impact on nonprofit organizations which "though not unique, require special consideration" (Gerard 1983:20) and also reflect the "genuine management complexity" (Billis 1989:25) of voluntary agencies. (These characteristics are discussed in more detail later.)

Meanwhile, at a more general level, it is suggested that if managers in voluntary organizations are not equipped with appropriate "tools" (Mason 1984) and a broad understanding of the organizational complexity of nonprofits, this does not facilitate them in their efforts to address fully the demands arising in relation to control and accountability. As Drucker (1989:89) notes, "good intentions are no substitute for management and leadership, for accountability, performance and results. Those require management".

How well equipped are managers in Irish voluntary organizations? Kreitner (1989:xxiii) suggests the need for "a solid gounding in management". Yet the fieldwork data revealed that CEO respondents had little formal education in management, in line with the observation of Mason (1984). Given that concepts of organizational theory cannot be learned through trial and error, yet understanding their organizational situation is the first step towards effective management and control (Daft 1986), it is suggested that the lack of appropriate knowledge on the part of the study sample of CEOs did not facilitate them in their task of implementing control and accountability.

While there was distinct evidence of a high level of commitment to the particular cause of individual agencies, this was considered sufficient to run each organization, a point disputed by many academic writers (Butler & Wilson 1990; Cyert 1975; Daft 1986; Drucker 1989, Young 1985). Yet, it was the broad management base on which implementation of control and accountability was dependent.

Next, turning to the particular characteristics of nonprofit organizations as detailed earlier in chapter 5, these are now examined in relation to their impact on control and accountability. It is recalled that six broad areas were identified as being of particular significance to voluntary organizations:

- their nonprofit status
- the service nature of operations
- their two distinct management systems
- governance issues
- staffing patterns
- environmental characteristics.

Cumulatively, these characteristics endorsed the complex nature of voluntary sector management, as suggested in the literature (e.g., Billis 1989). Each area is now reviewed briefly, in the context of the research findings.

The nonprofit status of voluntary organizations means that they lack the guidance of a single broad indicator of success such as profit provides (Maloney 1986) to indicate whether or not they are achieving their objectives (Anthony & Young 1988; Kanter & Summers 1987; Lovelock & Wineberg 1977; Ryan 1980). This difficulty is compounded by the service nature of

219

nonprofits which means that their "product" is intangible and therefore not easy to measure (Handy 1981; Gerard 1983; McLaughlin 1986; Murray 1987; Newman & Wallender 1978; Ryan 1980). Whereas service providers in the commercial sector face similar problems in measurement, unlike voluntary organizations, they do have the guidance of profit as an overall indicator of success. Therefore, taking the combined impact of these two characteristics into consideration - nonprofit and service provision - it is clear that voluntary organizations are faced with greater difficulties than their commercial counterparts in trying to establish overall measures of success.

This situation has implications for both control and accountability in a nonprofit setting. First of all in relation to control, it was established earlier (in chapter 6) that the starting point for control was to set standards against which performance could be measured (Gray & Smeltzer 1989). In turn, standards are derived from objectives (Koontz & Weihrich 1988) and the more specific and measurable an objective is, the more likely it can be used as a standard (Rue & Byars 1986). On the other hand, Anthony & Young (1984) counsel that if objectives are vague, no system can measure their attainment. Yet, findings from the fieldwork showed that, in nine of the ten organizations studied, objectives were stated in very general terms. This did not auger well as a basis on which to set standards. Not surprisingly therefore, the case studies endorsed the difficulties outlined by other observers (McLaughlin 1986; Newman & Wallender 1978; Ryan 1980) regarding setting standards in the service area.

In practice, instead of setting standards for control, the majority of the case study group relied on client feedback as indicating some "measure" of the achievement of overall objectives. However, given the reality of the situation for most clients of being restricted to one organization for a particular service, this did not put them in a strong position to voice negative feedback. In other words, they could not easily avail of Hirchman's (1970) "exit" option. Allied to this is the cautionary note voiced by Pride & Ferrell (1987:647) that "it is very easy for an organization to assume that it knows what the public needs or wants". These authors then give examples from the nonprofit sector which this assumption fails to support.

Only one organization, the Oak, was proactive in seeking feedback from clients. Its small client base made it feasible to write to individual clients on a regular basis to see if their needs were being served. This approach is in line with Parasuraman et al (1988) who suggest measuring consumers' perceptions of quality of service. In contrast, an organization such as the Larch or the Poplar, with a large client base, would find it costly to adopt a similar approach. This shows how organizational size can be a factor in developing appropriate controls.

In turn, the lack of specific standards impacted on accountability which was largely confined to the financial arena in the case-study sample, despite the emphasis by many commentators about its shortcomings in a nonprofit setting (Gray 1984; Jones & Pendlebury 1985; Laughlin 1990; Randall 1989). This illustrates the connection between internal control and external accountability and shows the shortcomings of viewing accountability in isolation from control. For, given the difficulties in relation to control, emanating from a failure to clarify objectives, the information was not available to report to outsiders, other than in very general terms, on non financial aspects of accountability such as process and programme achievements.

A third characteristic of nonprofit organizations is their dual management systems (Mason 1984). As inputs are provided by one group (donors) while services are provided to another (clients), this means that nonprofits, unlike commercial concerns, lack the direct link between inputs and outputs. Consequently, this gives rise to two managerial subsystems (Butler & Wilson 1990; Gerard 1983; Mason 1984; McLaughlin 1986) and necessitates two separate foci for control and accountability.

Difficulties in control can arise on the input side due to the fact that individual donors usually cannot be "invoiced" for a specific amount against which to measure receipts. So, most of the fieldwork cohort responded by acknowledging money once it had been received. Also, accountability to donors was mainly confined to the financial arena by provision of audited accounts. Yet, as referred to earlier, many writers stress that this in only a small part of the total pictureof accountability in nonprofit organizations, as donors need to know if their support is helping to achieve the organization's objectives (Dubin 1977), i.e., they need to know how the money received was used.

Turning to the output side, in an era of more critical consumerism (Leat 1988), accountability to clients is also considered to be necessary. Yet again, financial accountability was the main method of addressing this need, despite its shortcomings, as emphasised repeatedly by various commentators, as cited above.

The governance of nonprofits is another aspect which merits attention in the literature. Unlike commercial undertakings, voluntary organizations have no shareholders to form a board of directors (McLaughlin 1986), so their overall operation is overseen by a governing body (Billis & Harris 1986). Relevant observers indicate some problems surrounding these governing bodies, including general malfunctioning (Drucker 1990), lack of expertise

(McCrimmon 1979; Middleton 1987) and poor selection and training (Murray 1987).

In the case study cohort, evidence suggested that, by and large, identification with the particular interest of an organization was a guiding principle in selecting board members, rather than specialised skills, as recommended by Mullin (1980). Accordingly, there was little evidence to indicate the existence of appropriate expertise in meeting the demands of providing overall guidance for these organizations, both in the areas of control and accountability, and on broader issues, thus confirming the shortcomings identified by various reviewers, as indicated above. Also, in most organizations, there was a lack of "fresh blood" on boards and the majority of members did not receive training for their task, as recommended by McLaughlin (1986).

Regarding staffing, the field research confirmed that, in the case of both paid employees and volunteers, there was little by way of staff training. This does not provide an ideal basis from which to implement control and accountability. If staff members, both paid and voluntary, do not appreciate the complexity of implementing control and accountability, they are unlikely to be in a position to facilitate their implementation. Therefore, if the present rather basic approach to control and accountability in the case study group is to be improved, it is suggested that there is a need to institute formal staff training as, in the final analysis, "it is the behavioural response, not the mechanics of control, that really matters" (Newman 1975:43).

Finally, the environmental characteristics that impact on voluntary organizations also need to be addressed, as these organizations interact with their environment, providing output in the form of services to clients and obtaining input from donors to finance their service provision, thus confirming their open systems nature (Kast & Rosenzweig 1985).

Murray (1987:20) emphasises "the special needs and demands of many different funders" which require attention. The earlier review of accountability (in section 7.2) mapped concerns about fraud and malpractice both in the UK and the US voluntary sectors, leading to the need for greater accountability. Also, as detailed in section 7.3, the combination of changed patterns in voluntary organizations, a deterioration in the general economic climate, the heightened profile of the voluntary sector and changing funding patterns with more state input, has heralded increased demands for accountability. In addition, it is recognised that informing donors of the "outcome" of their "investment" is an effective way of maintaining their allegiance (Andreasen 1982; Lovelock & Wineberg 1977), endorsing the usefulness of accountability as a marketing "tool". This is particularly important in the current climate of "increasingly fierce competition" for funds (Irvine 1988).

Clients also merit attention. In an era of more critical consumerism and as part of a wider social movement towards participation, voluntary organizations are being challenged to move from doing things "for" clients to doing things "with" them (Leat 1988:12). In effect, this means being more accountable to clients.

These general concerns are reflected to a large extent in an Irish context. Public disquiet about the use of funds raised for charities is evidenced by the special government report on the matter (Report on Fundraising 1990). Difficulties in the economy have necessitated cutbacks in public expenditure while the unprecedented level of unemployment has led to an overall decrease in disposable income. This fact, combined with the advent of the National Lottery, has greatly increased competition for voluntary sector funding (Report on Fundraising 1990). A greater demand for participation is also discernible (CMRS 1992).

Cumulatively, these characteristics add up to demands for greater accountability on the part of Irish voluntary organizations. Yet, as highlighted repeatedly by contributors to the debate, e.g., Gray (1984), Laughlin (1990), fiscal accountability in nonprofit organizations is only a small part of the process. Accountability for process, programme and priorities (Leat 1988) needs to be added to complete the "ladder of accountability" (Stewart 1984). Despite this wider requirement, the case study organizations, by and large, confined their response to fiscal accountability. Recalling that "to be fully accountable implies the ability to exercise control" (Day & Klein 1987:227), this dependence on financial accountability was understandable, given the loose nature of internal control in these organizations which did not provide the necessary data to report on other aspects of accountability.

This brief overview of environmental characteristics shows how they can impact on voluntary organizations, giving rise to demands for greater accountability which, if they are to be met fully, are dependent on appropriate internal control.

Drawing together the main findings emerging from this exploratory study on management, control and accountability in Irish voluntary organizations, it is evident that the case study organizations, in common with their counterparts elsewhere, exhibit a range of organizational characteristics which present particular challenges for their management. Also, they operate in an environment which has always been broadly supportive of voluntary action. Yet, underpinned by harsh economic conditions and increasing competition, funding is becoming increasingly difficult. In addition, the lack of an overall policy framework for the Irish voluntary sector has meant that voluntary organizations have to operate in a policy vacuum. These environmental realities also impact on the management of these organizations. Therefore, both the internal and external contexts of these voluntary bodies present challenges for management.

The interview data yielded empirical evidence on management personnel in the study group, indicating a strong level of commitment in all cases. But against this background of concern, there was evidence to suggest limitations in formal management education and training, as predicted by informants in the preliminary fieldwork. Not surprisingly, this managerial background impacted on approaches to control and accountability where the keen appreciation of their need was not matched by responses at the "lived" level. The general situation obtaining in the ten organizations surveyed appears to fit in with the approach to organizational life, as described by Morgan (1986:16-7):

> We live in a world that is becoming increasingly complex. Unfortunately our styles of thinking rarely match this complexity. We often end up persuading ourselves that everything is more simple than it actually is, dealing with complexity by presuming that it does not really exist. . . . The real challenge is to learn to deal with this complexity.

The complexities inherent in the dynamic environment in which voluntary organizations now operate create new demands for their management. It is vitally necessary to move beyond what has been achieved and shed the familiarity of old routines, in order to develop effectively in the future.

It is suggested that being equipped with appropriate management "tools" and having a fuller understanding of the complex organizational reality of nonprofit undertakings, would facilitate managers of Irish voluntary organizations in meeting their demanding task.

Outline model showing key influences on the nature of management, control and accountability in voluntary organizations

An outline model based on insights gained from the series of case investigations conducted in this research, together with information gathered on the Irish voluntary sector, is now presented. This model shows the influence of environmental and organizational characteristics on management, control and accountability in Irish voluntary organizations.

The principal constituents of the model can be summarised as follows:

A voluntary organization is perceived as an open system with particular environmental and organizational characteristics.

Environmental characteristics can affect the system as follows:

- uncertainties can arise from multiple funding sources and/or competition for funds
- economic conditions can impact on the system, e.g., a recession can reduce funding while increasing demands for services
- increased interest in participation can lead to the need for greater involvement of clients
- socio-political influences can impact on the system, e.g., social policy can determine the sector's role in society; the regulatory climate for the voluntary sector and non supportive tax provisions can imposeconstraints on voluntary organizations, while the history of the sector and public attitudes towards it can determine its overall operational climate.

Therefore it is suggested that these environmental characteristics need to be taken into account in the management of voluntary organizations.
Organizational characteristics can impact on the system as follows:

- The combination of service provision (making achievements more difficult to quantify) with the lack of a profit yardstick with which to measure overall success, are features of voluntary organizations.
- The lack of a direct link between input (funding) and output (services) can create additional demands for nonprofit management.
- Governance and staffing patterns (often a mixture of paid and voluntary staff) are two other features in voluntary organizations.
- Geographical spread, the number of clients served, organization practice and sources of funding can also impact on voluntary agencies.

These organizational characteristics need to be considered in the management of voluntary organizations.
The control process in voluntary organizations can be influenced by both the environmental an organizational characteristics. In particular:

- On the input side, the uncertainty regarding funding can create additional control problems.

225

- On the output side, the service nature of provisions makes them less amenable to measurement and this is allied to the lack of an overall profit yardstick.
- The fact that often there is no direct link between funding and service provision also makes overall control more difficult.

Accountability to external constituents can also be influenced by both environmental and organizational characteristics.

- Demand for accountability is affected by the regulatory climate in operation.
- The ability to account for fiscal, process, programme and priority aspects of accountability is dependent on a level of internal control which can provide the necessary information.

This model identifies the complex set of environmental and organizational characteristics that impact on management, control and accountability in voluntary sector organizations. An outline of the model is shown in Figure 12.1.

The distinguishing feature of this model is that it presents an integrated approach to management, control and accountability in voluntary organizations, rather than dealing with each aspect in isolation. By mapping, Amacon, New Yorkout the key organizational and environmental variables that impact on nonprofit undertakings, this contingency model demonstrates the broader operational context that has to be considered by management in order to devise appropriate responses to the need for control and accountability. Going beyond the brief of other writers, some of whom have focused on the control area while others have concentrated on accountability, this model captures the interconnectedness of control and accountability in voluntary organizations, and shows how both are contingent on their internal and external operating situation.

Emerging from the model, it is suggested that management in voluntary organizations necessitates adopting a contingency approach (Kreitner 1989; Lawrence & Lorsch 1967) by taking into account both the particular

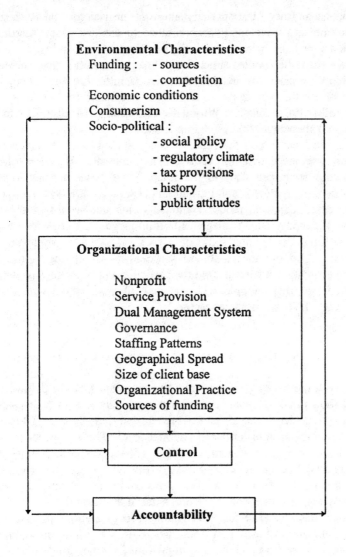

Figure 12.1 Key influences on the nature of management, control and accountability in voluntary organizations

environmental and organizational characteristics that impact on organizations in this sector and developing appropriate controls so that organizational achievements can be monitored and, in turn, accountability to external constituents can be implemented i.e., fiscal, process, programme and accountability for priorities. In addition, the model illustrates the complexity of management in the voluntary sector, thus endorsing the findings in the literature (Billis 1989; Butler & Wilson 1990; Mason 1984; McLaughlin 1986; Newman & Wallender 1978).

As established earlier, in the final analysis, implementation of control and accountability is dependent on management personnel. However, the case study findings suggested that, in the majority of cases, managers did not appear to have the required "solid grounding" (Kreitner 1989) in management. It is considered that this model could serve as one useful "tool" in the provision of appropriate management training as it provides a broad framework for understanding some of the key variables in voluntary sector management. Also the model should serve as a useful "map" for policy makers, in bringing to their attention the particular characteristics of voluntary organizations, as they grapple with the task of devising an overall policy framework for the Irish voluntary sector.

Suggestions for the Irish voluntary sector arising from the research

Based on both the background research and the more focused fieldwork, this study has shown that, in Ireland, voluntary organizations make a considerable contribution to society. It has been established that they are engaged in a wide range of activities at both local and national level. These are services which statutory authorities, operating in a difficult economic climate, either "could not or would not" supply (CSSC 1988:11). However, it also became apparent in the course of the research that there are certain shortcomings in the Irish voluntary sector, as it operates at present. First of all this section reviews some of the difficulties that arise for Irish voluntary organizations in their current operational climate. Following on from this, some suggestions are put forward as to how this situation could be improved in order to facilitate these organizations in their future efforts to enhance the social fabric of Irish society.

From the standpoint of the voluntary sector, at present it has to operate outside a defined policy context (Butler 1981; Lee 1987; NSSB 1982). Accordingly there is considerable disquiet about the lack of a clearly enunciated policy framework which would clarify precisely how voluntary organizations are meant to fit into the "overall scheme of things", as Butler

(1981) describes it. A related difficulty is the lack of consultation on the part of the statutory authorities regarding policy decisions that impact on voluntary organizations (CSSC 1988).

In effect this means that the relationship between the State and voluntary bodies is seen to be very one-sided, rather than being viewed as a partnership between the two parties. Currently the voluntary side does not have the status of a social partner which is afforded to other interest groups in society such as employers, trade unions and farming groups who are given a negotiating voice at national level, e.g., in the Programme for Economic and Social Progress (PESP 1991). In essence, to date there has been no formal recognition of of voluntary organizations as a distinctive group in Irish society.

Connected to this lack of a negotiating position, there is no formalised consultative mechanism in place which could facilitate dialogue between the statutory and voluntary sides and so enable voluntary bodies to play a part in policy development. In the absence of formal recognition and appropriate consultation, the approach of the statutory side to voluntary organizations is often characterised by an ad hoc response to demands arising from various voluntary bodies. For example, as mentioned earlier, the government's social employment schemes (SES), while of short term use to voluntary organizations, are inimical to the long term needs of these organizations as they hamper any attempt at long-term planning. This is just one example of how a government scheme designed to address the unemployment crisis as well as assist voluntary organizations, while of some benefit to these organizations, does not meet their long term needs.

The whole question of statutory funding is also high on the agenda of many voluntary bodies. As mentioned previously, in the general area of voluntary sector funding, statutory input is now considerable, amounting to over 200 million pounds annually (see Appendix I). However, six different government deparments are involved in the disbursement of these funds, either directly or through other statutory agencies, e.g., Health Boards. Again, in the absence of an overall guiding policy framework, there is no clear policy on how funds are to be allocated.

As this statutory finance, no matter how it is allocated, involves public money, there is a need on the part of the state to be accountable for it. In addition to this direct funding, the government also has a responsibility to monitor fundraising for charities donated directly by the public. Therefore the recommendations in the government report on fundraising (1990) regarding a tightening up of the present rather lax climate of control on charitable operations needs to be addressed.

While voluntary organizations may be dissatisfied about the current interaction with the statutory side, as described above, it must be acknowledged that they themselves are not without their shortcomings. For instance, it is recalled that various commentators (Curry 1980; IPAM 1986; Kennedy 1981; Lee 1987) mentioned the overall lack of co-ordination in the Irish voluntary sector as a whole. At an operational level, the research illustrated the complexity of both the internal and external contexts in which individual organizations currently function. However, the findings from the fieldwork suggest that many of those engaged in the sector do not appear to have had the benefit of formal training, particularly in the area of management. Also, smaller organizations, which find it difficult enough to generate funds for service provision, do not have the resources to finance training.

What can be done to address these perceived shortcomings? On the statutory side it is evident that there is a need to formulate an overall policy framework for the voluntary sector. It is considered that the lack of such a guiding policy is at the core of many difficulties currently being experienced in the voluntary sector. However, to avoid the one-sided relationship that is perceived to exist at present between the voluntary and the statutory side, it is suggested that some formalised consultative structure be put in place, in order to ensure that the voluntary side has an input into the drafting of this overall policy for the sector.

Once such a consultative mechanism is put in place, it would facilitate the participation of the voluntary sector in policy formation, on an ongoing basis and enable the statutory sector to learn from the experiences of voluntary organizations. In turn, this would facilitate the development of appropriate responses to the needs being identified at ground level by various voluntary bodies. In particular, the voluntary side can provide a vital channel through which the voice of those who experience exclusion and poverty is heard in the public arena.

From the point of view of the voluntary sector, such a consultative mechanism would enable it to establish a sectoral negotiating position with the statutory side, addressing broad issues that are relevant to the sector as a whole, e.g., the National Lottery problem; securing tax provisions that would be more conducive to generating support from the public; EC dimensions of voluntary action.

As highlighted earlier, currently, statutory support for voluntary organizations is spread over six different government departments. To facilitate the formulation of an overall policy framework, it is suggested that there is a need for one central source on the statutory side to deal with the voluntary side in a more co-ordinated manner. Such a central statutory unit

230

could address the ad hoc approach to funding by laying down general guidelines. In addition, it could progress the recommendations laid down in the government report on fundraising (1990) regarding overall control of voluntary organizations, by introducing a system of registration thus ensuring closer monitoring of voluntary activity and the need for accountability relating to both funds raised and the appropriateness of services provided. It is evident from the field research in this study that all the participant organizations are fully in agreement with the need for public accountability.

Also, as research on the Irish voluntary sector is very scant, this proposed central statutory unit could undertake or commission relevant research in order to assist the future development of Irish voluntary action. (Possible areas for research are detailed in the next section of this report.) For such a central unit to function effectively, it is recognised that adequate financial resources would need to be provided.

On the voluntary side, it was noted that it tended to be characterised by a lack of overall co-ordination, with many organizations buisily engaged in providing a service to a particular client group while not appearing to have any great level of awareness of the wider context of voluntary action. The research findings supported this view as most of the respondents showed little knowledge of broader developments e.g., the government report on fundraising (1990) or the ASC (1988) SORP on charity accounting. This situation indicates a need to develop fora where individual organizations and interest groups can come together at sectoral and national level in order to identify common ground and progress common issues.

Ideally it is suggested that there should be a national co-ordinating voluntary body to represent the sector as a whole. Such a body could represent the interests of voluntary organizations in regular consultations with the statutory sector. Also it could enable the voluntary sector to feature as one of the social partners in national fora set up to decide on social and economic policies at national level, e.g., The National Economic & Social Forum.

The present research also showed the complex management tasks involved in running voluntary organizations and findings suggested a lack of appropriate training to meet these demands. The proposed National Voluntary Body could examine the broad training needs in the sector and ensure the provision of suitable training to address the needs identified. Unlike the situation in the UK and the US, at present there are no educational courses available in Irish third level colleges which are specifically oriented towards the voluntary sector. Perhaps it is time that some such provision be made available here and a National Voluntary Body would be a a position to initiate and progress this requirement.

The recent response from one ad hoc group, representing over 60 voluntary groups, in drafting a charter from a voluntary sector perspective (CWC 1992) suggests that there is both an interest and a willingness in the sector itself in taking up the challenge of being one of the social partners in Irish society. However, it is considered that a more permanent representative body for the sector is required if this proposed partnership is to be sustained over time.

Once again, it is acknowledged that setting up such a national body would require resources which a hard-pressed voluntary sector is unlikely to have at its disposal. Therefore it is considered that there would be a need for the suggested central statutory unit to make resources available for the establishment of a corresponding body on the voluntary side. This organizational process would require both financial and infrastructural support, e.g., premises and back-up services. Yet, without the creation of such a co-ordinating national voluntary body, it is difficult to envisage the voluntary sector being in a position to enter into dialogue with the statutory side and so assume a partnership role.

To summarise this section, having reviewed the present shortcomings in the interaction between the statutory and voluntary sectors, it is considered that certain key provisions need to be put in place which would enable the voluntary sector to enhance its role in the broader societal context in which it operates. The need to develop an overall policy framework has been identified by many previous commentators and is endorsed by this researcher. It is suggested that a more focused input from both the statutory and voluntary sides is needed to facilitate this process. To implement this would involve the setting up of one central unit on the statutory side to formulate general policy in relation to the voluntary sector and co-ordinate the input from the various departments involved in supporting voluntary action. Likewise, it is considered that the voluntary side would need a corresponding co-ordinating national body to represent its overall interests in negotiating with the statutory side and also to foster training and development in the voluntary arena.

If the foregoing suggestions were implemented, it is considered that this would put the Irish voluntary sector in a better position from which to contribute to the development of Irish society in the years ahead.

Possible areas for future research

Prior to the present study, research in the Irish voluntary sector, especially in relation to management, was virtually in the realm of uncharted territory. It is hoped that, having made a start in the field of management, this will provide an impetus to further research. Possible topics include:

- Broader studies of management personnel in the voluntary sector, e.g. profiles of those involved in terms of background and training; assessment of training needs of managers; development of appropriate training, including programme content and methods of implementation
- An investigation of staffing patterns, e.g. mix of paid staff and volunteers involved
- Research on paid staff, including overall numbers involved, profiles, salary structures, training needs
- Information on volunteers, e.g. Who is involved? - age profiles; educational background; Why are certain categories under-represented? Types of activities undertaken by volunteers; Why do people volunteer? What is their initial motivation? What are their reasons for continuing or leaving? What are the perceived key benefits and drawbacks of volunteering? Management of volunteers: recruitment methods and their results. What methods of induction, training and development are used or needed?
- Studies of Boards of Management, e.g. composition - background of members; recruitment methods and criteria used; experiences of membership, benefits and drawbacks; training needs and provision.
- Research on the funding of voluntary organizations: patterns of funding, e.g. statutory/nonstatutory/mix of both and their impact; Statutory funding: how funding decisions are made; experiences of organizations seeking funding; monitoring of statutory funding; Commercial funding: overall scale and policies of individual companies on funding; Fundraising from the public: study of various approaches used and their advantages and disadvantages; the extent of competition for funds; an evaluation of the impact of tax concessions on donations; research on donors, including attitudes to donating; size and frequency of donations; selection of recipient organizations; expectations regarding accountability; methods of encouraging donating, e.g., pay-roll deductions.
- Service provision: perceptions of clients regarding level of service received; involvement of clients - present levels and possible methods of implementation.

It is considered that the availability of research on various aspects of voluntary action in Ireland, as outlined above, would contribute to the overall development of the sector and also be of practial interest to policy makers and to those working in the field.

Final reflections

In recent times and at an international level, the voluntary sector has re-emerged from its marginal position in society and is now playing a more significant role. This generally heightened profile of the sector is mirrored in an Irish context where, despite developments in State welfare, it has continued to make a valuable contribution in the provision of services to a wide range of people. Currently, in a climate of economic retrenchment, new and increasing demands are being made on Irish voluntary organizations and it is suggested that they will need increasing professionalism in order to meet these challenges.

In this context, management in the nonprofit sector has been identified as one area meriting greater attention. The era characterised by an approach of "give us some money and we'll do some good" (Dev Officer/Poplar) is now being replaced by the need for a more systematic approach to managing organizations. Faced with fresh challenges, it is no longer sufficient to strike camp and make no further progress. In a time of rapid change, voluntary organizations, in common with organizations in other sectors, have to adapt to these changes. The well-known observation of Cardinal Newman, made at a time of relative stability, that "to change is to grow; to be perfect is to have changed often", is even more apposite in the current climate where change is "so speeded up that we begin to see the present only when it is already disappearing" (Laing, quoted in O'Murchu 1987:11). In fact, Butler & Wilson (1990:165) identify the one consistent theme in their research as being "the sharply accelerating rate of change with which voluntary organizations must cope".

By exploring the areas of management, control and accountability in an integrated manner in the hitherto unexplored context of the Irish voluntary sector and presenting an outline model showing how environmental and organizational characteristics impact on these areas, it is submitted that this study provides an independent contribution to the ongoing wider debate on the voluntary sector. In addition, while acknowledging that "there is always a "more" that goes infinitely beyond what we have already grasped" (Hought 1986:21), it is hoped that the insights provided by this exploratory study advance in some measure the development of a more vibrant Irish voluntary sector in the years ahead.

APPENDICES

APPENDIX I

Breakdown of funding available to voluntary bodies from government departments in 1990/91

DEPARTMENT	YEAR	AMOUNT (million pounds)
Health	1991	132.4
Labour	1990	39.5
Environment	1991	16.9
Education	1990	14.5
Social Welfare	1991	2.4
Justice	1990	1.7
Total:		207.4

Source: Information Service, Department of Social Welfare (DSW 1992)

APPENDIX II

Organizations affiliated to UVOH

A.P.T.
Alzheimer Society of Ireland
Arthritis Foundation of Ireland
Association for Children and Adults with Learning Disabilities
Asthma Society of Ireland
Barnardos
Caring and Sharing Association (CASA)
Central Remedial Clinic
Cerebral Palsy Ireland
Cheshire Foundation in Ireland
Clashganna Mills Trust
Cope Foundation
County Wexford Community Workshop (Enniscorthy)
Cystic Fibrosis Association of Ireland
Disabled Drivers Association
Downs Syndrome Association of Ireland
Friedreich's Ataxia Society of Ireland
Galway County Association for Mentally Handicapped Children
Irish Association of the Sovereign Military Order of Malta
Irish Association for Spina Bifida and Hydrocephalus
Irish Deaf Society
Irish Epilepsy Association
Irish Guide Dogs Association
Irish Haemophilia Association
Irish Kidney Association
Irish Motor Neurone Disease Association
Irish Society for Autistic Children
Irish Wheelchair Association
KARE
M.S. Care Foundation
Multiple Sclerosis Society of Ireland
Muscular Dystrophy Ireland
National Association for the Deaf
National Council for the Blind of Ireland
National Federation of Arch Clubs

Order of Malta Workshops and Training Centre (Drogheda)
Polio Fellowship of Ireland
Rehabilitation Institute
R.P. Ireland - Fighting Blindness
Riding for the Disabled Association - Ireland
St. Michael's House
Sunbeam House Industrial Centre for the Mentally Handicapped
Volunteer Stroke Scheme
West Limerick Community Workshop

APPENDIX III

Fieldwork: Interview schedule

It is proposed to gather information on three broad areas as follows, from each of ten participating voluntary organizations:

a) General background information,

b) specific data on control,

c) approaches to accountability.

The proposed interview schedule for each area is attached.

GENERAL BACKGROUND INFORMATION   DATA

Name of organization: Establishing
                                                                               characteristics of
                                                                               each organization

Address:

Main services provided:

In what year was the organization established?

Is it a   (a) local or
              (b) national organization?

How many clients does it serve currently?:

STAFFING
                        Paid   Number
                              Full-time:
                              Part-time:

                        Volunteers
                              Full-time:
                              Part-time:

Is the organization affiliated to an umbrella body?

INCOME:

Overall income 1990:

What are the main sources of income?   Mix of statutory/
                                                                               other income

       Statutory sources:

       Voluntary:

GENERAL BACKGROUND INFORMATION	DATA

Is any `hidden' aid received, e.g.   free premises   see Leat et al
free phones   (1986:43)
free office eq'p't
other (specify)

Organization structure: formal/
informal

CEO PROFILE
     Age: 30 and under
              31 - 40
              41 - 50
              51 or over

General education:
         2nd level:
         3rd level: certificate
                          diploma
                          bachelors degree
                          masters degree
                          professional qualification
                          other (please specify)

Management training:

Management experience: No.years

                 overall
                 voluntary sector
                 commercial
                 other (specify)

ACCOUNTANT: PROFILE   DATA
     Age: 30 or under
             31 - 40
             41 - 50
             51 or over

Employment:
        Full-time
        Part-time
        Consultant
        Voluntary

General education:
        2nd level
        3rd level

                    diploma
                    bachelors degree
                    masters degree
                    professional qualification
                    other (specify)

Management education:

Management experience:
                    overall
                    voluntary sector
                    commercial sector
                    accountancy practice
                    other (specify)

BOARD OF MANAGEMENT : PROFILE   DATA

No. members:

Is there a financial sub-committee? Yes / No

Please classify Board members into occupations.

    CATEGORY   No.

    Co. executive
    Finance (banker/accountant)
    Small business
    Legal
    Medical
    Educational
    Religious
    Retired
    Other (specify)

How many have become Board members in the last 3 years?   Turnover

Are there any client representatives on the Board?   Consumer
                                                        rep'n?

Are there any funder representatives on the Board?

How often are meetings held? Monthly/quarterly/annually   Frequency

What is the average attendance?   90% or over
                                     75 - 89%
                                     50 - 74%
                                     Under 50%

Is training provided for Board members?

What selection criteria are used?

CONTROL

Control is about monitoring activities to ensure that they are being accomplished as planned.

General:	DATA

1. What is the general approach to control in this organization?

                                                     Overall approach to control

- How necessary do you consider it to be?

    vital/v.nec./nec./not v.important/unimportant

    Why do you hold this view?

- What difficulties does control give rise to?

- Is the overall approach to control:

    informal/day-to-day/formal   Informal/ formal?

DATA

2. What are the overall objectives of the organization?   Clarity of object

- Are there written objectives?   - overall

                              - departmental

- If not, how do people know what they are?

- Is there a written long-term plan for the organization?

3. What information do you get to let you know that the overall objectives are being achieved?   Coping with n/p status

- By what criteria is the overall effectiveness judged?

- How are overall achievements measured, i.e., what standards are used?

SPECIFIC: DATA

4. In the *personnel* area, how is the performance
   of individuals controlled ?   Control
                                                             of
                                                             personnel

- on a day-to-day basis ?

- do you have a formal appraisal system ?

- if `yes', how does it operate?

- what reinforcements are used?

- Staff training ?

              Full-time:

              Volunteers?

DATA

5. In the *financial* area, how are income and expenditure controlled?

Financial control?

- Are audited accounts prepared?

- Do you have a formal budgetary system?

  Formal?

  If `yes',

  - how does it operate?

- Is there only an overall budget, or do you have cost centres?

- How are standards set?

  Basis for setting standards?

  (a) on income side?

  (b) on expenditure side?

- Who is involved in setting budgets?

  Partici-pation?

  - CEO only
  - Department heads
  - Board
  - Budget committee
  - Other staff (specify)

If `no', how are income and expenditure controlled?

Measuring performance:

DATA

- Do you have a formal financial reporting system?

Measure-
ment

- Frequency? - weekly/monthly/quarterly/ annually

- Is it prepared on an overall or departmental basis?

- To whom are reports sent?

- Action:

- What follow-up action is taken if a variance shows up?

Follow-up
action?

- Who works out a plan for correction?

- How is this monitored?

OPERATIONS:

6. How do you judge the efficiency (inputs/outputs) of operations

Operations
control

- How do you judge the effectiveness (achievement of overall goals) of operations?

INFORMATION: DATA

7. What sort of information do you need to help   Infor-
   you run the organization?   mation

• How do you get this information?

EFFECTS OF CONTROL:

• Control can sometimes give rise to dysfunctional   Human
  effects.   factor
                                                         in
   Are you aware of: control

   (a) any resistance to control
        from any staff in particular?

   (b) manipulation of data?

ACCOUNTABILITY   DATA

1. In general what is your attitude to the issue of   Overall
   accountability to outsiders?   attitude
                                                             to a/c

2. Do you see any advantages arising from a/c?   Perceived
                                                             adv. &
                                                             disadv of
                                                             a/c

   • Any disadvantages?

   • What affect, if any, has a/c on your   Threat
     independence?   to indep?

3. To WHOM do you see the organization as being   Funders
   accountable?   only?

   • Is there any difference in a/c to different bodies?

DATA

4. Why does this a/c arise?

Proactive
or re-
active?

• any other reasons?

5. For *what* do you see the organization as being
accountable?

Money
only?

6. How does your organization address the need
for accountability?

Responses
to a/c

    (a) for funds received *in*

    (b) for services provided, re:

Focus of
a/c?

       - financial aspects

       - that objectives are being met

       - standards issues

       - appropriateness of the services offered.

7. Annual Report: does the organization prepare one?

    If *yes*

       - What are the broad areas covered?   Money
                                                          only?

       - To whom is it circulated?

       - Are other requests received?

8. Board representatives:

     - Have you considered having funders represented
      on the Board?

     - Clients?

9. Have you read SORP 2 on charity reporting?

    Views ?

10. Have you read the recent government report on fundraising?

    Views?

BIBLIOGRAPHY

Bibliography

ACTON R, Personal interview with Roger Acton CEO of the Union of
Voluntary Organisations for the Handicapped (UVOH),(Dublin Sept 26,1991)

AKENSON D, (1970), *The Irish Experiment*, Routledge Kegan Paul, London.

AMIR D & M AMIR, (1979), "Rape crisis centres: an arena for ideological
conflict", *Victimology* 4 247-57.

ANDERSON R, (1971), "Voluntary associations in history", *American
Anthropologist* 73 209-22.

ANDREASEN AR, (1982), "Nonprofits: check your attention to customers",
Harvard Business Review, May/June 105-10

ANDREWS F, (1950), *Philanthropic Giving*, New York: Russell Sage

ANHEIER H & M KNAPP, (1990), "Voluntas: an editorial statement",
Voluntas 1:1 1-12.

ANTHONY RN J DEARDEN & N BEDFORD, (1984), *Management
Control Systems*, 5th ed, Homewood Illinois, Irwin

ANTHONY RN & DW YOUNG, (1984), *Management Control in Nonprofit
Organizations*, 3rd ed, Homewood Illinois: Irwin

ANTHONY RN & DW YOUNG, (1988), *Management Control in Nonprofit
Organizations*, 4th ed, Homewood Illinois: Irwin

ARENSBERG CM & ST KIMBALL, (1968), *Family and Community in
Ireland*, Harvard Uni Press, Cambridge, Mass.

ARGYRIS C, (1952), *The Impact of Budgets on People*, Cornell University,
Ithaca, NY

ARGYRIS C, (1957), *Personality and Organization*, Harper & Row,
New York

ASC, (1984), "Accounting by charities: a discussion paper", Accounting

Standards Committee, London

ASC, (1984a), "Comments received on accounting by charities: a discussion paper", Accounting Standards Committee, London

ASC, (1985), "Accounting by Charities", Accounting Standards Committee, ED 38, London

ASC, (1988), "SORP 2: Accounting by Charities", Accounting Standards Committee, London

ASSISI SR M, (1967), *Sisters of the Holy Faith*, Three Candles, Dublin

AUSTIN M & J POSNETT, (1979), "The Charity Sector in England and Wales: Characteristics and Public Accountability", *National Westminster Bank Quarterly Review*, 40-51

AVES REPORT, (1969), *The Voluntary Worker in the Social Services*, Allen & Unwin, London.

BADELT C, (1989), "Government versus private provision of social services In", E James ed, *The Nonprofit Sector in International Perspective*, Oxford Uni Press, Oxford.

BADELT C & P WEISS, (1990), "Non-profit and government organisations in social service provision: comparison of behavioural patterns for Austria", *Voluntas*, 1:1 77-96

BAIRD L J POST & J MAHON, (1990), *Management: functions and responsibilities*, Harper & Row, New York.

BAKAL C, (1979), *Charity USA*, Times Books, New York.

BAKER TJ S SCOTT & I KEARNEY, (1989), "Quarterly Economic Commentary", August, ESRI, Dublin.

BALL C, (1979), "Whatever happened to voluntary bodies?", *Community Care*, Feb 22.

BANTON M, (1968), "Voluntary associations: anthropological aspects", *International Encyclopedia of the Social Sciences*, 16: 357-62, Macmillan & Free Press, New York

BARCLAY COMMITTEE, (1982), *Social Workers - Their Role and Tasks*, Bedford Square Press, London

BARLOW AC, (1981), *The Financing of Third Level Education*, ESRI, Dublin.

BARNARD C, (1938), *The Functions of the Executive*, Harvard Uni Press, Cambridge Ma.

BARNEY & GRIFFIN, (1992), *The Management of Organizations*, Houghton Mifflin, Boston

BARRETT SD, (1989), "Measuring Poverty in Ireland", *Economic and Social Review*, XX:4 353-60

BARRINGTON R, (1987), *Health Medicine and Politics in Ireland*

1900-1970, IPA, Dublin

BEN-NER A & T VAN HOOMISSEN, (1990), "The growth of the nonprofit sector in the 1980s: facts and interpretations", *Nonprofit Management and Leadership*, I:2 99-116

BERMINGHAM W & L O'CUANAIGH, (1978), *Alone*, Alone, Dublin.

BEVERIDGE LORD, (1948), *Voluntary Action: a Report on the Method of Social Advance*, Allen & Unwin, London

BILLIS D, (1984), "Voluntary sector management: research and practice", *PORTVAC, Working Paper 1*, LSE

BILLIS D, (1984a), *Welfare Bureaucracies*, Heineman, London

BILLIS D, (1984b), "Self help and service", *PORTVAC Working Paper 2*,LSE

BILLIS D, (1987), "Some puzzles and models of voluntary organisations", Paper presented at AVAS conference, Kansas

BILLIS D, (1989), "A theory of the voluntary sector: implications for policy and practice", Working Paper 5, CVO, LSE

BILLIS D, (1992), *Organising Public and Voluntary Agencies*, Rutledge, London.

BILLIS D & M HARRIS, (1986), "An extended role for the voluntary sector: the challenge of implementation", Working Paper 3, PORTVAC/CVO, LSE

BILLIS D & D YOUNG, (1990), Editors' notes, *Nonprofit Management & Leadership*, I:1 1-5

BINCHY H, (1963), "Social services in modern Ireland", *Studies*, 111:20172-9.

BINCHY H, (1967), "The role of the voluntary agencies", *Christus Rex* XXI:3, 253-62

BINNEY V, G HARKELL & J NIXON, (1985), "Refuges and housing for battered women in J Pahl ed", *Private Violence and Public Policy*, Routledge & Kegan Paul, London.

BIRD P & P MORGAN-JONES, (1981), *Financial Reporting by Charities*, ICAEW, London.

BIRKETT WP, (1988), "Concepts of accountability", Paper presented to the British Accounting Association Annual Conference, Trent Polytechnic

BLANCHARD J, (1963), *The Church in Contemporary Ireland*, Clonmore & Reynolds, Dublin.

BLAU PM, (1963), *The Dynamics of Bureaucracy*, Uni of Chicago Press.

BLAU PM & WR SCOTT, (1962), *Formal Organizations*, San Francisco,Chandler

BOLAND D, (1992), "289,000 people now without employment", *Irish Times* Aug 8

BOLSTER MA, (1978), *Catherine McAuley in her own Words*, Diocesan

Office for Causes, Dublin.

BORST D & P MONTANA, (1987), *Managing Nonprofit Organizations* AMACON, New York.

BOULDING KE, (1956), "General systems theory: the skeleton of science", *Management Science*, April 197-208

BOYDELL B, (1992), "Handel", *Irish Times*, Apr 11

BRENTON M, (1982), "Changing relationships in Dutch social services", *Journal of Social Policy*, 2:1

BRENTON M, (1985), *The Voluntary Sector in British Social Services*, Longman, New York

BRODY H, (1974), *Inishkillane*, Penguin, Harmonsworth

BROWNE N, (1986), *Against the Tide*, Gill & Macmillan, Dublin

BRUCE M, (1968), *The Coming of the Welfare State*, Batsford, London

BRUYN ST, (1966), *The Human Perspective in Sociology*, Prentice Hall, Englewood Cliffs NJ:

BUDGET BOOK, (1989), Stationery Office, Dublin

BURGESS EW, (1927), "Statistics and case studies as methods of sociological research", *Sociology and Social Research*, 12 103-120

BURKE H, (1976), *The Poor Law in Ireland in the Nineteenth Century*, Unpublished PhD thesis, University College Dublin, Dublin.

BURKE-SAVAGE R, (1965), "The Church in Dublin 1940-65", *Studies* LIV:216 297-338

BURRELL G & G MORGAN, (1979), *Sociological Paradigms and Organisational Analysis*, Heinemann, London

BUTLER F, (1981), "Voluntary inaction", *Community Care*, Feb 19 16-7

BUTLER RJ & DC WILSON, (1990), *Managing Voluntary and Nonprofit Organisations*, Routledge, London

BUTT & PALMER, (1986), *Value for Money*, 2nd ed, Blackwell, Oxford

CAF, (1987), *Charity trends*, Charities Aid Foundation, Tonbridge

CAF, (1992), Personal interview with a spokeswoman for CAF Oct 8

CALLAN T D HANNON B NOLAN & B WHELAN, (1989), "Measuring poverty in Ireland: a reply", *Economic and Social Review* XX:4 361-8

CAMMANN C & D NADLER, (1976), "Fit control systems to your mangerial style", *Harvard Business Review*, Jan-Feb 65-72

CANNIFFE M, (1992), "Conflicting interests slow work of expert group on agriculture", *Irish Times*, Sept 4

CARE OF THE AGED, (1968), *The Care of the Aged*, Stationery Office, Dublin.

CARNEY C, (1977), *Selectivist Social Services*, Unpublished PhD thesis University College Dublin, Dublin.

CARPER WB & WE SNIZEK, (1980), "The nature and types of organizational taxonomies", *Acadamy of Management Review*, V:1 65-75

CARROLL S & D GILLEN, (1987), "Are the classical management functions useful in describing managerial work?", *Academy of Management Review*, 12 41-9.

CASS RH & MANSER G, (1983), "Roots of Voluntarism" in B O'Connell ed *America's Voluntary Spirit*, Foundation Center, New York.

CATHOLIC TRUTH SOCIETY, (1931), *The Social Order: The Encyclical Quadragesimo Anno of Pius XI*, Catholic Truth Society, London.

CENTRAL BANK, (1989), *Central Bank Quarterly Report No 1*, Central Bank, Dublin

CENTRAL BANK, (1992), *Central Bank Quarterly Report No 1*, Central Bank, Dublin

CHILD J, (1984), *Organization*, 2nd ed, Harper & Row, London

CHILVERS D, (1987), ED 38: "Need for a charitable rethink", *Accountancy*, Feb 29-30

CHRISTOPHER J, (1991), "Another kind of 12 steps", *Initiative*, 7:2 4-6

CLANCY P, (1983), *Participation in Third Level Education*, Higher Education Authority, Dublin

CMAC, (1987), *Catholic Marriage Advisory Council of Ireland Annual Report 1986*, CMAC, Dublin.

CMRS, (1992), "Power participation and exclusion", Social Policy Conference CMRS, Dublin Sept 23

COMBAT POVERTY AGENCY, (1988), *Poverty and the Social Welfare System in Ireland*, Combat Poverty Agency, Dublin

COMPTROLLER & AUDITOR GENERAL, (1987), *Monitoring and Control of Charities in England and Wales*, HMSO, London.

CONN E, (1991), "The ecological organisation: a new perspective" *Management Education and Development*, 22:3 227-33

CONNORS T, (1980), *The Nonprofit Organization Handbook*, McGraw Hill, New York

COSTELLO A, (1985), *In God's Hands*, Veritas, Dublin

COUGHLAN A, (1966), *Aims of Social Policy*, Tuairm, Dublin

CROWSON RA, (1970), *Classification and Biology*, Atherton Press, New York

CSO, (1944), *Annual Report*, Central Statistics Office, Dublin

CSO, (1988), *Ireland: Population and Labour Force Projections 1991-2021*, Stationery Office, Dublin

CSO, (1989), Live Register- Monthly area analysis: July, Central Statistics Office, Dublin

CSSC, (1988), see KIRBY 1988

CSW, (1986), *Report of the Commission on Social Welfare*, Stationery Office, Dublin

CUMMINS M, (1989), "66% increase in cases of child abuse", *Irish Times*, 6 Sept

CURRY J, (1980), *The Irish Social Services*, IPA, Dublin

CWC, (1992), "Towards a charter for voluntary action", Discussion document Community Workers Co-operative, Dublin

CYERT RM, (1975), *The Management of Nonprofit Organizations*, Heath,Lexington, Mass.

DAFT RL, (1986), *Organization Theory & Design* 2nd ed, West, St Paul, Minnesota

DAIL REPORTS, (1974), 12 June, Col 961

DAIL REPORTS, (1975), 24 June, Col 1330

DAIL REPORTS, (1979), 28 Feb, Col 374

DARVILL G & B MUNDY, (1984), *Volunteers in the Personal Social Services*, Tavistock, London.

DAWSON K, (1989), "Challenge to Church as vocations plummet", *Sunday Tribune,* August 27

DAY P & R KLEIN, (1987), *Accountabilities*, Tavistock, London.

DERRICKSON M, (1989), *The literature of the nonprofit sector*, The Foundation Center, New York

DE TOCQUEVILLE [1835], (1983), "Of the use which the Americans make of public associations in civil life", in B O'Connell ed, *America's Voluntary Spirit*, The Foundation Center, New York.

DEUTSCHER I, (1973), *What we Say/What we Do*, Glenview Ill: Scott Foresman

DIAMOND T et al, (1986), *Charities Administration*, ICSA, Cambridge.

DI GIOVANNI J, (1992), "Shall you go to the ball?", *The Sunday Times* Style and Travel Section 4, April 26

DI MAGGIO P & W POWELL, (1983), "Institutional isomorphism", *American Sociological Review*, 48 147-56

DORR D, (1983), *Option for the Poor*, Gill & Macmillan, Dublin

DOUGLAS J, (1828), *Observations on the Necessity of a Legal Provision for the Irish Poor*, Wakefield, Dublin

DOUGLAS J, (1983), *Why Charity:the Case for a Third Sector*, Sage, Beverly Hills, CA.

DOUGLAS J, (1987), "Political theories of nonprofit organizations", in W Powell ed, *The Nonprofit Sector: a Research Handbook*, Yale Uni Press,New Haven, Conn.

DOWNEY HK & RD IRELAND, (1983), "Quantitative versus qualitative: the case of assessment in organizational studies", in J Van Mannen ed, *Qualitative Methodology*, Sage, Beverly Hills, CA.

DRUCKER P, (1989), "What business can learn from nonprofits", *Harvard Business Review*, Sept/Oct 88-93

DRUCKER P, (1990), "Lessons for successful nonprofit governance", *Nonprofit Management & Leadership*, I:1, 7-14

DSW, (1950), *First Report of the Department of Social Welfare 1947-1949*, Dublin: Stationery Office

DSW, (1992), *Charter for voluntary social services*, Unpublished report Information Service, Department of Social Welfare, Dublin

DUBIN RJ, (1977), "Determining results in the generosity business", in D Borst & PJ Montana eds, *Managing Nonprofit Organizations*, AMACON

DUFFY J, (1991), "Council of State's function still very confined", *Irish Times*, 21 Feb

DUNLEAVY E, (1989), "Frank Duff", *Maria Legionis*, 32:2, 13-8

DURKHEIM E, (1938), *The Rules of Sociological Method*, Free Press, New York

DURKHEIM E, (1951), *Suicide: a Study of Sociology*, trans G Simpson, Free Press, New York

EASLEY D & M O'HARA, (1986), "Optimal nonprofit firms", in S.Rose-Ackesman ed, *The Economics of Nonprofit Institutions: Studies in Structure and Policy*, Oxford Uni Press, New York.

ECAS, (1990), Euro Citizen Action Service - Information Phamplet, ECAS, Brussels

ECKSTEIN O, (1967), *Public Finance*, 2nd ed, Prentice-Hall, Englewood Cliffs NJ

EISENBERG P, (1983), "The voluntary sector: problems and challenges", in B O'Connell ed, *America's Voluntary Spirit*, Foundation Center, New York

ELLMAN M, (1982), "Another theory of nonprofit corporations", *Michigan Law Review*, 80 999-1050

ETZIONI A, (1961), *A Comparative Analysis of Complex Organizations*, Free Press, New York

ETZIONI A, (1964), *Modern Organizations*, Prentice Hall, Englewood Cliffs NJ.

FALK, (1987), "SORP 2 as a fundraising aid", *Accountancy*, Dec 77-8

FARLEY D, (1964), *Social Insurance and Social Assistance in Ireland*, IPA, Dublin

FAUGHNAN P, (1977), *The Dimensions of Need*, Irish Wheelchair Association, Dublin

FAUGHNAN P, (1990), *Voluntary Organisations in the Social Service Field*, Department of Social Welfare, Dublin

FAUGHNAN P & P KELLEHER, (1991), "The operation of the voluntary and community sector Draft Proposal", Community Action Network, Dublin

FAYOL [1916], (1949), *General and Industrial Management*, Pitman, New York

FEARNS P, (1984), *Business Studies*, 2 ed, Hodder & Stoughton, Sevenoaks

FILER COMMISSION, (1975), *Giving in America: Toward a Stronger Voluntary Sector*, Washington DC: Commission on private philanthropy and public needs

FILER COMMISSION [1975], (1983), "The Third Sector: Commission on private philanthropy and public needs", in B O'Connell ed *America'sVoluntary Spirit*, Foundation Center, New York

FINE GAEL/LABOUR, (1981), *Programme for Government 1981-86*, Stationery Office, Dublin

FOGARTY M   L RYAN & J LEE, (1984), *Irish Values and Attitudes* Dominican Press, Dublin

FRANCIS BRIGID SR, (1989), "Mother Mary Aikenhead", *The African Missionary Summer*, 16-7

FRASER D, (1973), *The Evolution of the Welfare State*, Macmillan, London

FREMONT-SMITH M, (1989), "Trends in accountability and regulation of nonprofits", in V Hodgkinson & R Lyman eds, *The Future of the Nonprofit Sector*, Jossey-Bass, San Francisco

GALBRAITH JK, (1978), "Economic development", in MR Rosenberg ed *Quotations for the New Age*, Citadel Press, Syracuse, NJ

GALLAGHER JP, (1975), *The Price of Charity*, Hale, London

GARDNER JW, (1979), "Presenting the Independent Sector", Remarks delivered at the Council on Foundations 30th annual conference May 16 Seattle: Washington

GARTNER A & F RIESSMAN, (1977), *Self-help in the human services*, Jossey Bass, San Francisco

GATEWOOD R & J LAHIFF, (1977), "Differences in importance of job factors between managers in voluntary and profit organizations", *Journal of Voluntary Action Research* 6:3-4 131-139

GERARD D, (1983), *Charities in Britain: Conservatism or Change?* Bedford Square Press, London

GIBBONS J, (1985), "Where The Money Really Goes", *Business & Finance*, August 8, 12-21

GIGILIONI GB & AG BEDEIAN, (1974), "A conspectus of management control theory: 1990-1972", *Academy of Management Journal*, 17:2 292-305

GILL J & P JOHNSON, (1991), *Research Methods for Managers*, Chapman, London.

GILL J & J PRATT, (1986), *Responses to Financial Constraints of Institutions of Higher Education in the Public Sector*, Department of Education and Science, London

GLADSTONE F, (1979), *Voluntary Action in a Changing World*, Bedford Square Press, London

GLADSTONE F, (1982), *Charity, Law and Social Justice*, Bedford Square Press, London

GLASER B & A STRAUSS, (1967), *The Discovery of Grounded Theory*, Weidenfeld & Nicolson, London

GLASSER R, (1975), *Reality Therapy*, Harper & Row, New York

GOETZ BE, (1949), *Management Planning and Control*, McGraw-Hill, New York

GOODMAN COMMITTEE, (1976), *Charity Law and Voluntary Organisations*, Bedford Square Press, London

GORDON CW & N BABCHUK, (1966), "A typology of voluntary association", in WA Glasser & DL Sills eds, *The Government of Associations*, Bedminster Press, New Jersey

GRAY R, (1983), "Accounting, financial reporting and not-for-profit organisations", *AUTA Review*, 15:1 3-23

GRAY R, (1984), "Uncharitable view of accounting", *Accountancy*, August 84

GRAY R D OWEN & K MAUNDERS, (1987), *Corporate Social Reporting: Accounting and Accountability*, Prentice Hall, Englewood Cliffs NJ

GRAY ER & LR SMELTZER, (1989), *Management: The Competitive Edge*, Macmillan, New York

GRAYSON LE & CJ TOMPKINS, (1984), *Management of Public Sector and Nonprofit Organizations*, Reston, Virginia

GREENE TF, (1972), *Nano Nagle*, Presentation Sisters, Cork

GREENPEACE, (1992), Publicity phamplet, Greenpeace, Dublin

GRINDHEIM JE & P SELLE, (1990), "The role of voluntary social welfare organisations in Norway: a democratic alternative to a bureaucratic welfare state?", *Voluntas*, 1:1 62-76

GUBA EG & YS LINCOLN, (1981), *Effective Evaluation: improving the usefulness of evaluation results through responsive and naturalistic approaches*, Jossey Bass, San Francisco

GUTHRIE D, (1979), "The place of voluntary organisations in Great Britain", *Journal of the Royal College of Physicians of London*, 13:4 237-8

GUTHRIE R, (1988), *Charity and The Nation*, Charities Aid Foundation,

Tonbridge Kent

HAAS J & T DRABEK, (1973), *Complex Organizations*, Macmillan, New York

HADLEY R & S HATCH, (1980), *Research on the Voluntary Sector*, Social Science Research Council, London

HADLEY R, A WEBB & C FARRELL, (1975), *Across the Generations: Old People and Young Volunteers*, Allen & Unwin, London

HALFPENNY P & C LESSOF, (1990), "The scale and determinants of volunteering in Britain", Paper presented at AVAS Conference, LSE, July

HALL PD, (1987), "A historical review of the private nonprofit sector", in W Powell ed, *The Nonprofit Sector: a Research Handbook*, Yale Uni Press, New Haven Conn.

HAMPTON DR, (1986), *Management*, 3 ed, McGraw-Hill, Singapore

HAND M, (1992), "Volunteers group to aid jobless", *The Sunday Tribune*, News Section 10 May

HANDY C, (1981), *Improving Effectiveness in Voluntary Organisations*, NCVO, London

HANDY C, (1983), "Organisations in search of a theory", NCVO worksheet NCVO, London

HANDY C, (1988), *Understanding Voluntary Organisations*, Penguin, Harmondsworth

HANNA E, (1988), *Poverty in Ireland*, Social Study Conference, Portlaoise

HANNAN D & L KATSIAOUNI, (1977), *Traditional Families*, ESRI, Dublin

HANSMANN H, (1980), "The role of nonprofit enterprise", *Yale Law Journal*, 89 835-901

HANSMANN H, (1987), "Economic theories of nonprofit organizations", in W Powell ed, *The Nonprofit Sector: a Research Handbook*, Yale Uni Press, New Haven Conn.

HARRIS LORD J, (1986), "Survivor grief following a drunk driving crash", Paper to World Congress of Victimology, Orlando

HARRIS M, (1987), Management committees: roles and tasks Working Paper 4 CVO LSE

HARRIS M & D BILLIS, (1985), *Organising Voluntary Agencies: A Guide Through the Literature*, Bedford Square Press, London

· HARTOGS N & J WEBER, (1978), *Impact of Funding on the Management of Voluntary Agencies*, Greater New York Fund/United Way, New York

HATCH S, (1980), *Outside The State*, Croom Helm, London

HATCH S, (1983), *Volunteers: Patterns, Meanings and Motives*, The Volunteer Centre, Berkhamsted

HATCH S & I MOYCROFT, (1979), "The relative costs of services provided by voluntary and statutory organisations", *Public Administration*, Winter 397-405

HEMPEL J, (1965), *Aspects of Scientific Explanation*, Free Press, New York

HENSEY B, (1979), *The Health Services of Ireland*, Stationery Office, Dublin

HICKS H & C GULLET, (1981), *Management*, 4th ed, McGraw-Hill, Singapore

HINTON N & M HYDE, (1980-81), "The voluntary sector in a remodelled welfare state", *The Year Book of Social Policy*, Routledge & Kegan Paul, London

HIRSCHMAN AO, (1970), *Exit Voice and Loyalty*, Harvard Uni Press, Cambridge Mass.

HITT MA, RD MIDDLEMIST & RL MATHIS, (1986), *Management: Concepts and Effective Practice*, 2nd ed, West, St Paul MN.

HODGKINSON V & E BORIS, (1990), "Useful data bases for practitioners and scholars of nonprofit management", *Nonprofit Management & Leadership* 1:1 79-85

HODGKINSON V & R LYMAN, (1989), *The Future of the Nonprofit Sector*, Jossey Bass, San Francisco

HODGKINSON V & M WEITZMAN, (1984), *Dimensions of the Independent Sector: a Statistical Profile*, Independent Sector, Washington D.C.

HOFSTEDE G, (1967), *The Game of Budget Control*, Tavistock, London

HOFSTEDE G, (1978), "The poverty of management control philosophy",*Academy of Management Review*, 3 July 450-61

HOFSTEDE G, (1981), "Management control of public and not-for-profit activities", *Accounting Organisations & Society* 6:3 193-211

HOLMQUIST K, (1990), "Group spent over 100,000 on overheads", *Irish Times* 6 June

HOPKINS B, (1980), *Charity Under Siege*, Wiley, New York

HOUGHT J, (1986), *What is God?*, Gill & Macmillan, Dublin

HURLEY DC, (1982), *Edmund Ignatius Rice*, Sadifa, Strasbourg

INGLIS T, (1987), *Moral Monopoly*, Gill & Macmillan, Dublin

INVESTMENT IN EDUCATION, (1965), Stationery Office, Dublin

IPAM, (1986), *To Scheme or not to Scheme?*, Independent Poverty Action Movement, Dublin

IRISH TIMES, (1988), "Gorta urges regulation of charities", *Irish Times*, 23 Aug

IRISH TIMES, (1989), "Scheme for young mothers launched", *Irish Times* 24 May

IRISH TIMES, (1992), "O'Connell criticises hospital services", *Irish Times*, Sept 1

IRVINE J, (1988), "Adopting a long term view", *Accountancy*, Dec 92-93

IWA, (1991), "Profile: the Rt Hon Earl of Dunraven", *IWA Newsletter*, 7 (Winter) 22-3

JACKSON PM, (1982), *The Political Economy of Bureaucracy*, Philip Allan, London

JAMES E, (1983), "How nonprofits grow: a model", *Journal of policy analysis and management* 2: 350-65

JAMES E, (1987), "The nonprofit sector in comparative perspective", in W Powell ed, *The Nonprofit Sector: a Research Handbook*, Yale Uni Press, New Haven

JAUCH LR & W GLUECK, (1984), *Business Policy and Strategy Implementation*, 4th ed, McGraw Hill, New York

JENKS C, (1987), "Who gives what?", in W Powell ed, *The Nonprofit Sector: a Research Handbook*, Yale Uni Press, New Haven Conn.

JOHNSON N, (1974), "Defining accountability", *Public Administration Bulletin* 17 Dec 3-13

JOHNSON N, (1978), "What sort of service?", *Social Service Quarterly*, 51:3 83-88

JOHNSON N, (1981), *Voluntary Social Services*, Blackwell & Robertson

JONES R & M PENDLEBURY, (1985), "What makes public sector accounting different?", *The Accountants Magazine* Nov 490-94

JORDAN VE, (1983), "We cannot live for ourselves alone", in B O'Connell ed, *America's Voluntary Spirit*, The Foundation Center, New York

JUDGE K, (1982), "The public purchase of social care: British confirmation of the American experience", *Policy and Politics*, 10 397-416

JURKOVICK J, (1974), "A core typology of organizational environment", *Administrative Science Quarterly*, 19 380-94

KANTER R MOSS & DV SUMMERS, (1987), "Doing well while doing good", in W Powell ed, *The Nonprofit Sector: A Research Handbook*, Yale Uni Press, New Haven Conn.

KAST FE & JE ROSENZWEIG, (1985), *Organization and Management*, 4th ed, McGraw-Hill, Singapore

KATZ A & E BENDER, (1976), *The Strength in Us: Self-help Groups in the Modern World*, New Viewpoints Books, New York

KATZ D & RL KAHN, (1978), *The Social Psychology of Organizations*, 2nd ed, Wiley, New York

KAVANAGH P, (1975), *The Green Fool*, Penguin, Harmondsworth

KENNEDY F, (1989), *Family Economy and Government in Ireland*, ESRI, Dublin

KENNEDY G, (1992), "Big increase in AIDS among heterosexuals", *Irish*

Times, Sept 17

KENNEDY R, (1973), *The Irish*, Uni of California Press, Berkeley

KENNEDY S, (1981), *Who should care?*, Turoe Press, Dublin

KENNEDY S, (1981a), *One Million Poor*, Turoe Press, Dublin KERR S, (1975), "On the folly of rewarding A while hoping for B", *Academy of Management Journal*, Dec 769-83

KILFEATHER F, (1992), "Charities seek to end prize limit restriction", *Irish Times*, Aug 15

KIRBY P, (1988), *Dublin: hard facts-future hopes*, Catholic Social Service Conference, Dublin

KLEIN R, (1974), *Inflation and Priorities*, Centre for Studies in Social Policy, London

KNAPP M, E ROBERTSON & C THOMASON, (1988), "Public Money Voluntary Action: Whose Welfare?" Discussion Paper 514/2 Personal Social Service Research Unit: University of Kent

KNIGHT B, (1984), "Management in Voluntary Organisations", ARVAC Occasional Paper No 6 ARVAC, Wivenhoe

KOONTZ H & RW BRADSPIES, (1972), "Managing through feedforward control", *Business Horizons*, 215:3 July 5-36

KOONTZ H, C O'DONNELL & H WEIHRICH, (1984), *Management*, 8th ed, McGraw-Hill, Singapore

KOONTZ H & H WEIHRICH, (1988), *Management*, 9th ed, McGraw-Hill, Singapore

KOTLER P, (1982), *Marketing for Nonprofit Organizations*, 2nd ed, Prentice Hall, Englewood Cliffs NJ

KRAMER R, (1981), *Voluntary Agencies In The Welfare State*, Uni of California Press, Berkeley

KRAMER R, (1987), "Voluntary Agencies and the Personal Social Services", in W Powell ed, *The Nonprofit Sector: a Research Handbook*, Harvard Uni Press, New Haven Conn.

KRAMER R, (1990), "Change and continuity in British voluntary organisations 1976 to 1988", *Voluntas*, I:2 33-60

KRAMER R & B GROSSMAN, (1987), "Contacting for social services", *Social Science Review*, March 32-55

KRASHINSKY M, (1986), "Transaction costs and a theory of the nonprofit organization", in S Rose-Ackerman ed, *The Economics of Nonprofit Institutions: Studies in Structure and Policy*, Oxford Uni Press, New York

KRASHINSKY M, (1990), "Management implications of government funding for nonprofit organizations: views from the United States and Canada" *Nonprofit Management and Leadership* 1:1 39-53

KREITNER R, (1989), *Management*, 4th ed, Houghton Mufflin, Boston

KUBLER-ROSS E, (1969), *On Death and Dying*, Tavistock, London

KUHNLE S & P SELLE, (1990), "Meeting needs in the Welfare State", in A Ware & R Goodi eds, *Needs and Welfare Provisions*, Sage, Beverly Hills

KUTI E, (1990), "The possible role of the nonprofit sector in Hungary", *Voluntas* 1:1 26-40

LANDRY C, D MORLEY, R SOUTHWOOD & P WRIGHT, (1985), *What a Way to Run a Railroad*, Comedia, London

LaROSSE R & J WOLF, (1985), "On qualitative family research", *Journal of Marriage and Family*, 47:3 531-41

LAUGHLIN R, (1984), *The design of accounting systems*, Unpublished PhD University of Sheffield

LAUGHLIN R, (1990), "A model of financial accountability and the Church of England", *Financial Accountability and Management* 6:2 93-114

LAVAN A, (1981), *Social Needs and Community Social Services*, Tallaght Welfare Society, Dublin.

LAWLER E & J RHODE, (1976), *Information and Control in Organizations*, Goodyear, Pacific Palisades California

LAWRENCE PR & D DYER, (1983), *Renewing American Industry*, The Free Press, New York

LAWRENCE PR & JW LORSCH, (1967), *Organization and Environment*, Irwin, Illinois

LAYTON D, (1987), *Philanthropy and Voluntarism: An Annotated Bibliography*, Foundation Center, New York

LEAT D, (1988), *Voluntary Organisations and Accountability*, NCVO, London

LEAT D, G SMOLKA & J UNELL, (1981), *Voluntary and Statutory Collaboration: Rhetoric or Reality?*, Bedford Square Press, London

LEAT D, S TESTER & J UNELL, (1986), *A Price Worth Paying?*, Policy Studies Institute, London

LECKY W, (1916), *A History of Ireland in the Eighteenth Century*, Longmans Green, London

LEE A, (1987), "The Role of the Voluntary Sector", Paper presented at National Social Service Board Conference, Burlington Hotel: Dublin 25th June

LEE J, (1973), *The Modernisation of Irish Society 1814-1918*, Gill & Macmillan, Dublin

LEE J, (1984), "Reflections on the study of Irish values", in M Fogarty et al, *Irish Values and Attitudes*, Dominican Publications, Dublin

LEGIO MARIAE, (1969), *The Official Handbook of the Legion of Mary*,

Concilium Legionis Mariae, Dublin

LePLAY F, (1855), *Les Ouvriers Europeens*, Alfred Mame, Tours France

LERNER M, (1983), "The Joiners", in B O'Connell ed, *America's Voluntary Spirit*, Foundation Center, New York

LEVITT T, (1973), *The Third Sector: New Tactics for a Responsive Society*, AMACOM, New York

LITTLER CR & G SALAMAN, (1982), "Bravermania and beyond: recent theories of the labour process", *Sociology*, May 253-62

LONDON RAPE CRISIS CENTRE, (1984), *Sexual Violence: the Reality for Women*, Women's Press, London

LORENTZEN H, (1990), "Welfare and Values: the adaption of voluntary religious service production to expanding welfare state standards", Paper presented at AVAS conference London:LSE July

LOVELOCK C, (1984), *Services Marketing*, Prentice Hall, Englewood Cliffs NJ

LOVELOCK CH & CB WEINBERG, (1977), *Cases in Public and Non-profit Marketing*, The Scientific Press, Palo Alto

LUPTON T, (1963), *On the Shop Floor*, Pergamon, Oxford

LYNAM R, (1983), "What kind of society shall we have?", in O'Connell ed, *America's Voluntary Spirit*, The Foundation Center, New York

MAC ARDLE D, (1965), *The Irish Republic*, 4th ed, Farrar Straus & Giroux, New York

MAC CRIMMON D, (1979), "Improving the efficiency of nonprofit organizations", *CA Magazine*, 112:8 101-3

MALONEY O, (1989), "Fair Profit", *The Furrow*, 40:8 467-70

MANLEY K, (1988), "Giving the whole story", *Accountancy*, Dec 94-6

MASON DE, (1984), *Voluntary Nonprofit Enterprise Management*, Plenum Press, New York

MATER ET MAGISTRA, (1961), "Encyclical of Pope John XXIII", English trans WJ Gibbons, in J Gremillion ed, *The Gospel of Peace and Justice*, Orbis, Maryknoll

MAWBY R & M GILL, (1987), *Crime Victims: Needs, Services and the Voluntary Sector*, Tavistock, London

McCARTHY J, (1989), "Time to unleash a charities watchdog", *Irish Independent*, Feb 22

McGRATH JE, (1982), "Dilemmatics: the study of research choices and dilemmas", in JE McGrath, J Martin & RA Kulka, *Judgement Calls in Research*, Sage, London

McGREGOR D, (1960), *The Human Side of Enterprize*, McGraw Hill, New York

McKELVEY B, (1975), "Guidelines for the empirical classification of organizations", *Administrative Science Quarterly*, XX:509-525

McKEVITT C, (1992), "Charities call out for new tax law as giving falters", *Sunday Tribune*, Aug 23

McLAUGHLIN C, (1986), *The Management of Nonprofit Organizations*, Wiley, New York

MECHANIC D, (1962), "Some considerations in the methodology of organizational studies", in HJ Leavitt ed, *The Social Science of Organizations*, Prentice Hall, Englewood Cliffs NJ

MELLOR H, (1985), *The Role of Voluntary Organisations in Social Welfare*, Croom Helm, London

MERVIS P & E HACKETT, (1983), "Work and workforce characteristics in the nonprofit sector", *Monthly Labour Review*, Apr 3-12

MIDDLETON M, (1987), "Nonprofit boards of directors:beyond the governance function", in W Powell ed, *The Nonprofit Sector: a Research Handbook*, Yale Uni Press, New Haven Conn.

MILES MB, (1983), "Qualitative data as an attrative nuisance: the problem of analysis", in J Van Mannen ed, *Qualitative Methodology*, Sage, Beverley Hills

MILLS PK & N MARGULIES, (1980), "Toward a core typology of service organizations", *Academy of Management Review*, V:2 255-65

MILLS C, RI MAWBY & I LEVITT, (1983), "Voluntary action in a complex society: a case study of the Plymouth night shelter.", Paper to social administration association conference, Cantebury Kent

MILOFSKY C, (1987), *Community Organizations - Studies in Resource Mobilization and Exchange*, Oxford Uni Press, New York

MINTZBERG H, (1979), "An emerging strategy of direct research", *Administrative Science Quarterly*, 24 582-9

MINTZBERG H, (1983), "An emerging strategy of direct research", in J Van Mannen ed, *Qualitative Methodology*, Sage, Beverly Hills

MORGAN G, (1986), *Images of Organization*, Sage, Beverly Hills California

MORGAN L, (1990), "Woman's refuge faces closure", *Irish Times*, May 23

MOYER M, (1983), *Managing Voluntary Organizations*, York University, Toronto

MULLIN R, (1980), *Present Alms: On the Corruption of Philanthropy*, Phlogiston, Birmingham

MULLINS L, (1985), *Management and Organisational Behaviour*, Pitman, London

MURRAY G J, (1969), *Voluntary Organisations & Social Welfare*, Oliver & Boyd, Edinburgh

MURRAY VV, (1987), "Why can't voluntary organizations be more businesslike?", *Canadian Business Review*, 14: 19-21

MURRAY V & P BRADSHAW-CAMBALL, (1990), "Voluntary sector boards: patterns of governance", Paper presented at AVAS conference LSE London, July

NAO, (1987), *Monitoring and Control of Charities in England and Wales*, HMSO, London

NATIONAL COUNCIL FOR THE AGED, (1988), *Years Ahead - a Policy for the Elderly*, Stationery Office, Dublin

NATIONAL COUNCIL FOR THE AGED, (1989), *Caring for the Elderly*, NCA, Dublin

NATIONAL INCOME AND EXPENDITURE, (1985), Stationery Office, Dublin

NCVO, (1984), *The Management and Effectiveness of Voluntary Organisations*, NCVO, London

NCVO, (1986), *Malpractice in Fundraising for Charity*, NCVO, London

NCVO, (1988), *What is Charity?*, NCVO, London

NELSON R & M KRASHINSKY, (1973), "Two major issues of public policy: public policy and organization of supply", in R Nelson & D Young eds, *Public Subsidy for Day Care of Young Children*, Heath, Lexington Mass

NESC, (1987), *Community Care Services*, National Economic and Social Council, Dublin

NEWMAN C, (1989), "Dail conditions are decrepit TDs claim", *Irish Times* Dec 1

NEWMAN W, (1975), *Constructive Control: Design and Use of Control Systems*, Prentice Hall, Englewood Cliffs NJ

NEWMAN W & HW WALLENDER, (1978), "Managing not-for-profit enterprises", *Academy of Management Review*, Jan 24-31

NICHOLAS D, (1988), "The Army's secret weapon", *Fundraising Management*, Nov 64-68

NIELSEN WA, (1983), "The third sector: keystone of a caring society", in B O'Connell ed, *America's Voluntary Spirit*, The Foundation Center, New York

NORMANTON EL, (1966), *The Accountability and Audit of Government*, Manchester Uni Press, Manchester

NORTON M, (1985), *Raising Money from Government*, Directory of Social Change, London

NSSB, (1982), *The Development of Voluntary Social Services in Ireland*, National Social Service Board, Dublin

NSSB, (1985), *Directory of National Voluntary Organisations*, National Social

Service Board, Dublin

NSSB, (1986), *Developing Social Services to Meet Community Needs*, National Social Service Board, Dublin

O'CONNELL B, (1976), *The Contribution of Voluntary Agencies in Developing Social Policies*, Council of Jewish Federations, New York

O'CONNELL B, (1983), *America's Voluntary Spirit: a Book of Readings*, The Foundation Center, New York

O'CONNELL J, (1988), Registered Irish Charities:motion, Seanad Report Nov 2, col 416-7

O'FAOLAIN N, (1990), "We can enjoy the challenge of change", *Irish Times* Dec 1

O'KEEFFE B, (1991), "For the disabled, employers are the handicap", *Irish Times*, Working and Living Supplement, 29 Nov

O'KELLY P, (1992), "IDA losing its authority?", *Sunday Tribune*, July 5

O'LEARY M, (1988), "The experience of poverty", in E Hanna ed, *Poverty in Ireland*, Social Study Conference, Portlaoise

OLENICK AJ, (1988), "How to improve nonprofit management", *Nonprofit World* 6:3 31-34

OLIVER J, (1982), "An instrument for classifying organizations", *Academy of Management Journal*, 25:4 855-66

O'MAHONEY A, (1985), *Social Need and the Provision of Social Services in Rural Areas*, An Foras Taluntais, Dublin

O'MEARA A, (1991), "Residential problem worsening for juvenile offenders", *Sunday Tribune*, Mar 24

O'MORAIN P, (1989), "Services for adult mentally handicapped in Ireland", *Irish Times*, 24 April

O'MORAIN P, (1989a), "MS centre brings relaxation relief to sufferers", *Irish Times*, Sept 26

O'MORAIN P, (1991), "Voluntary groups seek lottery funds", *Irish Times*, Jan 29

O'MURCHU D, (1987), *Coping with Change in the Modern World*, Mercier Press, Cork

O'NEILL M, (1989), *The Third America: the Emergence of the Nonprofit Sector in the US*, Jossey-Bass, San Francisco

O'REILLY M, (1865), *Progress of Catholicity in Ireland in the Nineteenth Century*, Kelly, Dublin

O'SULLIVAN C, (1990), Personal interview with Dr Claire O'Sullivan AIDS co-ordinator CSSC, Feb 10

OUCHI WG, (1979), "A conceptual framework for the design of organizational control mechanisms", *Management Science*, 25 833-48

274

OUCHI WG, (1980), "Markets bureaucracies and clans", *Administrative Science Quarterly*, 25 129-141

PARASURAMAN A VA ZEITHAML & L BERRY, (1988), "SERVQUAL: a multiple-item scale for measuring consumer perceptions of quality", *Journal of Retailing* 64:1, Spring 12-40

PATTON MQ, (1987), *How to Use Qualitative Methods in Evaluation*, Sage, Beverley Hills

PATTON C, (1990), "Big Batallions and Little Platoons", Seventh Arnold Goodman lecture, 7 June, Tonbridge: CAF

PEARSE J & R ROBINSON, (1989), *Management*, McGraw Hill, Singapore

PEILLON M, (1982), *Contemporary Irish Society*, Gill & Macmillan, Dublin

PESP, (1991), *Programme for Economic and Social Progress*, Stationery Office, Dublin

PETERS & WATERMAN, (1982), *In Search of Excellence*, Warner, New York

PETERSON S & V, (1973), "Voluntary associations is ancient Greece", *Journal of Voluntary Action Research*, 2:1 2-16

PETTIGREW AM, (1987), *The Management of Strategic Change*, Blackwell, Oxford

PHOENIX, (1992), David Cottrell's cancer `charity' 17 April 5

PICARDA H, (1977), *The Law and Practice Relating to Charities*, Butterworth, London

PIZZEY E, (1974), *Scream Quietly or the Neighbours Will Hear*, Penguin, Harmondsworth

POSNETT J, (1987), "Trends in the income of registered charities 1980-1985", in *Charity Trends*, CAF, Tonbridge

POULTON G, (1988), *Managing Voluntary Organisations*, Wiley, Chichester

POWELL W, (1987), *The Nonprofit Sector: a Research Handbook*, Yale Uni Press, New Haven Conn.

POWER B, (1980), *Old and Alone in Ireland*, Society of St Vincent de Paul, Dublin

PRESTON A, (1990), "Changing labour market patterns in the nonprofit and for-profit sectors: implications for nonprofit management", *Nonprofit Management & Leadership*, 1:1 29-38

PRIDE W & O FERRELL, (1987), *Marketing*, 5th ed, Houghton Mifflin, Boston Mass.

QUINLAN A, (1988), "Hillary praises voluntary groups", *Irish Times*, 5 Nov

QURESHI et al, (1983), "Motivations & rewards of helpers in the Kent community care scheme", in S Hatch ed, *Volunteers: patterns meanings and motives*, The Volunteer Centre, Berkhamsted

RAMANATHAN KV, (1982), *Management Control in Nonprofit Organizations*, Wiley, New York

RANDALL A, (1989), "Pressure to put more heart into accountability", *Accountancy*, Dec 70-2

RAYNEY P, (1988), "The fund raiser's guide to tax traps", *Accountancy*, Dec 99-101

READER'S DIGEST, (1990), "Honest policy", Aug 53

REDFIELD R, (1942), Introduction in GW Allport, *The Use of Personal Documents in Psychological Science*, Science Research Council, New York

REED A, (1990), "Charities must put their house in order", *The Independent* July 3

REESER C & M LOPER, (1978), *Management: The Key to Organizational Effectiveness*, Scott Foresman, Glenview Illinois

REPORT OF THE COMMISSION ON THE STATUS OF WOMEN, (1972), Stationery Office, Dublin

• REPORT ON FUNDRAISING, (1990), *Report of the Committee on Fundraising Activities for Charitable and Other Purposes*, Stationery Office, Dublin

REYNOLDS B & S HEALY, (1988), *Poverty and Family Income Policy*, CMRS, Dublin

RICHARDSON & GOODMAN, (1983), *Self help and social care*, Policy Studies Institute, London

ROBBINS D, (1990), "The core of the community: volunteers, voluntary organisations and the social state", Paper presented at EC conference Partners in Progress, Galway, July

ROBBINS J, (1980), *The Lost Children*, IPA, Dublin

ROBBINS SP, (1988), *Management: Concepts and Applications*, 2nd ed, Prentice-Hall, Englewood Cliffs NJ

ROBERTS J & R SCAPENS, (1985), "Accounting systems and systems of accountability - understanding accounting practices in their organisational contexts", *Accounting, Organisations and Society*, 10:4 443-56

ROBINSON D, (1971), "Government contracting for academic research: accountability in the American experience", in B Smith & D Hague eds, *The Dilemmas of Accountability in Modern Government*, Macmillan, London

ROBINSON D, (1979), *Talking out of Alcoholism: the Self-help Process of Alcoholics Anonymous*, Croom Helm, London

ROBSON S & G FOSTER, (1989), *Qualitative Research in Action*, Arnold, London

ROCKE W, (1992), "Marvellous response to Somalia tragedy from Irish public", *Sunday Press*, Sept 20

ROCKEFELLER JD, (1983), "The Third Sector", in B O'Connell ed, *America's Voluntary Spirit*, The Foundation Center, New York

ROETHLISBERGER FJ & WJ DICKSON, (1939), *Management and the Worker*, Harvard Uni Press, Cambridge Mass

ROSE-ACKERMAN S, (1982), "Charitable giving and excessive fundraising", *Quarterly Journal of Economics*, 96: 193-212

ROSE-ACKERMAN S, (1986), *The Economics of Nonprofit Institutions*, Oxford Uni Press, New York

ROSE-ACKERMAN S, (1990), "Competition between non-profits and for-profits: entry and growth", *Voluntas*, 1:1 13-25

ROSENBAUM N, (1981), "Government funding and the voluntary sector:impacts and opinions", *Journal of Voluntary Action Research*, 10 82-89

ROTTMAN D D HANNAN N HARDIMAN & M WILEY, (1982), *The Distribution of Income in the Republic of Ireland*, ESRI, Dublin

RTE, (1992), Look Here, Television programme presented by M Finnucane and Brian Dobson 8 pm Feb 26

RUDNEY G, (1987), "The scope and dimensions of non-profit activity", in W Powell ed, *The Nonprofit Sector: a Research Handbook*, Harvard Uni Press, New Haven Conn.

RUE L & L BYARS, (1986), *Management: Theory and Application*, 4th ed, Irwin, Homewood Illinois

RUTHERFORD BA, (1983), *Financial Reporting in The Public Sector*, Butterworths, London

RYAN JE, (1980), "Profitability in the nonprofit environment", *Journal of Systems Management* 31:8 6-10

RYAN L, (1979), "Church and politics - the last twenty years", *The Furrow* Jan 20-6

RYNNE S, (1960), *Father John Hayes*, Burns & Oates, London

SACHNOFF T, (1991), "Recovery pioneer to be honoured", *Initiative*, 7:2 6-7

SALAMON L, (1987), "Partners in public service", in W Powell ed, *The Nonprofit Sector: a Research Handbook*, Harvard Uni Press, New Haven Conn.

SALAMON L & A ABRAMSON, (1982), *The Federal Budget and the Nonprofit Sector*, Urban Institute Press, Washington DC

SAVAGE T, (1967), "Charitable works renewed", *Christus Rex*, XXI:3 283-90

SAYLES L, (1972), "The many dimensions of control", *Organizational Dynamics* 21-31

SEEBOHM REPORT, (1968), *Report of the Committee on Local Authority and Allied Social Services*, HMSO, London

SEED P, (1973), *The Expansion of Social Work in Britain*, Routledge Kegan Paul, London

SHEEHAN M, (1992), "Messiah fund doubles target", *Sunday Tribune*, Oct 4

SHERROTT R, (1983), "Fifty volunteers", in S Hatch ed, *Volunteers:Patterns meanings and motives*, The Volunteer Centre, Berkhamsted

SILLS DL, (1968), "Voluntary associations: sociological aspects", *International Encyclopedia of the Social Sciences*, 16: 362-379, Macmillan & Free Press, New York

SILVERMAN D, (1985), *Qualitative Methodology and Sociology*, Gower, Aldershot

SIMON JG, (1987), "The tax treatment of nonprofit organizations: a review of federal and state politics", in W Powell ed, *The Nonprofit Sector: a Research Handbook*, Harvard Uni Press, New Haven Conn.

SIMON JG, (1989), "Agendas for nonprofit research: a personal account", in V Hodgkinson & R Lyman", *The Future of the Nonprofit Sector*, Jossey Bass, San Francisco

SIZER J, (1977), *An Insight into Management Accounting*, Penguin, Harmondsworth

SMITH DH, (1980), "The impact of the non-profit voluntary sector of society", in T Connors ed, *The Non-profit Organization Handbook*, McGraw Hill, New York

SMITH D H, B BALDWIN & E WHITE, (1980), "The nonprofit sector", in T Connors ed, *The Nonprofit Organization Handbook*, McGraw Hill, New York

SOCIETY OF SAINT VINCENT DE PAUL, (1987), *In Giving we Receive*, Society of Saint Vincent de Paul, Dublin

• STEWART JD, (1984), "The role of information in public accountablity", in A Hopworth & C Tomkins eds, *Issues in Public Sector Accounting*, Philip Allan, London

STEWART J & S RANSON, (1988), "Management in the Public Domain", *Public Money and Management*, 8:1&2 13-9

STRIKE K, (1972), "Explaining and understanding: the impact of science on our concept of man", in LG Thomas ed, *Philosophical Redirection of Educational Research*, Uni of Chicago Press, Chicago

TASK FORCE ON THE CHILD CARE SERVICES: FINAL REPORT 1980 Stationery Office, Dublin

TAYLOR C, (1992), "Ahern takes tough line on trimming budgets", *Irish Times*, July 15

TAYLOR F, (1867), *Irish Homes and Irish Hearts*, Longmans, London

TAYLOR FW, (1911), *Principles of Scientific Management*, Harper, New York

TAYLOR SJ & R BOGDAN, (1984), *Introduction to Qualitative Research Methods*, 2nd ed, Wiley, New York

THANE P, (1982), *The Foundation of the Welfare State*, Longman, New York

THOMAS WI & F ZNANIECKI, (1918), *The Polish Peasant in Poland and America*, Knopf, New York

THOMPSON JD, (1967), *Organizations in Action*, McGraw-Hill, New York

TIME, (1990), "Milestones", *Time International*, July 23:70

TITMUSS RM, (1971), *The Gift Relationship: From Human Blood to Social Policy*, Allen & Unwin, London

TONNIES F [1887], (1955), *Community and Association*, Routledge & Kegan Paul, London

TOOLIN D, (1992), "The disabled must be unvolved in decisions that affect them", *Irish Times*, 8 May

TRIPP RT, (1976), *The International Thesarus of Quotations*, Penguin, Harmondsworth

TUTTY MJ, (1959), "Dublin's oldest charity", Paper presented to the Old Dublin Society, Nov 16

USEEM M, (1987), "Corporate Philanthropy", in W Powell ed, *The Nonprofit Sector: a Research Handbook*, Yale Uni Press, New Haven Conn.

UVOH, (1991), Pre 1992 budget submission, Union of Voluntary Organisations for the Handicapped, Dublin

VAN MANNEN J, (1983), *Qualitative Methodology*, Sage, Beverly Hills

VAN RIPER PP, (1966), "Organizations: basic issues and a proposed typology", in RV Bowers ed, *Studies on Behaviour in Organizations*, University of Georgia Press, Athens

VAN TIL J, (1988), *Mapping the Third Sector*, The Foundation Center, New York

VLADECK B, (1976), "Why nonprofits go broke", *The Public Interest*, 42 86-101

von BERTALANFFY L, (1968), *General Systems Theory*, Braziller, New York

WALKER P, (1981), "Institutions: a 19th century answer to a 20th century problem?", *Community Care*, 26 March

WALSH B, (1986), "The growth of government", in K Kennedy ed, *Ireland in Transition*, Mercier, Cork

WATERS J, (1992), "Voices raised for Somalia", *Irish Times*, Sept 29

WAX RH, (1971), *Doing Fieldwork: Warnings and Advice*, Uni of Chicago Press, Chicago

WEAVER W, (1983), "Pre-christian philanthropy", in B O'Connell ed, *America's Voluntary Spirit*, The Foundation Center, New York

WEBB EJ, (1966), *Unobtrusive Measures: Non-reactive Research in the Social Sciences*, Rand McNally, Skokie Ill

WEBB S & B, (1912), *The Prevention of Destitution*, Longmans, London

WEBB A & B WISTON, (1982), *Whither State Welfare?*, Royal Institute of Public Administration, London

WEBER M, (1947), *The Theory of Social and Economic Organizations*, T Parsons trans, Free Press, New York

WEISBROD B, (1975), "Towards a theory of the voluntary nonprofit sector in a three-sector economy", in E Phelps ed, *Altruism morality and Economic Theory*, Russel Sage, New York

WEISBROD B, (1977), *The Voluntary Nonprofit Sector: an Economic Analysis*, Heath, Lexington MA.

WEISBROD B, (1983), "Nonprofit and proprietary sector behaviour: wage differentials among lawyers", *Journal of Labour Economics*, July 246-63

WEISBROD B, (1986), "Towards a theory of the voluntary non-profit sector in a three-sector economy", in S Rose-Ackerman ed, *The Economics of Non-profit Institutions*, Oxford Uni Press, New York

WEISBROD B, (1988), *The Nonprofit Economy*, Harvard Uni Press, Cambridge Mass.

WEST EG, (1989), "The economics of charities: revised theory and new evidence", *Economic Affairs*, Feb/Mar 22-4

WHELAN B & R VAUGHAN, (1982), *The Economic and Social Circumstances of the Elderly in Ireland*, ESRI, Dublin

WHELAN B & CT WHELAN, (1984), *Social Mobility in the Republic of Ireland*, ESRI, Dublin

WHITE PAPER ON LOCAL GOVERNMENT ORGANISATION, (1971) Stationery Office, Dublin

WHYTE J, (1971), *Church and State in Modern Ireland*, Gill & Macmillan, Dublin

WILLIAMS GW, (1902), *Dublin Charities*, The Educational Repository, Dublin

WILLIAMS S, (1981), *Politics in for People*, Penguin, Harmondsworth

WILLIAMSON et al, (1982), *The Researh Craft*, Little Brown, Boston

WINKLER JT, (1987), "The fly on the wall of the inner sanctum observing company directors at work", in B Moyser & M Wagstaffe eds, *Research Methods for Elite Studies*, Croom Helm, London

280

WISH N, (1990), University and college-based nonprofit management programs in the United States, Paper presented at AVAS conference LSE London, July

WOLFENDEN COMMITTEE, (1978), *The Future of Voluntary Organisations*, Croom Helm, London

WOODFIELD SIR P et al, (1987), *Efficiency Scrutiny of the Supervision of Charities*, HMSO, London

WOODRUFFE K, (1974), *From Charity to Social Work*, Routledge & Kegan Paul, London

WOODWARD J, (1965), *Industrial Organization: Theory and Practice*, Oxford Uni Press, London

WORLD BANK, (1989), *World Development Report 1989*, The World Bank, Washington DC

WORSLEY P, (1977), *Introducing Sociology*, 2nd ed, Penguin, Harmondsworth

YEATES P, (1988), "Archbishop criticises cutbacks", *Irish Times*, 31 Mar

YOUNG D, (1983), *If not for Profit, for What?*, Heath, Lexington Mass.

YOUNG D, (1985), *Case book of Management in Nonprofit Organizations*, Haworth Press, New York

YOUNG D, (1987), "Executive leadership in nonprofit organizations", in W Powell ed, *The Nonprofit Sector: A Research Handbook*, Yale Uni Press, New Haven Conn.

ZALD M, (1970), *Organizational Change - the Political Economy of the YMCA*, Uni of Chicago Press, Chicago

ZALTMAN C, (1979), *Management Principles for Non-profit Agencies and organisations*, Amacon, New York